Political Disagreement, Violence and Nonviolence

Political Disagreement, Violence and Nonviolence

An Analysis of Political Ideologies and Their Distinctions between Kinds of Violence

Gregory McCreery

LEXINGTON BOOKS
Lanham • Boulder • New York • London

Published by Lexington Books
An imprint of The Rowman & Littlefield Publishing Group, Inc.
4501 Forbes Boulevard, Suite 200, Lanham, Maryland 20706
www.rowman.com

86-90 Paul Street, London EC2A 4NE

British Library Cataloguing in Publication Information Available

Library of Congress Cataloging-in-Publication Data

Names: McCreery, Greg, 1977- author.
Title: Political disagreement, violence and nonviolence : an analysis of political ideologies and their distinctions between kinds of violence / Greg McCreery.
Description: Lanham, Maryland : Lexington Books, 2023. | Includes bibliographical references and index. | Summary: "McCreery descriptively analyzes distinctions between kinds of violence, including nonviolence, as outlined by numerous philosophical theorists, arguing that a commonsense view of violence and nonviolence is based on paradigmatic cases. Beyond these what counts as kinds of violence and nonviolence is essentially contested due to political, ideological disagreements"-- Provided by publisher.
Identifiers: LCCN 2023010621 (print) | LCCN 2023010622 (ebook) | ISBN 9781793617217 (cloth) | ISBN 9781793617224 (epub)
Subjects: LCSH: Political violence. | Nonviolence. | Ideology.
Classification: LCC JC328.6 .M43 2023 (print) | LCC JC328.6 (ebook) | DDC 303.6--dc23/eng/20230330
LC record available at https://lccn.loc.gov/2023010621
LC ebook record available at https://lccn.loc.gov/2023010622

∞™ The paper used in this publication meets the minimum requirements of American National Standard for Information Sciences—Permanence of Paper for Printed Library Materials, ANSI/NISO Z39.48-1992.

To my wife, Sandra, whose enduring love and support have been tremendous. Without her, none of this would have been possible.

Contents

Acknowledgments

Much of this manuscript would not have been possible without the guidance of Stephen Turner, Charles Guignon, Martin Schönfeld, Joanne Waugh, and Michael Morris. Stephen Turner, in particular, has been an ongoing source of insight and inspiration. I can only hope that I am one day capable of achieving his success. I am indebted to all their advice, challenges, and teaching. I am also greatly appreciative of the patience and time taken by the editors at Lexington Books, particularly Joseph Parry and Anna Debiec. So many things impeded upon my ability to finish this in a timely manner, and the experience of publishing this with Lexington Books was truly valuable, particularly because of the editors' willingness to work with me. Last, but certainly not least, I am very appreciative of my friends' and family's jovial engagement with my combative questions and disagreements, particularly my wife, Sandra, and mother, Leslie.

Preface

The United States of America's House Committee's Congressional Hearing on the controversial event, which took place at the Capitol in Washington, DC, on January 6, 2021, serves as an excellent example of what this book concerns. Though there may be agreement that an event did occur, exactly what happened and what it means is contested by politicized groups that think of this event from opposed ideological perspectives. While a joint session of Congress gathered to count electoral votes, President Donald Trump's supporters gathered to listen to him and others give speeches, proceeded to march on the Capitol, and ultimately, some participants broke their way into the Capitol, harming police officers, some of whom would later die. Disagreements abound concerning this event, particularly concerning whether it involved violence, to what extent the entire event can be described as violent, whether that violence was legitimate, and whether it constituted a protest, a riot, an insurrection, or possibly even an excursion of "tourists," as Georgia representative Andrew Clyde suggested on May 12, 2021. This example reflects the argument outlined in this book because it demonstrates that there are disagreements concerning what counts as violence, what counts as *kinds* of violence, and whether those kinds of violence are legitimate. These disagreements are unavoidable because they occur in relation to opposed, irreconcilable political ideologies held by politicized groups, *even if there is agreement that something violent occurred.* Furthermore, if there is such disagreement, then this suggests that a politically neutral conception of violence is likely impossible.

It is not difficult to find examples of such disagreements. Another one concerns the murder of George Floyd and the Black Lives Matter protests that occurred in various cities and towns across the United States in relation to Derek Chauvin's killing of Floyd on May 25, 2020. Even if there is agreement that violence occurred when Floyd was killed, or that some of the protests that followed were peaceful, while others turned violent, whether the violence of Chauvin kneeling on Floyd for around seven minutes was justified raises ideological, political disagreements. Likewise, the question concerning whether the Black Lives Matter protests against police brutality were legitimate generates ideological, political disagreement. For example, a related disagreement concerns Kyle Rittenhouse's murder of Joseph Rosenbaum and Anthony Huber, as well as his injuring of Gaige Grosskreutz on August 25, 2020, at a Black Lives Matter protest in Kenosha, Wisconsin, in the United States. Not everyone agrees that Rittenhouse was justified in using violent force, presumably in self-defense, despite the fact that a jury of his peers found him not guilty on November 19, 2021. Even if there is an agreement that violence occurred, the agreement ends there. Based on whether one perceives Rittenhouse's actions as self-defensive, or as defensive of local businesses, or as offensive, aggressive, and a violation of the rule of law, one's perspective tends to place oneself within a politicized group that shares ideological assumptions about violence, about who can use violence, about when violence counts as self-defensive, and about when violence is justifiable and when it is not.

Historically speaking, John Brown's raid on the munitions store at Harper's Ferry, Virginia, in the United States, from October 16 to 18, 1859, which he had hoped would spark a slave rebellion, was likewise an event in relation to which disagreements arose due to political, ideological disagreements. For example, in his book *Weird John Brown: Divine Violence and the Limits of Ethics*, Ted A. Smith outlines how Brown's actions were contested from the start, due to political and religious disagreements concerning the institution of slavery, the relationship between Brown's actions and "higher law," and how and whether slavery ought to be abolished and what the means to abolition ought to be.[1]

Another contested example of what counts as violence can be seen with Kevin J. O'Brien's argument that climate change is itself violent, which is found in his book *The Violence of Climate Change: Lessons of Resistance from Nonviolent Activists*.[2] Not only do some question whether climate change is even real, but others might deny that a nonhuman meteorological phenomenon could even be violent in the first place. O'Brien argues that "to see climate change as violence is to see it as the product of a destructive system that degrades human lives, other species, and the world upon which all living beings depend."[3] Someone might simply disagree with this claim because this conception of violence includes *too much* as counting as violence, given that this isn't a case of an intentional, instrumental use of means by a human agent for the sake of causing harm or destruction. However, if some things are violent despite the fact that they are not direct uses of means for the intentional purpose of causing harm or destruction, then where is the line drawn between what counts as violence and what does not?

Much of the disagreement that occurs concerning these examples raises questions: What is violence? Is there a correct definition for violence? Is violence exclusively a product of human actions? Does violence only harm bodies? Do we have to be able to see violence for something to count as violence? Can it be known for certain whose violence is defensive? If so, what factors and conditions must exist for an instance of violence to count as self-defense? When a group of people are united in action, does the violence of two or three of them turn the action of the whole group into a violent one? Does liberation justify the use of violence? Is violence a necessary condition for liberation? If one ideal, such as liberation, can justify violence, then what other ideals justify violence? What ideals do not justify violence and why not? Does the effort to defeat violence justify uses of violence? If that is the case, then can violence be defeated, if violence is the means to defeating violence? On what authority is the justification for uses of violence to defeat violence based? If the use of violence to defeat violence merely ensures that violence continues nonetheless, can nonviolence succeed where violence fails to be useful as a means to eradicating violence? Can the nonviolence of a group itself be experienced as violence, if that nonviolence only works as a means to bringing about a change that is not desired by the adversaries against whom the group nonviolently acts? These are not new questions, but they are serious ones, particularly because discussions concerning violence often have to do with death and injury. There are real-world consequences to the ways in which violence is conceived, distinguished into kinds, believed to be legitimate, and thought of as the means to defeating violence. Such questions arise throughout much of the history of scholarship on violence and nonviolence, as theorists attempt to resolve one of the fundamental issues that plagues humanity, which is the tendency of humans to resort to violence or to demarcate some instances of violence (and of nonviolence) as justified and legitimate, while others are defined as unjustifiable and illegitimate, despite that most people appear to agree that violence is wrong because it harms, kills, disrupts, and destroys. This raises other questions: Is the assumption that violence is wrong simply an ideological mask worn to hide an underlying understanding that violence is not altogether wrong? Is violence *the way* of humanity or is it only one way among others? In order to begin to address these and related questions, this book considers various ways in which violence and nonviolence are conceptualized and justified from opposed perspectives, addressing many of the traditionally influential theorists who address violence and nonviolence, explicitly or implicitly. In doing so, I mean to reveal fundamental, ideological, political disagreements and how these arise in relation to opposed ideologies that politicized groups tend to share. If I am correct, the result is that, even if there is a widespread, shared belief that it is common sense that violence is wrong and ought not to occur, this agreement ends quite quickly once the means to defeating violence are addressed, particularly due to opposed political ideologies. This is not to suggest that some single political ideology could eliminate disagreements concerning instances of violence, because political ideologies are not static but change in relation to situated contexts, which themselves generate disagreements due to opposed interpretations of those contexts. Instead, disagreements concerning instances of violence demonstrate that a politically neutral conception of violence is likely impossible. A politically neutral conception of violence would be one that reflects an objective, factual understanding of violence in all its kinds that does not bias any perspective, ideology, or political philosophy. A politically neutral conception of violence could be utilized to scientifically study violence, but given the recurrence of human conflicts, particularly political, ideological conflicts, it is unlikely that such a conception of violence is possible. To claim to have a politically neutral and correct view of violence is itself a sort of bias. Any scientific approach toward studying violence is bound to be laden with assumptions about violence, primarily that it is wrong and ought not to occur. This may appear to be a politically neutral stance on violence. However, as soon as we agree that violence is wrong and ought not to occur, there arises political, ideological disagreements concerning what in fact counts as violence, what in fact ought not to occur, and what in fact the means are toward eliminating the violence that ought not to occur.

The same is the case with nonviolence. It might be assumed that nonviolence is at least better than violence, but what counts as nonviolence and what conditions justify its uses are bound to generate disagreements. So a political, ideologically neutral conception of nonviolence is likely to be impossible. From here, I outline some basic ways to begin thinking about violence, nonviolence, and their kinds and, afterward, I define what I mean by the concepts of relationality, ideology, and the political.

First, it is significant to note that disagreements concerning violence and nonviolence arise due to opposed perspectives. From some perspectives, violent actors are considered heroes, freedom fighters, and patriots, and from other perspectives, they are traitors, terrorists, insurrectionists, and criminals. These concepts are themselves complex, insofar as how they are defined or characterized suggests a concrete, comprehensive understanding of what the concepts refer to, but opposed groups can simply usurp concepts for their own ideological purposes. For example, the idea of freedom can easily be utilized by two opposed groups in their actual, physically embodied confrontations. Both groups can think to themselves, "we are free, and we have the true idea of freedom," denying the freedom of the opposed group, who might be characterized as terrorists, traitors, and so on. From their opposed perspectives, they might agree that freedom is of value, and given this, they might think and act upon the notion that "there is no freedom for the enemy of freedom," denying one another's pursuit and embodiment of freedom. Both groups might *think* freedom and agree that terrorists, traitors, etc. are in the wrong, but the groups think these *from their own perspectives*, with their own background ideological assumptions. The concepts of freedom, terrorism, traitors, etc. held by each group can then serve as a reason for justifying their own violence *against* the other. Though opposed in their political views, members of opposed groups can describe themselves by using the same concepts that imply a positive connotation (heroes, freedom fighters, etc.), while describing the opposition by using concepts that imply a negative connotation (traitors, terrorists, etc.). Furthermore, from some perspectives, the systemic structure of the law, the economy, and justice itself can be understood as violent, while others might outright oppose the claim that a system, economy, or justice could themselves be violent. My intention is not to argue for how we should characterize any individual's actions, or group of actors, or historic events, or systems, or structures but is instead to deconstruct influential political ideologies that provide grounds for disagreements concerning violence and nonviolence by accounting for their opposed perspectives.

Second, despite what may seem to be common sense, violence and nonviolence are complex. Even if what counts as violence and as nonviolence seems obvious and commonsensical, commonsense notions concerning what counts as violence and as nonviolence are not as common as might be expected, particularly once political, ideological descriptions and assumptions are considered. For example, it might be common sense that shooting an attacker when being attacked is an act of justifiable self-defense, but as soon as we consider who the attacker is, why the attacker attacked, who the victim is, and why they defended themselves, a vast amount of space opens into which political, ideological disagreements flow. It might be initially assumed that it is common sense that violence is wrong, but once the background ideological frameworks of theorists are considered, we quickly see that the wrongness of violence is not commonsense. An analysis of disagreements reveals the significant, nonneutral, political character of ideological conceptions of violence and nonviolence. In this sense, I mean to contribute to the study of violence and nonviolence the difficulty that researchers face when analyzing these and intend to expand upon the already significant amount of literature that exists by incorporating many of the major arguments that have been produced concerning violence and nonviolence, though not all, for the sake of demonstrating that there is no politically neutral conception of violence and nonviolence. For researchers, it is paramount to account for the political, ideological assumptions that ground a theorist's distinctions between kinds of violence and nonviolence, particularly because how a theorist suggests that violence and nonviolence work as means to ends reveals that theorists are not really committed to the view that violence is essentially wrong. Researchers have to account for their own biases concerning violence and nonviolence. Most any argument that concerns violence and nonviolence, including my own, is perspectival, complex, and nonneutral because the potential for politicized group formation in relation to any ideological comprehension of violence and nonviolence is going to generate disagreements.

Third, any analysis of violence and nonviolence must produce some understanding of what can be characterized and evaluated as violence and as nonviolence, and this, it is hoped, can reveal the extent to which there is *some agreement* concerning what counts as violence and as nonviolence, no matter how minimal that agreement might be. For example, this agreement is likely to rest upon the *normal* view that violence is wrong. This view is normal insofar as it is typically unusual for a person to consider violence as not wrong, particularly when violence is used against a person. However, even if there is agreement, this will not be a politically, ideologically neutral agreement. An understanding of violence and nonviolence requires acknowledging this. I will not attempt to produce a politically, ideologically neutral conception of violence and of nonviolence because I don't think that doing so is possible. If I tried to do that, I would be producing a political, ideological account of how violence and nonviolence *should* be conceived, providing another ground for disagreement. Instead of attempting that, I approach conceptions of violence, nonviolence, and their kinds, as produced by numerous theorists, so that the inevitability of disagreement may rear its head. Nonetheless, my argument will likely generate disagreement, given that some theorists will likely claim to have a correct distinction between nonviolence, violence, and kinds of violence. Perhaps commonsensical grounds for dealing with violence and nonviolence are possible because it is normal to evaluate violence as wrong, but due to disagreements that emerge from such so-called commonsensical grounds, I find this unlikely. Given the political and ideological disagreements that occur, it is difficult to conclude that any general agreement can permanently provide ground for understanding and dealing with violence and nonviolence. However, the wrongness of violence tends to be the most common view, and it is in relation to this wrongness that disagreements concerning violence and nonviolence make sense. There is certainly little hope for violence to be understood simply as wrong and nonviolence as not wrong because violence itself can be characterized as that which defeats the wrongness of violence, and nonviolence itself can be evaluated as wrong by those against whom nonviolence is directed.

Fourth, this appears to imply that there is a possibility for an *endless disagreement*, given that definitions and characterizations produced by theorists that aim to capture the uniqueness of all the kinds of violence and nonviolence ultimately, at the same time, *evaluate* what counts as violence and nonviolence, and thus disagreement emerges typically due to how politically, ideologically influenced evaluations oppose one another. It may be obvious that violence is *wrong* and that nonviolence is *not wrong*, and this seems to be common sense (or that it *should* be common sense). If there is agreement, then this is likely where it occurs. Many people likely evaluate violence as wrong, but that doesn't mean that they won't turn to violence when they find themselves in a situation in which violence becomes a possible course of action, or that is interpreted as the only course of action that can be taken even as a last resort. The numerous authors addressed here, in this context, often assume violence is wrong but almost immediately then justify instances of kinds of violence. It is not my intention to attempt to define whose characterizations of justifiable violence are correct or best. Instead, I mean to show, in part, that any attempt to address violence seems to inevitably play into treating violence as *not entirely wrong*, which undermines the commonsense view that violence is wrong, revealing that perhaps it is not common sense that violence is wrong, and this seems to be the source of the endless disagreements that emerge in analyses of violence and nonviolence. If some violence is not entirely wrong, then theorists can structure their ideological, political frameworks such that these hinge on how this not entirely wrong kind of violence works toward group visions of a good life, such as seen in liberal, Marxist, fascist, and other sorts of political theory.

Fifth, the same can be said of nonviolence. Though nonviolence contrasts violence, which seems to imply that nonviolence is not wrong, once nonviolence is analyzed, particularly in terms of its efficacy as a political action directed *against* an adversary, nonviolence can turn out to be wrong *from the perspective of that adversary*. What counts as nonviolence is likely to generate an endless disagreement. The predicament here is how to address violence and nonviolence without resorting to relativistic, parochial claims, particularly when dealing with political structures, governments, regimes, and groups of individuals. Perspectival, nonneutral disagreements tend to make it seem as though we perhaps don't know much about violence and nonviolence but simply disagree. However, political and ideological disagreement concerning violence and nonviolence does not imply disagreement concerning the wrongness of violence and that nonviolence is not as wrong as violence. In order to address violence and nonviolence, it has to be established that, generally speaking, violence is wrong and nonviolence is not as wrong, because (again) it is only with this assumption that the disagreements make sense at another level of evaluation of violence, kinds of violence, and of nonviolence. These are not my evaluations of violence and nonviolence, but instead, arguably speaking, violence and nonviolence are generally experienced as wrong and not wrong, respectively. However, how true can this be, if some believe that instances of some violence are legitimate and justifiable, and some believe that instances of some nonviolence are illegitimate and unjustifiable? What can we really assume about violence and nonviolence in commonsense terms? It may turn out that we cannot assume much of anything to be true about a theorist's claims concerning violence and nonviolence if their perspective is simply a reflection of the parochial, political ideology to which they most strongly relate. And again, this implies that my own argument cannot achieve objective truth, which is why I mean to avoid claiming that it does.

Sixth, theorists commonly aim to produce conceptions of ways in which group formation occurs, often in opposition to other possible ways that group formation can occur, and in doing so, they typically end up evaluating kinds of violence as justifiable and as unjustifiable, as legitimate and as illegitimate, particularly in relation to other things, such as security, freedom, equality, power, and justice. A paradox emerges when it is claimed that violence is wrong, and it is then claimed that violence is justified as the means to defeating the wrongness of violence. This suggests that, though violence is wrong, when it is used by *particular people in particular ways for the purpose of defeating some other particular kind of violence that is evaluated as wrong in a worse way, the wrongness of violence transforms into its being evaluated as justifiable and legitimate because the wrongness of this violence defeats the wrongness of that violence.* This sort of reasoning is specious. If it is so simple to justify the use of violence by producing ideological, political characterizations of kinds of violence, doesn't this itself reveal that violence is here to stay? For as long as humans engage in actions that can be experienced or interpreted as kinds of violence, other humans will want to stop them, and not even nonviolence can produce a sort of permanent success, given that nonviolence itself can be and has been interpreted as violence.

Now, this seventh point reflects my only attempt to characterize violence and nonviolence, though this is not meant to make an objectively true claim about violence and nonviolence. The most general sense in which violence itself can be described is such that *violence makes way*, in the sense that it cuts through, divides, disrupts, and disturbs. However, it is incorrect to assume that these descriptors indicate that violence is only destructive because violence can also be constructive and constitutive of who and what people, institutions, organizations, and states are, such as in terms of what they become as a result of a momentous violent event. The point is that violence *moves through*. Violence occurs and has consequences. This characterization is necessarily vague and probably allows for too much to count as violence, but it is also useful insofar as this characterization captures much of the nuance found when sifting through definitions and characterizations of violence. For example, when a person exclaims, "Make way!" they are coming through, regardless of what may be, and their coming through will disturb, disrupt, and destroy whatever *was* beforehand, but the result is *something else*, which was constituted based on the past occurrence of the violence that moved through. Violence is like someone recklessly, unapologetically pushing through a crowded room, despite the resistance of the bodies encountered. Similarly, when a fist punches into a face, the contact made is one that impacts the face, making it other than what it would have been had the fist not punched the face. In the first example, there need not be an intention to harm, while in the second there is, but in both cases something happens and *what is* has been changed such that it is no longer what it was, but it becomes different in relation to what had occurred due to the violence. Also consider that a rape is a sexual act that is resisted by the victim but occurs nonetheless, without consent. A person can't want or consent to a rape because, on this view, then the rape would not cut through, divide, disrupt, destroy, and so on. A murder similarly occurs without consent, and a killing would not be considered a murder if the victim desired to be killed, but rather something akin to assisted suicide. A war or invasion likewise makes way through a territory, disrupting what was, and in relation to the war or invasion, people become something other than what they were before. Violence might be that to which we seem to initially say, "No!" because the wrongness of it is not something that one desires to experience. However, instances of violence are often affirmed and are also sometimes considered constitutive of systems, structures, regimes, and government. Violence, in this sense, is a double-edged sword that *makes its way through* but at the same time *leaves a trail of consequences* that emerge because of the violence. Violence makes way, cutting through, but in doing so, it creates a result, which may be a harm, but even that harm can be experienced as constitutive of who or what someone or something is, after the harm occurred. This is not a neutral, objective conception of violence but one that is so vague and general that, though it helps to characterize violence, it fails to do so in a way that can concretely establish what violence itself is as a matter of fact, particularly because numerous things "make way" that we would typically not describe as "violence," such as a knife cutting through butter. However, one can certainly take an approach toward cutting butter with a knife that others from their own perspective might interpret as quite a violent act of cutting butter.

Continuing with this seventh point, nonviolence, which is supposed to be the opposite of violence, also appears to work such that it *makes way*. Nonviolence is a political action that typically aims to address or bring attention to an injustice for the sake of gaining support and ultimately eliminating the injustice. Literature concerned with nonviolence tends to portray nonviolence as not just any action that is nonviolent but one that has a *goal*. This goal tends to be political, insofar as it concerns human relationships. Insofar as a nonviolent political action has a goal and aims toward this goal *as an action*, adversaries may experience the otherwise nonviolent political action as not authentically nonviolent. The adversary can experience the nonviolent action that cuts through and makes way on the streets, in town halls, and at lunchroom counters, destroying or disturbing *what was* (particularly that which the adversary embraces as that which should not be destroyed or disturbed) as violence. Again, this is not a politically, ideologically neutral conception of nonviolence, particularly because there are numerous things that "make way" in relation to a cause that we would not typically characterize as a nonviolent political action. One might have the purpose of driving to the market and do so "nonviolently," but that does not make the driving itself a case of nonviolent political action. Whether the drive is nonviolent also hinges upon how the driving is interpreted, given that a person can quite aggressively drive through traffic without producing what we would typically consider to be harms, rather than going with the flow of traffic, though whether this aggression is violent or nonviolent depends upon one's nonneutral perspective and the situation in which the drive occurs.

So, eighth, common to both nonviolent political actions and to violence is that their *making way* can result in harms, but whether these harms are experienced as harms, and furthermore as violence or as nonviolence, depends on one's political, ideological assumptions. Harm is not always recognized as harm, and sometimes harm can be constitutive, contributing to who or what someone or some group is, and thus, harm is not exclusively destructive. Sometimes it is not until much later that harm is detected, and sometimes the harmful experiences we endure lead to us becoming who and what we are. That is, violence cannot be distinguished from nonviolence by simply looking for whether harm has occurred.

These eight claims together constitute the logic of this argument: there is nonviolence and violence. They can be characterized as distinct, but they are not necessarily distinct. They do things and consequences result, and people produce rationalizations that tend to prefer or to denigrate instances of such actions. This results in controversy and disagreement. Altogether, any understanding of violence and nonviolence must account for the fact that violence and nonviolence are conceived of from perspectives, which makes such conceptions complex, while involving some basic agreement, but also involves endless disagreement, particularly in relation to groups that form in relation to shared visions of some good life that must be achieved, which involves distinctions between positively and negatively evaluated kinds of violence and nonviolence, and violence and nonviolence generally "make way" and produce harms, though harms themselves cannot establish a distinction between violence and nonviolence. From here, I introduce how I think of violence *relationally* by referencing various theorists on the relationality of violence and will do the same in relation to what I mean by *political ideology*. I then outline the overarching argument in more detail, before laying out the structure and content of the book.

Violence and nonviolent political actions are *relational*. Neither occurs in a vacuum, divorced from relationships. Not even the violence of a suicide is nonrelational because the suicidal person utilizes violence in relation to themselves, their situation, and others. It is the relationality of violence and nonviolent political actions that can make sense of what they are within a dynamically unfolding, situated context. It is also this relationality that contributes to violence and nonviolence being nonneutrally understood. How a violent or nonviolent action is evaluated will typically depend upon how one interprets the action in relation to other things. It is often asked, "Why did this violence (or nonviolence) occur?" and some might think that there is no reason for the action, or that violence is "nonrational" in the sense that it is nonsensical, but on the contrary, there is almost always the possibility of discovering some reason why violence (and nonviolence) occurred, and we can find this by considering the things to which the violence (or nonviolence) relates. However, in some cases, it perhaps can occur that the reason for an instance of violence (or nonviolence) is less than obvious to such an extent that, in some cases, a reason might not be uncovered, but this is probably because of the failure to find the reason and not because there is no reason. Likewise, when someone says that an act of violence is "inexplicable," this claim tends to function rhetorically and is probably intended to focus attention only on the wrongness of the violent action (it happened for no discernible *good* reason) rather than allow for a reason that could explain the violent action. To understand a violent or nonviolent action, by considering the relationships within which it has occurred, we can at least begin to understand reasons that explain why it occurred. For example, a so-called *random*, violent attack on people simply shopping at their local market explains the reason for the violent action. The appearance of its randomness can suggest that the perpetrator had a reason to randomly attack random people they are otherwise unfamiliar with simply for the sake of the attack. The attack itself serves as the reason. This is not a circular claim but instead only means to indicate that, in some cases, when we ask why someone attacked a group of individuals that the attacker otherwise does not know, the answer can be that the attacker simply wanted *to attack someone for the sake of doing so*. In some cases, violence occurs for the sake of violence.

In other cases, the reason is often much more obvious. For example, one country attacks another because its leaders openly and explicitly decide to do so in order to gain resources, to defend their country, or possibly simply to demonstrate power and domination over others. The relationships and how they unfold between two countries would need to be assessed. A serial killer chooses their victims because of what and who they are and how the killer relates to the victims. Some perpetrators of violence might legitimately have mental issues that somehow result in them violently relating to others, and these mental health issues can themselves still provide reasons for why the person acted as they did. Of course, mental health can be used as an excuse, that is, as a reason to excuse the violent actions of a perpetrator. So what might at first appear to be a reason that at least excuses the violent action could turn out to be a reason that covers up other, more fundamental reasons for the person's violent action, such as if the perpetrator had a motive and their mental status was not *the reason* for their violent act.

Likewise, though possibly less often, nonviolent civil disobedience might occur simply for the sake of engaging in such an action, though more often it is typical that nonviolent actors make their causes explicitly public by means that include chanting, signs, posters, letters written to members of government, and so on. The point is that, whenever nonviolence or violence occur, they occur in relation to other things, even if they occur in relation to nonviolence or violence themselves, for their own sake. Neither nonviolence nor violence would be what they are as *meaningful* actions and events without their being related to something.

This relationality of violence and of nonviolence is also *political*, insofar as humans are involved in relationships to one another as *vulnerable, physical bodies*, but also insofar as humans in their relationships together strive for goals in terms of a shared conception of some good. Judith Butler emphasizes this vulnerability of the human body in her article "Violence, Mourning, Politics."[4] The body is primary and vulnerable to violence in relation to others, and this relationality is revealed by how, when we lose someone, we lose something of ourselves:

> Each of us is constituted politically in part by virtue of the social vulnerability of our bodies—as a site of desire and physical vulnerability, as a site of a publicity at once assertive and exposed. Loss and vulnerability seem to follow from our being socially constituted bodies, attached to others, at risk of losing those attachments, exposed to others, at risk of violence by virtue of that exposure.[5]

To this statement, it should be added that a nonviolent political action can have a similar effect in relation to vulnerable bodies, even if the people who inhabit those bodies are upholding some status quo injustice, such as racists and sexists intend to do. Even if their vulnerability is based on upholding an injustice, this does not mean that they are not also vulnerable as bodies that exist in relation to others. Relationships constitute who and what each person is, and in these relationships, violence and nonviolence affect a person. In this sense, the body is and is not one's own due to the exposure to the threats that others can be.[6] A person is also vulnerable as a body from the very start, insofar as a person is relationally reliant on others from birth, and thus, the pervasively possible threat of violence (and of nonviolence) influences the constitution of who one is as an embodied individual.[7] Butler adds that

> Relationality [is] not only . . . a descriptive or historical fact of our formation, but [is] also . . . an ongoing normative dimension of our social and political lives, one in which we are compelled to take stock of our interdependence. According to this latter view, it would become incumbent on us to consider the place of violence in any such relation, for violence is, always, an exploitation of that primary tie, that primary way in which we are, as bodies, outside ourselves and for one another.[8]

Butler here defines violence as essentially "an exploitation of that primary tie" that a person has in relation to others as bodies. This is not a neutral definition of violence, given the emphasis on bodies as primary. Also, not every vulnerability is recognizable, and it is in the recognition of a vulnerability that a vulnerability begins to take shape.[9] I take from this the view that, as bodies, individuals exist relationally in vulnerable ways, and these vulnerabilities affect relationships, just as relationships themselves can affect vulnerable bodies, whether those relationships are violent or nonviolent ones. However, it's not as if humans are always a threat to one another in their relationships as vulnerable bodies. Others only produce a potential threat.

I want to retain this view that relationality and the body are primary because this helps to make sense of the politicization of individuals into groups that embrace particular ideological views that influence justifications for particular uses of kinds of violence against other kinds of violence. Also, nonviolent threats to vulnerable bodies might sound incorrect, but simply imagine how organizations that intend to uphold sociopolitical or economic injustices can also engage in nonviolent disobedience for their own goals. It's not as though only those who have right or justice on their side engage in nonviolent political actions, given that "right" and "justice" are themselves concepts that can be understood in a variety of ways. Though nonviolence is often said to be directed against injustices, this need not be the case because what counts as an injustice can itself be contested, and this suggests how nonviolent political actions can themselves be experienced as violent by an adversary.

Butler also addresses this vulnerability of the body in her chapter "Rethinking Vulnerability and Resistance" from the book *Vulnerability in Resistance*.[10] She writes,

> It is not just that this or that body is bound up in a network of relations, but that the body, despite its clear boundaries, or perhaps precisely by virtue of those very boundaries, is defined by the relations that make its own life and action possible. . . . We cannot understand bodily vulnerability outside this conception of social and material relations.[11]

That is, how bodies exist as vulnerable can only make sense if we account for their relationships. If relationships are constitutive of who and what a person is, or at least some relationships are needed for a person to flourish, then any relationship that violates this flourishing could be described as violent, even if it's an otherwise nonviolent relationship. Furthermore, Butler argues that there is an experience of a "linguistic vulnerability," which implies that "who we are, even our ability to survive, depends on the language that sustains us." Name calling, for example, "act[s] on us." She explains that "there is a distinct performative effect of having been named as this gender or another gender, as part of one nationality or a minority, or to find out that how you are regarded in any of these respects is summed up by a name that you yourself did not know and never chose." As a result, "we cannot cast off abiding and governing images, norms, and ideals such as these without losing a sense of who we are."[12] That is,

> We cannot talk about a body without knowing what supports that body and what its relation to that support—or lack of support—might be. In this way, the body is less an entity than a relation, and it cannot be fully dissociated from the infrastructural and environmental conditions of its living.[13]

In other words, humans exist in dependency relationships and, due to these, humans are vulnerable due to the variety of relationships that contribute to their being who and what they are. For example, "when we are unsupported, when those infrastructural conditions characterizing our social, political, and economic lives start to decompose, or when we find ourselves radically unsupported under conditions of precarity or under explicit conditions of threat," we begin to lose something of what we are.[14] Butler adds that we should "understand embodiment as both performative and relational, where relationality includes dependency on infrastructural conditions and legacies of discourse and institutional power that precede and condition our existence."[15] Again, these dependency relationships reveal vulnerabilities that are a part of who we are. That is,

> We are invariably acted on and acting, and this is one reason performativity cannot be reduced to the idea of free, individual performance. We are called names and find ourselves living in a world of categories and descriptions way before we start to sort them critically and endeavor to change or make them on our own. In this way we are, quite in spite of ourselves, vulnerable to, and affected by, discourses that we never chose.[16]

As vulnerable subjects, we are always already subjected to a discourse of categories and conceptualizations that precede and partially contribute to who and what we are, while at the same time, insofar as we exist, we stand in relation to and contribute to this discourse. Last, "as much as 'vulnerability' can be affirmed as an existential condition, since we are all subject to accidents, illness, and attacks that can expunge our lives quite quickly, it is also a socially induced condition, which accounts for the disproportionate exposure to suffering, especially among those broadly called the precariat for whom access to shelter, food, and medical care is often quite drastically limited."[17] In short, Butler's point is that

> vulnerability is not a subjective disposition. Rather, it characterizes a relation to a field of objects, forces, and passions that impinge on or affect us in some way. As a way of being related to what is not me and not fully masterable, vulnerability is a kind of relationship that belongs to that ambiguous region in which receptivity and responsiveness are not clearly separable from one another, and not distinguished as separate moments in a sequence; indeed, where receptivity and responsiveness become the basis for mobilizing vulnerability rather than engaging in its destructive denial.[18]

This relationality constitutive of vulnerable, embodied existence is inextricable to being human, and violence and nonviolence each affect this relationality, revealing the vulnerability of such embodied existence. The name calling that Butler refers to won't necessarily be commonly described as violence, but if it exploits a person's vulnerability in some way, then what might otherwise be nonviolent can turn out to be violent.

I also address the relationality of violence in my "On the Politicization of Violence Within Reductive and Non-reductive Accounts of Violence," notably utilizing the work of authors, such as Edith Stein, Alfred Schütz, and Michael Staudigl, among others.[19] The argument of this article follows the claim that each individual has a "Paradigm Case Core Conception of Violence" (hereafter, PCCCV), which is an individual's unique way of conceiving of violence "constituted by what each [individual] experiences and interprets as cases of violence."[20] This view sounds correct insofar as not every individual experiences the same set of instances of violence, but instead, for each individual, their "PCCCV is a continuously developing, inductive list of instances of actions, events, and relationships that an individual interprets as . . . violence." Because each PCCCV exists based on an inductive gathering together of experiences had, each is necessarily incomplete because an individual can always experience instances of violence not previously experienced and can thus expand their PCCCV. Furthermore, despite that everyone has their own PCCCV based on their own limited number of experiences, an intersubjectively shared PCCCV is possible, and the PCCCVs of individuals can "overlap," producing a potential for politicized group formations, though it is unlikely that any two PCCCVs could be precisely the same. However, even if such groups form, "no two individuals have exactly the same PCCCVs [*sic*], since each has unique experiences of and relationships to phenomena interpreted as violence."[21]

Following Michael Staudigl, I emphasize that "experiences of violence are *contextual, perspectival, and relational*."[22] I reference Staudigl's description of how the body's experience of kinds of violence affects what things mean and how the meaningfulness of things affects the body's experience of violence:

> *Physical* violence . . . not only affects the objective body, but also the lifeworldly idealizations of our "I can" and therefore our habitual openness to the world. Conversely, *psychological* (e.g., verbal) violence always has an effect on our bodily movement in our surrounding social world and on our "orientation" in it. *Structural* violence . . . interferes in the habit formation of the subject, thereby creating "docile bodies" that silently accept the discriminating social (e.g., legal) structures that shape them and their possibilities of (self-)perception, interpretation, and action. As for *cultural* violence, it attacks the "collective bodily existence" of the subject, i.e., the silently shared patterns of its inter-corporeal existence alongside which the individual "I can" primordially develops and realizes itself in a pre-given cultural nexus. Thus, . . . different forms of violence attack the different ways in which we realize and understand ourselves as irreducibly embodied beings.[23]

In this sense, from Staudigl, violence is "*both affective/bodily and symbolic/meaningful*," which I interpret such that "violence always affects, is related to embodiment, and bestows sense, or is itself meaningful, even as that which destroys."[24] Furthermore, in relation to the phenomenological accounts of "Edith Stein on the body and empathy as conditions for intersubjectivity," and Alfred Schütz on "commonsense constructs," "typicalities," and "the taken for granted," I mean to "reveal what is shareable among PCCCVs . . . [and] how we influence the development of one another's PCCCVs via empathic relationships, contributing to shared conceptions of violence."[25] Ultimately, I argue that "*because we cannot get at violence itself, and can only interpret violence in its relations, which involve humans, we therefore cannot avoid politicizing our conceptions of violence in our empathic, intersubjective relationships*." For example, from Schütz, I point to how "shared 'common-sense thinking' constitutes a 'we' insofar as the 'we' is 'everyone whose system of relevances is substantially (sufficiently) in conformity with yours and mine.'"[26] Any knowledge of what is typical or paradigmatic "is contingent; there are only interpreted facts [that are either understood from within their context or as 'detached from their context by an artificial abstraction']. The objective, anonymous knowledge held by a 'we' is historically contextualized."[27] Based on this view, I argue that "the extent to which PCCCVs are shareable [or overlap], even within a group such as a political party, is limited because each individual experiences their own unique, contextualized life, sometimes empathizing with the experiences of others."

I also point to Stein's description of "empathy as an embodied individual's non-primordial experience of another's primordial experience," such that, "through empathy, . . . a relationship between I and you, a 'we' is experienced" due to having an idea of "*what it is like*" for an embodied individual to experience something.[28] Through empathy, intersubjectivity is possible because one individual can understand that another individual experiences the *same* world, but in a *different* way.[29] I contend that "in addition to first-hand experiences [of violence], I can empathize with the experiences of violence that others have without replacing my own understanding of violence with theirs, but instead, adding what I experience to my own understanding of violence." This shows that a PCCCV must be an incomplete, "inductive list of paradigmatic cases of violence," because it is always possible to experience novel kinds of violence not experienced before, particularly through the empathic relationship to another's experiences or due to having such experiences oneself. This does not imply that, over time, we altogether develop some ideal PCCCV that ultimately arrives at a final definition of violence because full agreement on what violence itself is cannot be possible because "individuals typically are already oriented toward their own understanding of what counts as violence" and they need not empathize or can even refuse to understand what another experiences as violence. Based on these things, I argue that "because of the primary role played by empathy in intersubjective, embodied relationships that occur within historically embedded and influenced socio-economic contexts in which individuals relate to individuals, communities, structures, parties, institutions, organizations, systems, and states, we should expect that conceptions of violence are typically, non-neutrally political."[30] There is not likely to ever be one universally accepted way to define and to evaluate instances of violence, no matter whether these are physical, structural, psychological, cultural, or symbolic. It is unlikely that all or even most individuals would ever totally share one conception of what violence itself is. I state,

> *Alone*, we each understand violence in relation to what we have experienced, what we take as typical, or for granted, or as commonsense, and *together* we empathically construct intersubjective understandings of violence, but we cannot escape the political nature of violence insofar as violence is relational, contextual, and perspectival, and we are always already influenced by others, including predecessors, parties, public institutions, governmental organization, and communities in general.[31]

Rather than further discuss my argument that outlines a diverse set of theorists whose work on violence is either "reductive" (in the sense that the theorist typically only focuses on violence as instrumental) or "nonreductive" (in the sense that a theorist conceives of violence as not only instrumental), it suffices to acknowledge the four points that I claim should be taken from my argument. First, "we should avoid reducing the concept of violence" to the assumption that it is only instrumental and always wrong because violence can be "constitutive of things [such as structures and systems], and not always in instrumental, or wrong ways."[32] Second, political disagreements concerning what counts as violence reveal that, "from perspectives, violent actions and events are defined *in relationships to other things*, which do not themselves define violence. Violence is a relational phenomen[on]." Third, McCreery "generate[s] an inductive list constitutive of a PCCCV." The list is descriptive and inductive and is only one possible PCCCV among many:

> Violence can be instrumental, and rational in relation to short-term goals . . . , violence can be neurologically defined in relation to prototypical instances [of violence], and pragmatically justifiable, though wrong . . . , violence can be normatively justifiable as defensive violence, despite its wrongness . . . , violence can be liberal or Marxist, an imposed expectation, a negation of consciousness, and evil . . . , violence lacks a universal form but can be generalized as a violation, or as an impairment of human life, violation of integrity, violation of vulnerabilities . . . , violence brings about negative effects, is unnatural, unlawful, decomposed, an unconditioned affirmation of freedom, an affirmation of a right, Manichaean, a demand, non-physical, linguistic, symbolic . . . , violence can be constitutive of meaning, destructive of meaning, subjectifying and de-subjectifying, and is always related to the body . . . , violence is hubristic, relational, and phenomenal . . . , and . . . nonviolence cannot be clearly distinguished from violence conceptually, or in practice.[33]

The point that I make in relation to this necessarily incomplete list is that, whether an individual agrees with none of it, some of it, or all of it, the individual takes a political stance in relation to others with whom the individual may or may not agree, particularly in relation to actions and events interpreted as violence. "Interpretations of and responses to violence are politically non-neutral, as each individual or community interprets individual instances of violence in their own ways, influenced by their situatedness in an unfolding historical context of empathic, intersubjective relationships."[34] Within relationships, individuals emerge as who and what they are, sometimes sharing conceptions of things counting as violence, particularly insofar as individuals are embodied and, as such, vulnerable. Relationality, the political, embodiment, and vulnerability themselves together constitute a basis for understanding disagreements concerning violence. Likewise, the same is true of nonviolence.

My fourth point is that even if we can empathize with how others understand and distinguish between kinds of violence, this "does not in principle mean that one shares with the other precisely the same PCCCV, or political ideology." And this leads me to argue that a politically neutral definition of violence is probably impossible because any individual's PCCCV arises from within their own "historically-influenced, intersubjective contexts." In the end, I mean to nonreductively define violence "as that which *makes way* for a flood of meaning and interpretations, or that opens up a void into which individuals assert their interpretations, contributing to the sense [that is, the meaning] of violence." This "makes way" is what I referred to earlier. This implies that, even if all people understand violence instrumentally, and as that which produces some sort of harm, we should at the same time always keep in mind that what counts as violence and as distinctions between kinds of violence are essentially contestable, particularly because violence can also be conceived of in noninstrumental ways that also "make way," even nonviolently. This is important, in my view (and will be expanded upon later), primarily because *we should always remain open to the fact that what we might initially consider to be an instance of justified violence or nonviolence could always turn out to be other than what we first think it to be.*[35] In short, it is wise to be cautious of one's own assumptions concerning violence (and nonviolence) because such assumptions are likely to have been influenced by one's empathically enabled, intersubjectively politicized experiences that occur in relation to others concerning what is "typical" of or "taken for granted" about violence. That is, "*we cannot get at violence itself, and can only interpret violence in relations*," which means that we "*cannot avoid politicizing our conceptions of violence in our empathic, intersubjective relationships*."

Now, in terms of political theory, violence understood as a relational phenomenon helps us to understand disagreements between political theories insofar as, commonly, political theorists aim to produce conceptions of political communities that *share a vision of some good*, a part of which involves the absence of violence, or at least some kinds of mechanisms that aim to ensure that violence occurs to the least extent possible or is directed against those who threaten the political community, internally or externally. Such mechanisms include militaries, police, and even basic agreements, as they are found in traditional notions of social contract theory, which are addressed later. Humans are not minds floating around in bodies relating to one another at some mental level, or at least humans aren't primarily minds, but rather human existence is embodied, and it is in relation to human bodies that the threat of the wrongness of violence is most obvious. The suppression of the threat of violence is often that which serves as a unifying principle within political theory. As bodies, humans relate in their everyday actions, doing as humans do. In their relationships, the political emerges. *The political is anything that involves a group of humans in relationships in which decisions occur concerning how those relationships ought to be.* Typically, those relationships are not considered violent ones, and how the political is conceived by a theorist is also typically in terms of how to avoid and suppress violent relationships. What counts and does not count as violence, and as kinds of violence, is a politically ideological disagreement, which is likely impossible to resolve, particularly because the political itself is soaked with disagreement, and from political, ideological perspectives, violence is not only defined but is also evaluated in ways that oppose one another. Tyrannical regimes, fascist regimes, liberal regimes, communist regimes, and so on are each theorized in ways that operationalize violence and nonviolence by defining kinds of violence that serve as a sort of lynchpin within a theory. As will be discussed later, political ideologies, insofar as they define distinctions between kinds of justifiable violence and unjustifiable violence, produce the conditions for an ongoing disagreement, despite the general, commonsensical view that violence is wrong.

In terms of *ideology*, this concept has been utilized in various ways since its inception, so I explain the way in which I use the term when I refer to "political, ideological disagreements." George Lichtheim provides an outline of the ways in which "ideology" has been used over the course of history in his *The Concept of Ideology*.[36] I only highlight some of the more general developments indicated by Lichtheim in order to point to a variety of ways that the concept of "ideology" has been conceived of and used, particularly in relation to its positive and negative connotations. Initially, Antoine Destutt de Tracy coined the term *idéologues* while a member of the *savants*, who were tasked with managing the Institut de France, which was meant "to provide France with a nation-wide system of higher learning committed to the philosophy of the Enlightenment."[37] These *idéologues* impressed Napoleon Bonaparte, who became an honorary member of the Institut in 1797. Given his support, they in turned helped him to ascend to power. However, Bonaparte would later turn against them when the teaching of liberal and republican ideas was seen by him as a threat to his despotic rule. These ideologists "were liberals who regarded freedom of thought and expression as the principal conquest of the [French] Revolution." Lichtheim describes a "twofold character of the liberal 'ideology,' as a system of normative ideas and as an incipient critique of the very notion of absolute norms," which is found in Destutt de Tracy's work as a "*Science des idées*," which aims to "describe the natural history of the mind" based on biological terms rather than religious ideas.[38] Foregoing much of the detail of Lichtheim's historical outline, the point is that the *idéologues*' influence reflects a confidence in "the power of rational thought."[39] This positive connotation implied by the concept of "ideology" would soon change, as it did when Bonaparte turned against the *idéologues*, but particularly due to Georg Wilhelm Friedrich Hegel's "German ideology," which was "a reaction against the theory and practice of the French Revolution."[40] Hegel's critics would later return to the French Enlightenment's "naturalist critique of theology and metaphysics." Lichtheim argues that "the problem of ideology (in the sense of 'false consciousness' or 'imperfect consciousness') arises for Hegel because in his view individuals, and even entire nations, are instruments of history, executors of a process whose meaning is concealed from them, and which becomes selfconscious [*sic*] only *post festum* in the philosopher who sums up the sense of the epoch."[41] Hegel's critics saw "his teachings on Right and the State . . . as the 'ideology' of the political status quo: its intellectual projection and justification."[42] Speculative philosophy was seen as the obstacle to philosophy achieving its goals of "liberty and rationality," which led to Karl Marx (in part influenced by Ludwig Feuerbach) conceiving of ideology as a combination of "Hegel's insight into the transitory character of the successive manifestations of Spirit, and Feuerbach's materialist inversion of Hegel, with its stress on the this-worldly character of natural science." Like Hegel, Marx believed "that cognition gives access to universal truths not present in immediate experience," such that "history makes sense" because "the historical process vindicates Reason because it can be understood."[43] Marx conceived of ideology in terms of "false consciousness," as opposed to "true consciousness which will enable men to understand their role" in history.[44] Every time period has its "ideology," which is historically found in the ways philosophers respond in their efforts to understand reality: "Marx . . . held that the philosophy of every age is the 'ideological reflex' of determinate social conditions." In this sense, approaches to understanding human reality in its historical contexts are "ideological" because "participants fail to comprehend the situation in which they are involved."[45] So "ideology" refers to humans attempting to but struggling to think the reality of their lived existence. That which lacks "true consciousness" is ideological and, thus, the term bears a negative connotation.

From Friedrich Nietzsche's work, Lichtheim emphasizes how, for Nietzsche, "*unmasking*" occurs when ideologies are critiqued so that their illusions can be revealed.[46] "History for [Nietzsche] . . . is a masquerade . . . in the sense that men drape their 'real' biological drives and goals in idealist costumes. All thought is ideological; its unconscious function is to serve the life process." Nietzsche, in Lichtheim's view, considers the distinction "between 'objective' and 'ideological' thinking [to be] . . . meaningless: all thought is a species of poetry, and the real Being of the world remains irreducible to discursive reasoning." In this sense, it can be said that the possibility of "true consciousness" is itself ideological. Lichtheim also points to Max Weber, arguing that there are two meanings of "ideology" because "the term . . . can signify both the consciousness of an epoch and the 'false consciousness' of men unaware of their true role."[47] However, with Weber, ideology is relativized in relation to how each culture will have "its own norms and values which enter into the perception of what is called 'reality.'"[48] Lichtheim argues that the "problem of 'false consciousness' arose from the awareness that the various possible standpoints [from which 'the rationality of history [could] be perceived by the intellect'] were inadequate as well as incompatible."[49] That is,

> The attempt to discern a logic of history [over the past two centuries] was more than an idle play with concepts: it responded to a practical purpose which in our own age has become more urgent as the globe shrinks, and historically divergent and disparate cultures press against one another. Because these pressures are experienced as ideological conflicts among people holding different and incompatible aims in view, it remains the task of the critical intellect to evolve modes of thought which will enable men to recognize the common purpose underlying their divergencies. . . . In this perspective, *the transformation undergone by the concept of ideology appears as an index to the tension between the actual historical process and a critical consciousness nourished by the traditions of classical rationalism.*[50]

In relation to our contemporary period, Lichtheim argues that "ideology" is "synonymous with any kind of consciousness that can relate itself to the ongoing activity of a class or group effective enough to make some sort of practical difference."[51] So "an understanding of what is involved in the concept of ideology is thus at the same time an exercise in that historical imagination which enables us to see our predecessors as men engaged in an enterprise whose outcome still concerns us."[52] Though I have avoided the rich detail that Lichtheim covers in his article, the point should be clear. Ideology concerns ideas and their pragmatic effectiveness in the lived world. *The attempt to understand what humans are, what their goals can be, and how to make this understanding "fit" the lived, unfolding historical process is what makes a political theory ideological.* In this sense, a political theory is always already ideological.

In relation to violence and nonviolence, we can consider how such phenomena are situated within various political theories to unveil the ideological views of a theorist concerned with envisioning some shared conception of a "good." For example, in Thomas Hobbes's *Leviathan*, as is addressed later, he is clearly concerned with how the presumably frightening violence of humanity's natural condition serves as a causal mechanism that springs individuals forth toward the decision to submit obediently to the decisions made by a sovereign in exchange for protection from that violence.[53] Hobbes's idea of humanity's natural condition serves as a premise from which an entire perspective on government's role in relation to its subjects derives. There is, in this sense, a "science" or *logos* of ideas. The logic of an idea, such as Hobbes's view that humans are naturally selfish, implies an entire network of ideas constitutive of a political philosophy. Hobbes operationalizes the violence he conceives of as essential to humanity's natural condition. This operationalization grounds his entire work. Disagreement with his conception of humanity's natural condition implies possible disagreements with much of the rest of his work. As will be addressed throughout this book, we can dissect theoretical approaches to understanding violence and nonviolence in this way. Theorists tend to define and operationalize basic conceptions of violence and nonviolence and outline how these imply networks of ideas constitutive of their political philosophies, in relation to which political group formations occur within the scope of a conception of some shared "good" that ought to be achieved. Analysis of this tendency enables the unveiling of fundamental, nonneutral, politically ideological disagreements concerning violence and nonviolence.

This understanding of ideology as a sort of science of ideas concerned with how human understanding can best reflect actual, human existence and relationships as they unfold in history is basically confirmed in 2006 by Bo Stråth, who outlines a way to think of what ideology itself is in his *Ideology and History* such that "ideologies can be seen as cognitive structures with legitimizing functions."[54] Stråth outlines relevant works from numerous authors very closely to what Lichtheim does. His main points concerning what an ideology is and what it does are sufficient to address. In Stråth's view, ideology is, in various ways, seen as representing something, making it appear, though how representation occurs and what it is "has become problematic to say the least."[55] As examples, Stråth points out that "the language of globalization and the ideas of clashes of civilizations are sufficient evidence of the role of ideologies, in the form of master narratives, with totalizing ambitions or pretensions of being *the* explanation of the world." Stråth claims that

> instead of taking ideologies as pre-given they must be critically deconstructed and contextualized. Their emergence must be historicized and their appearance must be understood much more in terms of opposition, discontinuities and contradictions, internally as well as externally, than in terms of cohesion and continuity.

This is what I mean to do in this book. By critically examining the role played by violence and nonviolence within the work of a political theorist, we can uncover fundamental disagreements that arise from disparate political ideologies, which demonstrate the essential contestedness of the concepts of violence and nonviolence that exists beyond paradigm cases of violence and nonviolence. Stråth adds that "the critique of ideologies becomes part of the ideological debates and the deconstruction of myths becomes at the same time the construction of new myths. In such processes of de- and re-construction there is no final end and history has no direction but becomes contingent and open."[56] So my argument will inevitably fall into this trap, becoming a part of the ideological debate, and perhaps constructing a new myth concerning violence and nonviolence. Either way, I mean to openly acknowledge this trap. By considering the contestable character of the concepts of violence and nonviolence, beyond paradigm cases, my argument cannot itself avoid participation in this contestedness. However, I do mean to avoid relativizing violence and nonviolence too much, which is why it is important to emphasize that violence is commonly considered by most people to be concretely wrong, particularly in terms of paradigm cases of violence, such as rape, murder, torture, and so on. Likewise, a nonviolent protest is typically not necessarily evaluated by everyone as wrong, given paradigm cases of protesters simply "sitting-in" or walking down a street for the sake of demonstrating their interest in the achievement of some cause. In other words, we generally agree that there are things that are definitely, in their concrete existence, violent and others that are definitely, in their concrete existence, nonviolent, but the disparate and opposed political ideologies demonstrate that agreement stops with the paradigm cases.

As an example of a "strong ideology" that strives to be a master narrative that describes the world as it is, Stråth points to nationalism, which has had "many different forms of expression and political action guidelines across the European surface based on a great variety of ways to mix socialist, liberal and conservative ideological arguments."[57] Also, ideologies can be and are used to communicate and mobilize communities, though not necessarily in only one way.[58] As Stråth puts it:

> Instead of treating ideologies as more or less fixed, socially shared, belief systems persistent over longer times and with more or less cohesive and consistent groups of adherents, they should be historicized and contextualized through an analytical focus on the speech act situations where power positions are established through the appropriation of key concepts and their ensuing interpretative power. This perspective on historians and ideologies contains an ideology-critical deconstructivist dimension.[59]

A simple example of how key concepts are appropriated, contextualized, and interpreted in various ways that establish "power positions" is the concept of "freedom," which is contested insofar as freedom for some people means something like the ability to be and express themselves as they consider themselves to be, such as in terms of race, ethnicity, culture, and gender, while others appropriate freedom as indicative of how they should be free from those who express themselves in ways that they dislike or disagree with. Ideology functions such that commonly utilized ideas are embedded within theoretical frameworks that expand from what those ideas are characterized as, what they mean, and how they ought to be brought into practice in the world, or not. Then they are acted upon, just as a particular kind of nationalism or freedom can result in politicized group formations that themselves constitute enacted movements that have real consequences in the world.

Stråth also addresses ideology in his chapter "Ideology and Conceptual History," published in the *Oxford Handbook of Political Ideologies*.[60] Again, Stråth's argument is similar to Lichtheim's, so it suffices to indicate his main points on what ideology is. For one thing, Stråth argues that "ideology escapes definition" because how it is used changes in relation to context and historical developments.[61] In order to analyze "ideology from the viewpoint of conceptual historical methodology," it must be recognized that the term "ideology" has been given meaning in a "contentious process" from the start, which is because "politics in democratic societies [which are 'based on general agreement on certain key concepts like democracy, freedom, solidarity, welfare, progress, etc. but on deep disagreement when it comes to giving substance and content to these concepts'] is not about consensus but about conflict and the search for compromises." When Napoleon used the term politically and polemically against the *idéologues*' arguments, their "ideas became synonymous with illusion and self-deception." To arrive at facts, ideology was critiqued, and the term began to imply "a particular form of illusion, a belief in the power of ideas in politics and world history." So rather than only indicating a science of ideas, the term "ideology" also came to be "a condescending catch-word that served to demarcate political enemies."

Then, over the course of the nineteenth century, "ideology became a label for unrealistic theories that tried to intervene in the spheres of government and political action," though the term still "retained its original meaning of a scientific discipline." The term "ideology" continued to be used derogatively such that it was typically used to label enemies rather than oneself or one's group. From 1900, however, the concept of "ideology" itself would become value neutral, and "value was infused" when terms were amended to it, such as "socialist, liberal, conservative, nationalistic, false, and right."[62] The result was that "ideas and ideologies were increasingly understood as the products of groups, part of cultural milieus that shaped and were shaped by human activities," which means that "they had to be taken seriously." Thus, "from this point on ideologies were analyzed in the discipline of history of ideas as long, coherent chains of thought." Fascism, Nazism, and Stalinism, for example, "were fundamentally built on ideologies," and democratic ideologies could be analyzed in relation to those in order to find similarities and differences.[63] A part of this includes the emergence of "the end of ideology school," which saw the defeat of totalitarian regimes "as marking the end of attempts for world ideological domination."

Stråth outlines how "totalitarian" was conceived as an ideology by Giovanni Amendola (in 1923), Giovanni Gentile (in 1946), Benito Mussolini (in 1935), Franz Borkenau (in 1938 and 1940), Isabel Patterson (in 1943), E. H. Carr (in 1946), Karl Popper (in 1945), and Hannah Arendt (in 1967).[64] He argues that "the converging view on totalitarian ideology about a totalitarian society combined a fierce and aggressive nationalism, a cult of the leader, terror and physical violence, and a myth of juvenile regeneration that resurrected past glories [which] . . . gave rise to fascism, Nazism, and Stalinism."[65] Furthermore, "the fall of the Soviet empire . . . was seen in ideological terms as a new divide," though some, such as Francis Fukuyama (in 1992), argued that ideologies were disappearing along with history. In contrast to this, "a new strong master narrative emerged around a semantic field of concepts such as globalization, neoliberalism, market economics, freedom, and citizenship." Common to the prominent ideologies of the twentieth century was that they had "a clear teleological message concerning a goal-bound process."[66] So there were ideologies concerned with a "unified world," but then there were ideologies concerned with "a clash of civilizations and wars of religion," as well as "the European ideology based on imaginings of a European identity and European unity and diversity." When Stråth published his article in 2010, "The war of religions ideology remains strong and has undergone further evolution in the direction of nationalism, populism, and racism." His main point is that "from the perspective of conceptual history there is no reason to believe in the end of ideologies or the end of history. Ideological attempts to master the world form a story with permanent challenges and no end, where ideology must be seen in plural." However, in the 1980s, there was a linguistic turn that "connected to a new methodological and epistemological approach," and ideologies from then on would be analyzed in relation to "struggles for discursive power based on the appropriation of the priority of interpretation of key political concepts and the occupation of semantic fields." As Stråth puts it, "the goal was the right to define and identify problems and their solutions. . . . In such contexts patterns of affirmations, negations, and repressions were apparent in processes by which one definition emerged as more or less dominant." From this, "the result was . . . a conceptualization of a field that always contains multiple and contested meanings." Concepts, such as freedom, security, rights, etc., are commonly utilized by adherents to an ideological way of thinking, but in different ways within arguments that oppose one another. So even if such concepts and their definitions were supported by a general public, division resulted, given other ways in which such concepts can be conceived of and defined.[67] So in Stråth's view, "ideology is a concept that is still very much alive. . . . The term is seen simultaneously as an instrument that provides orientation and initiates political action and as an instrument to control the world manipulated by the powers that be or want to be." Ideologies, in this sense, "do not represent an objective external reality," but they still aim to "make sense of the world" while remaining "contested categories in a flux." So, again, there is no one way to define "ideology" because it has been employed in various ways since its start, but we can analyze how an ideology, in terms of the "science of an idea," plays out within the historical context in which it emerged as a way of thinking about reality, though no such ideology ever perfectly matches reality. With conceptions and definitions of violence and nonviolence, this is where the political ideology of a people matters most. In relation to the legitimacy of an act of violence or nonviolence, given the core ideas of a people who share some ideological vision of a good that they believe should be achieved among themselves, an entire network of implications follows, and this often orientates and incites action toward a goal. This does not mean that their ideological vision of a good reflects true reality but could still be clouded in illusion and falsehoods. In the United States, in relation to the events of January 6 and the "Stop the Steal" ideology, for example, the claim that the election was stolen from Donald J. Trump continues to orient and incite the actions of "MAGA" ["Make American Great Again," that is, Trump's well-known campaign slogan] even if numerous judges have found little evidence of fraud that would have changed the results of the election in Trump's favor. Despite that some of those judges were appointed by Trump himself, his supporters continue to believe and act upon the ideological belief that the election was stolen. Those who do not support Trump and deny the truth of this ideology might refer to it in a condescending way, arguing that it is an illusion, based upon unrealistic theories, clouded by delusional conspiracy theories.

For a third account on what "ideology" is, Hannah Arendt (who, being Jewish, fled the Nazis from Paris in 1941) provides an explicit demonstrations of how totalitarian ideology functions as the science of an idea that leads those who embrace it to the point of willingly sacrificing themselves for the sake of the ideology. In "Ideology and Terror: A Novel Form of Government," Arendt argues that an ideology basically explains everything that pertains to the view of the person who has the ideology.[68] For example, if a person believes that there is a *historical* war between economic classes, or a *natural* war between races, then we can make sense of a person's view and actions who believes in such ideologies. So an ideology is the logic of an idea that studies the history of the idea's implications, while treating history as following some "law."[69] However, because ideologies concern historical transformations, they are not scientific. Instead, the idea of an ideology becomes a means of explanation and can be used to understand history based on the logic of the idea, and a movement results.[70] In other words, there is first an idea and from this idea, a premise can be derived, and this brings an actual, enacted movement of people to fruition such that whatever they do occurs in relation to the logic of the idea to the extent that anything that contradicts the logic of an idea is prohibited and, thus, the logic of the idea becomes productive. In short, an ideology follows from the assumption that one idea explains everything from a premise and everything is interpreted in relation to the one idea such that no experience may teach anything that opposes the logic of the idea. In this sense, because ideologies subject everything to an idea, they are totalitarian.

Arendt's examples, Joseph Stalin and Adolf Hitler, demonstrate how the idea that underpins an ideology is converted into a foundation for a totalitarian body politic.[71] For both, either History or Nature decides who should die, in terms of a class war or a race war, respectively. Furthermore, commitment to an ideology implies commitment to other things, particularly the preparation of individuals to be either victims or executioners in relation to the ideology. This occurs to the extent that, for example, the Bolshevik's purge forced fearful victims to confess to crimes they never committed. Furthermore, once a person submits to the logic of an ideology, their freedom is lost due to being tyrannized by the logicality of the ideology. Such a person is dominated by the premise of the idea and they are no longer free to think, but instead, they are made to feel responsible for the ideology's movement as History or as Nature. Due to the terror that is the essence of totalitarian governments, individuals are lonely and lack relationships with others that are meaningful from outside of the logic of the totalitarian ideology because the terror that is at the core of this ideology ruins the possibility of meaningful relationships between fearful people.[72] Such totalitarian governments also prefer individuals who fail to distinguish between truth and falsity or who think that there is no such distinction. Such individuals only conform and obey. When isolated in their loneliness, individuals are also impotent and unable to act in concert. In the sense of Arendt's view of "the political," if individuals are unable to act in concert, then they lack political power and are reduced to *animal laborans*, that is, people who merely labor and who are valued only because they labor because they are unable to fabricate anything new that would change the world. Isolation is insufficient though because we often work in isolation, so it is really loneliness that is experienced as totalitarianism's tyranny over individuals. Isolated from one another by a totalitarian government that promotes fear, private life is further destroyed as individuals become lonely and experience not belonging to the world. So fearful loneliness is the foundation or the terror that is the essence of totalitarian government and its ideology. The lonely experience superfluousness and uprootedness as they experience not belonging to the world and not having a place in it, respectively. This loneliness is not solitude, however, because in solitude, one at least has oneself, while in loneliness, one loses one's own self and loses trust in oneself, which weakens the possibility of forming meaningful relationships with others. This loneliness experienced prepares individuals for totalitarian domination because then such individuals are prepared to embrace a logic of totalitarian ideology. Doing so occurs because individuals then believe their lives to be meaningful in relation to the totalitarian ideology. Lonely individuals turn to the principles of totalitarianism because it gives their lives meaning in relation to the movement of History or Nature, but their lives are only meaningful in relation to totalitarianism and not in relation to other humans. Individuals are not even allowed to be isolated because in isolation a person might think for themselves and make decisions that oppose the totalitarian government. Totalitarianism is total in the sense that it does not allow for such social conditions but instead means to keep individuals in a condition of loneliness so that they only relate to the logic of the totalitarian regime's ideology. That is how the logic of an idea plays out, in Arendt's view. From the basic notion that Nature or History itself is a movement, particularly in terms of how a race or class will inherit the future, an entire network of other ideas is implied, such as that one must not turn against Nature or History because then one would become a victim of the movement. So the point to take away from Arendt is that, based on the logic of a core idea, an entire network of ideas and actions follow, and this is what is meant by "ideology" in this book. I mean to argue that, due to opposed political ideologies, around which groups form in relation to a shared vision of some "good," which is based on some core idea or ideas, no conception of violence or of nonviolence is politically neutral, except perhaps the basic notion that violence is wrong and that nonviolence is not entirely wrong, or at least is not *as wrong as* violence.

An excellent example of how the logic of an idea implies a premise from which a movement follows is found Arendt's *Race-Thinking before Racism*:

> Race-thinking, with its roots deep in the 18th century, emerged during the 19th century simultaneously in all Western countries. Racism has been the powerful ideology of imperialistic policies since the turn of our century. It certainly has absorbed and revived all the old patterns of race opinions which, however, by themselves hardly would have been able to create or, for that matter, to degenerate into racism as a "*Weltanschauung*" or an ideology. For the "idea" of race does not belong in the history of ideas, and not until the end of the last century were dignity and importance accorded it as though it had been one of the major spiritual contributions of the Western world.[73]

Arendt goes on to outline how race-thinking developed into racism as an ideology, but her point is as previously stated, namely that the idea of race plays out as a premise that implies an entire series of considerations, policies, and action. In terms of an ideology, she points to how some opinions that made a significant impact "proved strong enough to attract and persuade a majority of people."[74] An ideology is unlike an opinion, though, insofar as an ideology "claims to possess either the key of history, or the solution of all the 'Riddles of the Universe,' or the intimate knowledge of the hidden universal laws which are supposed to rule nature and man." In this article, Arendt again points to two prominent ideologies, namely, "the ideology which interprets history as an economic struggle of classes, and the other that interprets history as a natural fight of races." As such, we can retrospectively see how history has led to the present condition in which these ideologies continue to function "as . . . political weapon[s] and not as . . . theoretical doctrine[s]."[75] Ideologies certainly change over time, but they remain alive because they are in "immediate contact with political life."

However, as Arendt says, "Ideologists who pretend to possess the key to reality are forced into changing and twisting their opinions about single instances according to the latest events and never can afford to come into conflict with their ever-changing deity: reality. It would be absurd to ask reliability of people who by their very convictions are bound to justify any given situation."[76] So, like racism and its origins in race-thinking, which Arendt argues had more to do with social hierarchies and economics than with race itself, a seed can be planted in relation to an idea that is then defined dynamically in relation to the unfolding conditions in which the ideology is utilized. Today, for example, we might look at how concepts pertaining to globalism, nationalism, patriotism, freedom, rights, equality, security, terrorism, violence, nonviolence, the "far right," the "far left," and so on are consistently upheld but not as static ideas and instead as ideas that play out over time, based on what they imply, and they don't necessarily imply one way of thinking or acting. If racism is something understood and embraced, racial conflict follows. Likewise, if a conception of violence or of nonviolence is defined or characterized in a particular way, then this implies a series of consequences. For example, if a theorist only defines violence instrumentally, then this will essentially lead that theorist's ideology to come into conflict with other theorists who refuse to only reduce violence to its instrumentality. In relation to whether one agrees or not that violence is only instrumental and is never noninstrumental, political groups form in relation to some shared conception of a "good." Those who reject the possibility of systemic or structural, noninstrumental violence may overlook injustices and violations of human rights as a result, dismissing them as nonsensical because such things don't fit with their ideological beliefs. Politicized groups may not see it as evident or necessary to bother with addressing claims concerning noninstrumental violence, and hence the political, ideological disagreements emerge with the possibility of leading to actual conflict.

The point is that violence and nonviolence are contested concepts for which no nonneutral definition is possible. The argument of the book is as follows: It is common that violence is viewed as wrong, particularly insofar as it harms the vulnerable body. As embodied persons, individuals mean to protect themselves from this wrongness of violence. People desire security. To make sense of how individuals can protect themselves from violence, theorists conceive of means to this end, such as in terms of social contract theories and nonviolent political action. However, in doing so, theorists at the same time introduce systems, structures, states, organizations, and institutions that themselves can be defined or characterized as violent, insofar as their effect upon embodied individuals is harmful physically, psychologically, economically, socially, culturally, religiously, or in some other way. The very answers that theorists often give as solutions to violence can themselves, from other perspectives, turn out to be violent. The wrongness of violence is seen as that which must be stalled, thwarted, and destroyed, and other *kinds* of violence are defined as legitimate means to defeating the wrongness of violence. Defensive violence, military violence, police violence, and so on are often defined and characterized as the means by which the wrongness of violence itself is defeated. Individuals either agree with these definitions and characterizations or not, based on whether they embrace their underlying ideologies, that is, how an idea of violence is characterized or defined and how that then plays out in efforts to defeat or transform some kind of violence. Insofar as individuals agree on some things, they are potentially politicized as a group or community in opposition to those who disagree and who are themselves potentially politicized as a group or community. So the ways in which these ideologies of violence nonneutrally play out in relation to opposed, politicized groups can be analyzed, revealing the weaknesses of such political ideologies, insofar as they fail to "solve" the problem of violence that a theorist means to address. Each individual in their embodied existence relates to others with whom they either agree or disagree that particular instances of kinds of violence are legitimate and justifiable. Each individual also has a limited experience of instances of violence. Firsthand experiences of a variety of kinds of violence are likely less often shared than secondhand experiences of violence as witnesses and are even more likely less often shared than thirdhand experiences of violence that occur through mediums, such as photographs, the internet, television, and so on. That is, hearing about or seeing violence that is not immediately experienced, but is instead experienced through some medium, is probably more common than secondhand experiences in which one directly and immediately experiences violence, which is probably more common than one's actual engagement in a firsthand experience of violence as a perpetrator or victim. Either way, the limited number of experiences of violence, and the variety of ways in which violence is experienced, means that when one person *thinks* violence, they are likely not thinking *the same* as another person does when they *think* violence, though they are likely to be thinking of the *wrongness*. Therefore, this being the case, and because the wrongness of violence is indeed commonly a reason for avoiding violence, *distinguishing kinds of violence as legitimate and justified can never be a politically neutral distinction to make.* Groups of individuals, based on what they agree upon in terms of their rejection of the wrongness of violence, can and do form together in opposition to other groups of individuals who themselves agree upon their rejection of the wrongness of violence, but from their own, opposed perspective.

In the following, the first chapter outlines definitions for a commonsense view of violence produced by Joshua Greene and Jason Brennan, arguing that there are incontestable instances of violence that are *almost* universally agreed upon, such as when an adult intentionally smashes a child's head against a table, purposefully causing harm. It is also claimed that, because political, ideological distinctions between kinds of violence arise from the creation of moral equivalences to a commonsense view of violence, political ideology is the source of disagreement concerning what violence is and what instances of violence are. The second chapter argues that conceptions of violence and of the political are essentially contested. Walter Bryce Gallie's criteria for what counts as an essentially contested concept are utilized in order to argue that violence is an essentially contested concept at the level of the political, though not at the level of the commonsense view of violence that is based on the wrongness that is commonly attributed to violence. In fact, the paradigm cases that the commonsense view of violence pertains to serve as the core cases that are then interpreted as kinds of violence at the ideological level. To define violence as altogether wrong or to define kinds of violence as acceptable and others as wrong is itself a politically ideological move to make, such as when liberalism defines its own uses of violence as justified and legitimate and its enemy's violence as unjustifiable and illegitimate. The World Health Organization and Vittorio Bufacchi's definitions for violence are presented, as are the definition for terroristic violence defined by Thomas Nagel. Verena Erlenbusch's critique of a liberal view, such as that of Nagel and the World Health Organization, is addressed as a reflection on the fact that, beyond the commonsense view of violence, violence is an essentially contested concept for which an ideologically, politically nonneutral definition is unlikely. The third chapter outlines numerous definitions produced by various philosophers, historians, and theorists, such as Machiavelli, Arendt, Hobbes, Kant, Treitschke, Weber, Bakunin, Sorel, Žižek, and Benjamin. Their definitions demonstrate their political ideological assumptions, demonstrating an ongoing disagreement, in the sense of Rancière's formulation for what counts as a disagreement such that each theorist defines kinds of violence from the perspective of their own political ideology. They all might agree that a single act is violent, under the commonsense view of violence, but they disagree concerning what kind of violence it is. So though they may point to the same events and actions as examples of violence, what they mean fundamentally differs due to their respective political ideologies. This disagreement shows that there is no neutral justification for the neutrality of a state, particularly if a neutral state must defend itself. The state is instead defined in historically contextual terms of how the state relates to kinds of violence, and the distinctions between kinds of violence are not themselves politically, ideologically neutral. So the concept of violence, beyond the commonsense view that is based on paradigm cases of violence, is an essentially contested concept for which a nonneutral definition is unlikely. Beyond the commonsense view, political ideology is inextricably bound up within distinctions between kinds of violence. The fourth chapter[77] then examines arguments concerned with the question of whether nonviolence counts as a kind of violence. If distinctions between kinds of violence are essentially contested and nonneutrally defined, and nonviolence is defined as distinct from violence, then it follows that nonviolence is an essentially contested concept for which no nonneutral definition is possible, at least beyond a commonsense view of nonviolence. A commonsense view of nonviolence is the assumption that nonviolence is not violent in the way that the commonsense view defines violence based on paradigm examples of violence. That is, nonviolence occurs when there is no action or event that most people would define as a violent one. Definitions for nonviolence, civil disobedience, nonviolent political actions, and nonviolent direct actions are then outlined. These definitions aim to show that the doctrine of nonviolence does not merely refer to nonviolent acts but to a strategy that is a means to defeating kinds of violence. Given that what counts as the nonviolence that defeats violence is ideologically a matter of disagreement, nonviolence, in this sense, can count as a kind of violence. The final chapter concludes, raising questions concerning how violence can be valued other than as wrong, the degree to which a state cannot neutrally justify its neutrality, and the degree to which, beyond the commonsense view of violence, there ever could be agreement concerning what counts as kinds of violence.

NOTES

1. Ted A. Smith, *Weird John Brown: Divine Violence and the Limits of Ethics* (Stanford: Stanford University Press, 2015).

2. Kevin J. O'Brien, *The Violence of Climate Change: Lessons of Resistance from Nonviolent Activists* (Washington, DC: Georgetown University Press, 2017).

3. Ibid., 4.

4. Judith Butler, "Violence, Mourning, Politics," *Studies in Gender and Sexuality* 4 (2003): 9–37.

5. Ibid., 10.

6. Ibid., 15.

7. Ibid., 20.

8. Ibid., 16–17.

9. Ibid., 30.

10. Judith Butler, "Rethinking Vulnerability and Resistance," in *Vulnerability in Resistance*, ed. Judith Butler, Zeynep Gambetti, and Leticia Sabsay (Durham: Duke University Press, 2016), 12–27.

11. Ibid., 16.

12. Ibid., 17.

13. Ibid., 19.

14. Ibid.

15. Ibid., 21.

16. Ibid., 24.

17. Ibid., 25.

18. Ibid.

19. Gregory McCreery, "On the Politicization of Violence within Reductive and Non-reductive Accounts of Violence," *Human Studies* 43 (2020): 269–89.

20. Ibid., 269. This book discusses the paradigm case core conception of violence at length.

21. Ibid., 270.

22. Michael Staudigl, "Topics, Problems, and Potentials of a Phenomenological Analysis of Violence," in *Phenomenologies of Violence*, ed. Michael Staudigl (Leiden: Brill, 2013). See also Michael Staudigl, "Towards a Relational Phenomenology of Violence," *Human Studies* 36 (2013): 43–66.

23. McCreery, "On the Politicization of Violence," 283; Staudigl, "Topics, Problems, and Potentials," 52.

24. McCreery, "On the Politicization of Violence," 283–84.

25. Ibid., 271. See also Edith Stein, *The Collected Works of Edith Stein, Volume Three: On the Problem of Empathy*, trans. W. Stein (Washington, DC: ICS Publications, 1989). Also see Alfred Schütz, "Common-Sense and Scientific Interpretation of Human Action," in *Collected Papers 1: The Problem of Social Reality*, ed. M. Natanson (Boston: Martinus Nijhoff, 1962).

26. McCreery, "On the Politicization of Violence," 272.

27. Ibid., 272. McCreery quotes from Schütz.

28. Ibid., 272–73.

29. Ibid., 273.

30. Ibid., 274.

31. Italics added.

32. Ibid., 287.

33. To produce this inductive list of characterizations of violence, McCreery references numerous theorists, many of whom are addressed later in this book.

34. Ibid., 288.

35. Ibid., 289.

36. George Lichtheim, "The Concept of Ideology," *History and Theory* 4 (1965): 164–95.

37. Ibid., 165.

38. Ibid., 167.

39. Ibid., 169.

40. Ibid., 170.

41. Ibid., 172.

42. Ibid., 173.

43. Ibid., 174.

44. Ibid., 175.

45. Ibid., 176.

46. Ibid., 183.

47. Ibid., 184.

48. Ibid., 185.

49. Ibid., 193.

50. Ibid., 193; italics added.

51. Ibid., 194.

52. Ibid., 195.

53. Thomas Hobbes, *Leviathan: With Selected Variants from the Latin Edition of 1668*, ed. Edwin Curley (Indianapolis: Hackett Publishing Company, 1994).

54. Bo Stråth, "Ideology and History," *Journal of Political Ideologies* 11 (2006): 23.

55. Ibid., 38.

56. Ibid., 39.

57. Ibid., 39–40.

58. Ibid., 40.

59. Ibid.

60. Bo Stråth, "Ideology and Conceptual History," in *Oxford Handbook of Political Ideologies*, ed. Michael Freeden, Lyman Tower Sargent, and Marc Stears (New York: Oxford University Press, 2013), 3–19.

61. Ibid., 3.

62. Ibid., 10.

63. Ibid., 13.

64. Ibid., 13–14.

65. Ibid., 14.

66. Ibid., 15.

67. Ibid. 16.

68. Hannah Arendt, "Ideology and Terror: A Novel Form of Government," *The Review of Politics* 15, no. 3 (July 1953): 303–27.

69. Ibid., 316.

70. Ibid., 316–17.

71. Ibid., 315.

72. Ibid., 310, 322–23.

73. Hannah Arendt, "Race-Thinking before Racism," *The Review of Politics* 6, no. 1 (January 1944): 36–37.

74. Ibid., 38.

75. Ibid., 39.

76. Ibid., 59.

77. I draw on ideas and passages that appeared in "The Efficacy of Scapegoating and Revolutionary Violence," in *Philosophy, Culture, and Traditions: A Journal of the World Union of Catholic Philosophical Societies*, ed. William Sweet, 10 (2014): 203–19. I am grateful to the editors of the journal for permission to draw on this material.

Chapter One

A Commonsense View of Violence

1.1 INTRODUCTION: A COMMONSENSE VIEW OF VIOLENCE

There is a difference between a commonsense view of violence and distinctions between kinds of violence. A commonsense view, in the sense meant here, typically defines violence as a physical means intentionally used by a person to produce physical or psychological harms, destruction, or death. It is common sense that most agree that such an action or event is an instance of violence. For example, most agree that intentionally smashing a person's head against a table for the sake of causing harm is an instance of violence. Most people react to such actions and events by defining them as violent ones. Likewise, hitting, punching, slapping, beating, torturing, raping, murdering, shooting, exploding, and other things that harm, destroy, or kill a person or group of people, physically or psychologically, fall under this commonsense view of violence. These are paradigm cases of violence. Furthermore, most people evaluate such actions as wrong.

Disagreements arise when we claim that, although violence is wrong, an instance of violence is not wrong because it is justified, or when distinctions between kinds of violence are defined. The issue is that, though there is common agreement that violence, in paradigm cases, is wrong, indeed is the paradigm of wrongness, there is disagreement concerning what kinds of violence are not wrong, and how kinds of violence are to be distinguished. For example, one might claim that defensive violence is not wrong but is legitimate and legal, but another can question whether an instance of violence is defensive, and thereby can define the violence as illegitimate and illegal. So there is common agreement on the wrongness of the paradigm cases of violence, but there is disagreement concerning what counts as equivalent to the paradigm cases of violence.

A commonsense view of violence is based on the uncontested fact that there are paradigm actions and events that all agree are instances of violence. The paradigm cases serve as those kinds of actions that are raw examples that are commonly agreed upon as counting as instances of violence. The action or event is itself, at the same time, conceptualized as "violent." However, as noted in the previous paragraph, there is disagreement concerning when violent actions and events are equivalent to things like self-defensive violence, legitimate violence, and oppressive violence. An argument should be produced in order to demonstrate that a violent action is equivalent to self-defensive violence, but only examples can be given, inductively showing that major accounts of this kind are political. When a person has demonstrated that an act of violence is equivalent to self-defensive violence, for example, the person has produced a justification for that act of violence by claiming that it is not equivalent to paradigm cases. Though violence is entirely wrong, according to a commonsense view, the act of violence that is defined as morally equivalent to self-defensive violence is justified. Justifications built upon equivalence claims like this one move away from the paradigm cases that define violence as wrong. As another example, when a theorist defines some violence as legitimate, the theorist defines its legitimacy in moral equivalence relationships to other things, such as freedom, justice, or the existence of a state. These moral equivalence definitions for kinds of violence produce definitions for violence that do not unite the concept of a kind of violence to the act of violence in the same way that paradigm cases do. Instead, because violent acts and events are defined as equivalent to other things, which are then defined so that these violent acts and events are justified, these definitions serve as grounds for disagreements. Unlike the paradigm cases, for which the act or event itself is that which defines them as paradigm cases, distinctions between kinds of violence extend the concept of violence, relating instances of violence to some things, while detaching some other instances of violence from those same things.

For example, in the context of slavery in the United States, John Brown's 1859 raid of Harper's Ferry in Virginia, which involved violence in the form of people being shot, in accordance with the paradigm examples of violence, can be defined as a justified kind of violence by producing moral equivalence relationships to other things, such as self-defense. The violent actions of Brown and his raiding party could be defined as terroristic, or as emancipatory by relating it to other things, such as to an attack on the United States, or to the higher and antiviolent good of the abolition movement, respectively. The violent actions of the soldiers, likewise, can be defined as oppressive or as legitimate in relation to the experiences of slaves or to the United States, respectively. So a paradigm case core conception of violence is that which is agreed upon, and distinctions between kinds of violence extend this view of violence to other things, producing moral equivalence relationships between some acts of violence and some other things.

Ted A. Smith discusses at length how, despite the general agreement that violence occurred at the raid on Harper's Ferry, John Brown's actions were understood in disparate ways.[1] In *Weird John Brown: Divine Violence and the Limits of Ethics*, Smith refers to Marilynne Robinson's novel *Gilead*, in which the old man narrator "remembers his grandfather had provided a safe house for Brown. . . . For the grandfather's generation, Brown was the prophet who made the faith come alive. Brown's violence was a kind of sacrament, making manifest the presence of God in the world. For the next generation, though, Brown was the fanatic who had caused violence on a massive scale."[2] Robinson also, according to Smith, points to the generation that follows this one and how this "third generation . . . displays more ambivalence, neither celebrating Brown nor rejecting him but trying to make sense of him. The narrator himself is part of this generation. He refuses his grandfather's flat identification of Brown's violence with the work of God and his father's refusal to entertain any possibility of divine violence."[3] Furthermore, according to Smith, Brown himself described "the violence that he did and the violence done to him as part of a process in which the land was purged of its sins with blood. For Brown, the significance of violence extended beyond any chain of this-worldly cause and effect. It was part of an eschatological history of redemption. Brown's critics have seized upon this remark as a sign of fanaticism."[4] So it should be clear that this one example indicates an agreement that a paradigm case of violence had occurred during the raid on Harper's Ferry, but the agreement ends there, not only between Brown and his critics but across generations.

The point here is that there is a paradigm case core conception of violence, and there are distinctions between kinds of justifiable violence. Individuals can agree that a paradigm case of violence has occurred, but the agreement ends there. I hope to show that, in the case of all the standard major philosophical accounts of violence, these distinctions between kinds of violence are produced by theorists in relation to political ideologies that oppose one another. As indicated in the preface, an ideology is the "science of an idea" and how it serves as a premise that leads to holding particular views and engaging in actions in relation to the ideology. An ideological belief in white supremacy, for example, leads a person to have certain beliefs about things and to engage in kinds of actions that relate to their ideological belief. Insofar as such ideologies are shared among collectives of individuals, they are political. Altogether this shows that, despite agreement upon paradigm cases of violence, violence, in the standard philosophical literature, is an essentially contested concept due to the dependence of each conception of violence on opposed political ideologies that fundamentally disagree within one another.

Though there is generally no disagreement at the level of the paradigm case core conception of violence, distinctions between kinds of violence are essentially contested. Furthermore, agreement with a distinction between kinds of violence is a belief in that distinction and does not eliminate the essential contestedness of conceptions of kinds of violence that are not themselves the paradigm cases of violence. In other words, agreement with a distinction between kinds of violence suggests one's political ideology, though not necessarily. Agreement with a distinction between kinds of violence does not, in principle, mean that one shares the same political ideology as the person who defines distinctions between kinds of violence. Political ideology reflects a belief in a distinction between kinds of violence. However, because there are various, opposed ways that kinds of violence can be defined in moral equivalence relationships to political ideologies, definitions of kinds of violence are not neutral. A neutral definition would be one that does not favor any political ideology. Because distinctions between kinds of violence are produced from the perspectives of theorists situated historically in their respective contexts, a neutral definition is not possible. This suggests but cannot establish that a neutral distinction between kinds of violence cannot be achieved, given opposed distinctions between kinds of violence. The argument here is necessarily inductive, based on the extant theories of violence. But the pattern strongly suggests that no alternative account of violence that extends beyond the paradigm cases will not also be dependent on political ideologies. So, in short, my thesis is that, in consideration of a necessarily incomplete set of examples of definitions that define violence as equivalent to other things, it is likely that no defined kind of violence is politically neutral, except, perhaps, the paradigm case core conception of violence, which defines actions as violence based on the wrongness of intentional uses of physical means for the sake of causing physical or psychological harms or destruction. This list is necessarily incomplete because novel ways of defining violence can always be produced by defining violence as equivalent to other things. Because this list of definitions is necessarily incomplete, the conclusion cannot be proven with certainty. However, in relation to one another, definitions for kinds of violence show that the concept of violence is essentially contested. And because any essentially contested concept is not politically neutral, no definition for violence is politically neutral.

In order to analyze commonsense views of violence, the definitions of commonsense views of violence produced by Joshua Greene and Jason Brennan are discussed next. Greene argues that the human brain neurologically defines what counts as commonsensical, "prototypical" violence, and Brennan focuses on what he considers to be the commonsensical wrongness of violent killings. Brennan means to argue that private citizens are justified to use defensive violence against government agents and officials, even in liberal democracies. Once their arguments are discussed, then it is shown that their definitions agree at the level of the paradigm case core conception of violence but disagree when their respective discussions concerning violence move beyond the paradigm conception of violence, thereby becoming non-neutral, politically ideologically speaking.

1.2 JOSHUA GREENE ON THE MORAL PSYCHOLOGY OF PROTOTYPICAL VIOLENCE

In his book *Moral Tribes: Emotion, Reason, and the Gap between Us and Them*, Greene argues that humans have a "dual-process" moral brain, neurologically at work, automatically producing emotional gut reactions, on the one hand, and manually reflecting upon those automatic reactions, rationally calculating what should be done, on the other.[5] He means to argue that the dual-process theory indicates that humans should adopt "deep pragmatism," that is, a utilitarian, manual-mode approach to compromising and cooperating with collectives of people ("Them") who are not of our tribe ("Us").[6] In order to show that people neurologically, automatically, and emotionally react to uses of personal, violent force in particular, Greene utilizes the Trolley Problem, which was first introduced by Philippa Foot, and later discussed by Judith Jarvis Thomson.[7]

For our purposes here, only two versions of the Trolley Problem are needed, namely the switch dilemma and the footbridge dilemma. In the switch dilemma, a trolley is running down a track toward five people, and the subject has the option of throwing a switch so that the trolley goes onto an alternative track but kills one person. In the footbridge dilemma, a trolley is running down a track toward five people, and the subject is standing on a footbridge next to a man wearing a backpack and has the option of pushing this man in front of the trolley so that his backpack and body stop the trolley from killing the five people. In both cases, one person is killed so that five can live. A utilitarian, rational calculation would have the subject decide to save the five people in both cases. However, participants in studies are typically unwilling to push the man from the bridge (only 31 percent said they would push the man), but are typically willing to throw the switch (87 percent said they would throw the switch).[8]

Using the data he gathers, Greene argues that the different responses produced by subjects are due to the human brain's ventromedial prefrontal cortex (VMPFC) and amygdala, which are responsible for emotional responses.[9] Greene had people read and respond to the switch and footbridge dilemmas while their brains were scanned using functional magnetic resonance imaging (fMRI). In the switch dilemma, there is only the utilitarian commitment to serve the greater good, which is an unemotional calculation. However, in the footbridge dilemma, because the subject is directly pushing the man with the backpack to his death, the automatic, emotional response to this action provides an explanation for why people are typically unwilling to push.

In both dilemmas, there is an increase of activity in the VMPFC (an emotional response is triggered), but in the case of the footbridge dilemma the increase is greater and the result is less people willingly pushing one person to his death in order to save five.[10] In contrast, in the switch case, there was increased activity in the dorsolateral prefrontal cortex (DLPFC), which is responsible for cognitive control ("the ability to orchestrate thought and action in accordance with internal goals").[11] In the switch dilemma, despite that the studied subjects *know* that they are killing one person to save five, 87 percent of them find this acceptable *because they do not touch the person who is killed.*[12] In contrast, in the footbridge dilemma, the subjects directly touch the victim who is pushed to his death, which explains why only 31 percent are willing to push.[13] The footbridge case is "personal," and the switch case is not. In the end, Greene argues that the studies show that "emotional responses *cause* people to say no to the footbridge dilemma."[14]

The evidence produced from these studies leads Greene to argue that his dual-process moral brain theory is confirmed. The human brain has automatic, emotional settings and a "manual mode" that is cognitive control.[15] The automatic settings are efficient and inflexible because they immediately respond to stimulants and consistently respond in the same way. The manual mode is inefficient but flexible because it more slowly thinks through what the person experiences and can do to achieve goals, evaluating positives and negatives in utilitarian terms. Emotions are fast and automatic in the sense that a person cannot choose to have an emotion but can only trigger that emotion by thinking of things that bring the emotion about.[16] Emotions, however, also exert pressure on what a person does, or is willing to do, despite what the manual-cognitive-decision-making mode would tell the person to do.[17] Reasoning and emotions are not independent from another because emotions can influence what a person decides to do, and decisions can trigger emotions. However, a person can reject emotional urges through the use of manual-mode cognitive control.[18]

What is common among people, Greene assumes, is that they generally want to have *positive experiences* and tend to have the same kinds of automatic, emotional, moral settings, such as "empathy, anger, disgust, guilt, shame, and discomfort with certain forms of personal violence."[19] Pushing a man from a bridge is a use of personal, physical force, which is commonly, negatively reacted to. Pushing a man from a bridge is not an experience that people typically want to have (69 percent of the time, according to results of the footbridge dilemma). The significant factor that makes a difference toward why people are willing to switch the trolley to a different track and kill someone to save five but are not willing to push a man from a footbridge to save is "the direct application of *personal force* (pushing vs. hitting a switch) and whether the victim is harmed as a *means versus side effect*."[20] That is, the studies show that what matters is how these factors are combined. Eighty-seven percent of people approve of using personal force that indirectly kills someone as a side effect (the switch dilemma). When a person is directly harmed as a means but not through a use of personal force and instead as a side effect (such as when the switch is thrown and the trolley kills one instead of five), this is also acceptable to most people. However, "if you harm someone as a means *and* you use personal force, then the action seems wrong to most people," as with the footbridge dilemma.[21] Commonly, the use of personal force in order to cause direct harm upon another person produces an emotional reaction that influences the decision not to use personal force that will cause direct harm. These are paradigm cases of violence. Most people agree that these acts are violent, and most people refuse to engage in them because most people consider such acts to be wrong.

An issue that arises, for Greene, concerns the fact that many of the things we do *not* do result in harm to others. However, he argues that people typically consider harms caused by direct actions, and as results of uses of means, to be worse than harms of omission, which occur when certain actions are not performed.[22] His reason for this lies in the means versus side effect distinction. For example, people would typically not directly starve a person to death but will allow it to happen anyway, fully knowing that there are starving people in the world. Such people do not act toward alleviating starvation and thereby indirectly, and possibly unintentionally, cause harm, but this harm is a side effect of each person's pursuit of his or her own goals. Omissions, such as not feeding starving people, may produce worse harms than direct actions, such as directly starving one or a few people, but Greene's point is that the brain plans and is goal oriented, which means that it is not thinking of all the things omitted from the plan and its possible side effects. Instead, the brain only thinks of a limited number of actions performed as a means to goals. A person's ability to think of only a limited number of things when planning actions as means to goals indicates that a person is unable to think of all the things she is *not* doing or that *might* happen as side effects.[23] This indicates that "harmful omissions don't push our emotional moral buttons in the same way that harmful actions do."[24] Omissions are not directly enacted, so they do not trigger the automatic, emotional response. So, commonly, in Greene's view, people automatically, emotionally respond to direct uses of personal force as a means to producing harm and not to omissions or side effects.

Greene's evidence for the existence of a commonsense view of violence arises from his inference that humans commonly have an *alarm system* that automatically tells them what *not* to do and that protects people from the vengeance of others, and stops them from engaging in indiscriminate uses of violence, thereby supporting cooperation. "An automated antiviolence system in our brains" makes it possible for people to inspect action plans, assessing possible means to goals, for the sake of avoiding being casually violent because, emotionally, people take seriously their own direct uses of personal violence as means to goals.[25] This alarm system stops us from engaging in what could be dangerous plans.

Greene adds that "to say that this automatic alarm system responds to violence probably gets things backwards. . . . [Instead,] our conception of violence is *defined* by this automatic alarm system."[26] That is, people like the 69 percent of subjects who automatically, emotionally reject the violence of pushing a man from a footbridge have an emotional response that defines what counts as violence. Increased activity in these areas, when deciding what to do with the footbridge dilemma, means the brain neurologically and emotionally responds in a causal way. However, neurologically, we are not all the same.[27] As his studies show, if some part of the brain has been damaged, then whether a person rejects uses of personal force depends upon whether the person's emotions are functioning "normally" in the way the emotions of the 69 percent, who rejected pushing the man from the footbridge, function.

The antiviolence alarm system, Greene adds, "may respond more to harms caused using personal force not because personal force matters per se, but because the most basic nasty things that humans can do to one another (hitting, pushing, etc.) involve the direct application of personal force."[28] "The most basic nasty things" are included in the things people can do, and these are the negatively evaluated, rejected instances of "the direct application of personal force," which implies that there is nothing nastier than this direct use of personal force that a person could do. In this sense, "our alarm gizmo responds to actions that are *prototypically violent*—things like hitting, slapping, punching, beating with a club, and . . . pushing."[29] This prototypical violence that our brain's "alarm gizmo" automatically, emotionally responds to is a direct use of means of personal force for the sake of causing harm. Prototypical violence corresponds to what has been thus far referred to as paradigm cases of violence.

However, Greene adds that anyone whose "antiviolence gizmo" does *not* function in this way is abnormal.[30] "If you don't *feel* that it's wrong to push the man off the footbridge, there's something wrong with you," he writes.[31] The "antiviolence gizmo" *normally* functions as a part of the planning of means toward goals, tracking direct uses of personal force and the active harms that may result, such that the passive, indirectly produced harms that result from side effects and omissions matter less. This is a neurological claim, and not a prima facie moral or political one. Most people, normally, refuse to perform actions that require their own personal use of direct force for the sake of causing harm. This refusal is the core response that identifies the immediate negative evaluation of violence, on which all accounts of violence depend.

For example, one person is sacrificed in the switch dilemma, but Greene does not criticize those who decide to throw the switch as having something neurologically wrong with them. He assumes that what is normal, neurologically speaking, is what most people exhibit. In the switch case, the death of one person is a side effect, and because this does not produce increased activity in the areas of the brain responsible for emotion, it is "normal" for people to decide to throw the switch. However, by claiming that there are normal people, he implies a group of abnormal people. Despite that 31 percent were willing to push the man from the footbridge, these people are abnormal and have something wrong with them, neurologically speaking.

1.3 DOES THE AUTOMATIC ANTIVIOLENCE SYSTEM PROVIDE A COMMONSENSE DEFINITION FOR VIOLENCE?

The prototypical violence defined by Greene fits a paradigm case core conception of violence. If one responds to prototypical violence, automatically and emotionally rejecting it, then one is normal, descriptively speaking, and also has a normal, commonsensical view that intentional (direct) uses of physical means (personal force) for the sake of producing physical harms should not be used. However, Greene does not address psychological harm. Psychological harm might not be thought of as a consequence of one's actions. Instead, the harm might result from the use of hurtful words. Such harms might be kinds of "side effects," and so perhaps they produce no emotional impact when one decides how to act or speak, but Greene's studies do not address this.

If there is an alarm gizmo that automatically, emotionally responds to intentional, active, and direct uses of personal force that results in harm, then this provides evidence for a commonsense view of violence. However, even if there is a normal, commonsense view of what counts as violence at the neurological level of an automatic, emotional rejection of kinds of actions that characteristically involve a use of personal force as a direct means to harming someone, the commonsense view and the automatic, emotional rejection of kinds of violent actions do not address the fact that prototypical violence is also that which can be defined as a normal, good, legal, and legitimate means to use. This also does not capture other ways that harms are produced unintentionally and nonphysically. Distinctions between defined kinds of violence do capture these other ways of defining kinds of violence. That is, distinctions between kinds of violence do explain how what might otherwise count as abnormal uses of personal force for the sake of causing harm can count as normal, and even as desirable. So the automatic alarm gizmo corresponds to a paradigm case core conception of violence, which can count as a commonsense view, but beyond this, the automatic alarm gizmo does not explain how instances of paradigm cases of violence are normatively justified.

In Greene's study, 69 percent refused pushing the man in front of the trolley, and 31 percent chose to push the man because the wrongness of the action did not produce emotions that were strong enough to lead them to *decide* not to push the man. This decision to save five by pushing one takes place manually, as a rational utilitarian calculation, but Green argues that this is abnormal, given the results of his research. If Greene is correct that emotions cause decisions, then those who decided to push the man from the footbridge were either able to transform a negative emotion associated with pushing the man into a positive one, or they were unable to have the emotional response in the first place. If the studied subjects did have the negative emotion, then it seems that the goal of saving the other five people overrode the strength of this emotion, but the neurological studies do not explain why or how this happens. At the level of the definition of prototypical violence and a commonsense view of violence, this revaluation of the negative emotional response to an act of violence into something positive is neurologically abnormal. However, at the level of distinctions between kinds of violence, these kinds are evaluated as not entirely wrong in ways that transform the abnormal into a justified kind of violence, which appears to be just what the 31 percent did when they decided to push the man to his death.

Greene bases his distinction between normal and abnormal responses to violence on the authority of his scientific studies. His focus on prototypical violence, as defined by the automatic antiviolence system, limits his ability to make sense of why people still choose to use and justify violence. He can only claim that those who push the man from the bridge are abnormal, if they do not feel that it is wrong to do so.

Like the paradigm case core conception of violence, Greene negatively evaluates violence based on the increased activity in the VMPFC that occurs in 69 percent of the studied patients. The paradigm case core conception of violence evaluates violence as wrong but does not need neurological evidence of increased emotional activity in the brain in order to do so. The paradigm case core conception of violence is defined by those actions and events that most people consider to be wrong. Greene argues that a person is abnormal if they do not feel that it is wrong to push the man. This may be descriptively accurate. Normatively, the wrongness of the pushing of the man from the bridge does not necessarily follow from his evidence. There is only increased activity in the VMPFC, which amounts to brute scientific data that might explain why people choose not to perform certain actions. Whether or not this data indicates the normative wrongness of prototypical violence itself is not necessarily within the scope of his data. So when Greene says that those who do not feel this wrongness are abnormal, he points to the paradigm case core conception of violence, but why we need this neurological evidence in the first place is questionable, given the ordinary agreement concerning paradigm cases of violence.

Because the automatic antiviolence system demonstrates increased emotional activity in the VMPFC, it is not clear that it defines prototypical or a commonsense view of violence in the way Greene claims. What would be interesting is to see what happens when the studied participants are asked by researchers about performing actions that are not captured by the paradigm case core conception of violence, but that might still be claimed to count as violence. For example, some might claim that violence occurs when a person draws a cartoon of something offensive (such as of a religious figure performing a perverted act), or when someone is unable to afford the medication that would save their life. Perhaps the choice would be for the participant to decide whether to draw the cartoon, or whether to withhold the funding that the person needs to afford their medication. The point is that it is not clear that this automatic antiviolence system would reject these actions, which some people might count as kinds of violence. The trolley problems already involve what many would consider an act of violence that falls under the paradigm case core conception of violence. So it is not clear that the automatic antiviolence gizmo can tell us very much about violence beyond the paradigm case core conception. Perhaps it does, perhaps not, but the paradigm case core conception of violence persists. Most people would agree that pushing a person to their death is itself a violent act and wrong, and whether or how they emotionally respond to having to decide to kill a person may be relevant to understanding why violence is wrong, but this emotional response does not itself explain cases of some people "abnormally" choosing to engage in violence by pushing the man to his death in order to stop the trolley and save five people.

In the next section, Jason Brennan's argument concerning the justification for uses of defensive violence is discussed, particularly in light of the distinction between violence as a wrong and violence as not wrong. As soon as we begin to distinguish between whether violence is wrong or not wrong, we are no longer defining violence itself and have moved beyond the paradigm case core conception of violence. Given that distinctions between kinds of violence no longer address violence itself, there is disagreement between opposed distinctions between kinds of violence, politically ideologically grounded in the way that distinctions between kinds of violence are related to other things. The automatic alarm gizmo does not address or explain how kinds of violence are evaluated as justifiable.

1.4 BRENNAN ON KILLING AS DEFENSIVE VIOLENCE

Jason Brennan produces a definition for a commonsense view of violence in his article "When May We Kill Government Agents? In Defense of Moral Parity."[32] Brennan's definition differs from the one given earlier, particularly in that he is only concerned with showing that, though violence is altogether wrong, it is sometimes permissible in liberal democratic societies for private citizens to kill government agents, leaders, and police officers in self-defense or in the defense of others. He writes, "violence in self-defense and defense of others is warranted, on commonsense moral grounds, only to protect oneself or others from severe harm or injustice."[33] Though he assumes "commonsense moral grounds," Brennan is not defining violence itself in terms of a commonsense view. Instead, Brennan begins from a normative evaluation of violence, namely that it is acceptable when used defensively.

Here, we see what Brennan considers to be commonsensical:

> Killing is wrong. However, a person can become liable to be killed by performing certain wrongful or unjust actions. A person is liable to be killed when he is doing something deeply wrong, unjust, or harmful to others, and when killing him would serve a defensive purpose, such as self-defense, the defense of others, or to prevent him from causing greater injustice. Killing is also restricted by a doctrine of necessity: at minimum, when a nonlethal alternative is equally effective at stopping someone from committing injustice, it is not permissible to kill him.[34]

Brennan begins with the general assumption that "killing is wrong" but then immediately indicates when killing is not wrong. Killing, of course, is a paradigm case of violence and not violence itself, according to the paradigm case core conception of violence. Killing is a paradigm case of violence, but as an example, it is not a definition for violence. So Brennan begins from a general assumption that killing is wrong and immediately posits an exception to "killing is wrong." A person may be killed if the person has performed a "wrongful or unjust action," and self-defense or the defense of others by means of a killing is necessitated as a last resort. The wrongfulness of killing can be justified when used defensively against a person who does wrong to others. Self-defense and the defense of others, when no other alternative is available, are the conditions that qualify an action counting as an exception to the rule that "killing is wrong." However, the commonsense view of violence as described by Brennan does not define violence itself as wrong. He only states that killing is wrong. Brennan assumes a commonsense view that is supposed to provide a point of agreement upon which he can argue in favor of a justification for defensive violence. Brennan's claim that there is a "common moral ground" assumes normative evaluations of violence that are beyond the paradigm cases of violence.

Brennan adds that there is a liberal democratic assumption that only government agents and officials may kill for the sake of defending lives from threats, to uphold the law, and to attain justice. In liberal democratic societies, Brennan argues, the typical assumption is that killing is wrong, but because these societies assume that killing should never occur, they assume that "only nonviolent resistance to state injustice is permissible . . . [and that] we must defer to democratic government agents, even when these agents act in deeply unjust, harmful, and destructive ways."[35] Brennan's intention is not to urge people to kill government agents but is instead to show that government agents can be justifiably killed. He means that, even if we should aim to nonviolently combat injustices, it is incorrect to infer that citizens can never justifiably kill state leaders, agents, and police. So he appears to want to show that the commonsense view of defensive violence in liberal democratic societies is incorrect in its assumptions.

In Brennan's view, the exception that allows for killing to count as "defensive," and as not wrong, applies in all cases and not only in those cases when a defensive killing is used by a person against private citizens. If a government official, agent, police officer, etc. is not killing for the sake of defending themself or others, then those against whom the intention to kill is directed are justified to kill in defense of themselves and others. This suggests that even a commonsense view of violence that allows for self-defense itself requires political premises in order to distinguish genuine self-defense from self-defense that is not properly regarded as self-defense because it is illegitimate. With this concept of defensive violence, we come to political questions.

In terms of legitimacy, from the perspective of the state, the state can (because it is "permitted" in Brennan's sense of the term "legitimacy") make the claim that private citizens can justifiably use violence in self-defense and defense of others against other private citizens but not against government agents.[36] However, the authority of the state's legitimate claim is lacking, in his view, because private citizens will not necessarily, obediently submit to it, particularly when needing to defend themselves or others from government officials and agents whose violence is not self-defensive or in defense of others. Brennan writes, "it is a part of commonsense moral thinking . . . that we are presumed not to have a duty to follow unjust orders. This duty must be justified."[37] That is, it would be unjust for a government to demand that private citizens obediently submit to government agents, police officers, and military personnel when they kill private citizens. The state bears the burden of providing justification for why citizens must obediently submit to its government officials and agents who aggressively, and not defensively, kill private citizens, but the state's justification might not bear weight when a government agent or official is aggressively aiming to kill oneself or others.

Brennan argues that violence is only justifiable, and not wrong, when used defensively. However, that a use of violence could count as defensive in the first place, and as *not* wrong, is a matter of disagreement because the justification for a use of violence against government agents is political. Not everyone will agree. Political formations of collectives of individuals can arise in relation to disagreement concerning whether the violence used against a government agent is defensive. This violence is not wrong, but it is justified, according to Brennan, if it is used in response to unjust acts, where "justice" is defined in the political sense relating to just authority, which is itself defined in accordance with Brennan's political ideology. If it cannot always be shown for certain that a private citizen or government official was using defensive violence, then whose violence counts as defensive, and as not wrong, is an issue that is not easily settled.

For example, the issue concerning whose violence is defensive is irrelevant, at least for pacifists, because an authentic pacifist's strict commitment to peace and nonviolence would not endorse any kind of violence as justified, whether it is defensive or not. Defensiveness does not indicate that an instance of violence is not wrong because violence is completely wrong, in a pacifist's view. The pacifist's commitment to nonviolence, to peace, and to the view that violence is only wrong means that the pacifist disagrees with every justification for violence. Brennan's so-called commonsense moral thinking is contestable. Whose violence counts as defensive and as not wrong is contestable. Beyond his defined commonsense view, Brennan's view encounters disagreements concerning kinds of violence, wrong and not wrong ones, and defensive and aggressive instances of it.

The view that violence is wrong is the view of the paradigm case core conception of violence, but political ideologies appropriate this wrongness when they justify kinds of violence. Disagreements emerge when, from the perspectives of political ideologies, violent acts and events are defined by theorists as equivalent to other things for the sake of justifying those actions and events. The violence that is claimed to be not wrong and defensive is defined as an instance of killing a government agent in self-defense or in defense of others. The relationship between killing being not wrong when used defensively but wrong otherwise is a condition for disagreement.

1.5 THE OBSCURITY OF DEFENSIVE VIOLENCE

One approach toward determining whose violence is defensive is to attempt to answer the question, who started it? Is the government official, police officer, or military personnel violently defending themself and others from a private citizen, or is the private citizen using defensive violence against the violence of these government officials, officers, and personnel? Any answer to these questions will favor one side over another and requires an analysis of what happened, in what order, and such analyses cannot always perfectly reproduce a sequence of events. This was my point in the preface, concerning Kyle Rittenhouse's killing of Joseph Rosenbaum and Anthony Huber and shooting of Gaige Grosskreutz. Whether or not these were cases of legitimate, justified self-defense is contestable. Rittenhouse can claim self-defense and tell a story about what occurred that video recordings may corroborate, but whether this was an authentic case of self-defense is going to generate disagreement, particularly because most people are mere thirdhand witnesses who can only listen to testimonies and watch available videos. Most people *were not there* but still develop their own perspective based on what they see and hear with the potential to form politicized collectives of individuals based on an ideological belief that Rittenhouse's shooting, injuring, and killing of others was defensive.

Aside from the Rittenhouse case, there are other issues that arise when claiming that an act of violence was defensive. If there are others who can be referenced as those for whom the violence is defensive, then the difficulty of knowing whose violence is defensive increases. Simply imagine a heated exchange between involved individuals taking place such that one party claims to be defending a group of people from the other party, and this other party claims to be defending the very same people. If violence is not only defensive when self-defensive but also when used to defend others, then claims can be made concerning whose violence was defensive in relation to some group of people whose situation required defensive violence. Whose violence counts as defensive, then, is a ground for political disagreement.

The point is that, though a commonsense view of morality may consider violence to be wrong, except when used defensively, it does not itself distinguish between defensive and aggressive violence. Whether an act of violence is defensive depends on how that action is evaluated, and such evaluations will relate events together in ways that could be related in other ways. For example, if a government official intentionally and aggressively causes psychological harms to private citizens by threatening them with physical violence that is not actually used, and these are not immediately obvious to others because they are psychological harms that these others have not themselves experienced, then for the private citizens who suffer these harms, their own violence may count as defensive violence from their own point of view, but not from the point of view of those who did not experience those psychological harms. Likewise, a victim of rape and sexual assault, particularly women, who kills the rapist may consider their own killing to be defensive, but a judge might decide that the killing of the rapist was not defensive, for whatever reasons, but namely because the judge relates the events together in a different way. For those who use violence (in the sense that a commonsense view defines it), they might evaluate its use as a defensive one, despite its wrongness, while others see it as not being a defensive use of violence, and simply as "wrong," because they evaluate the event differently, from an opposed perspective or from another context. When this is the case the violence is and is not defensive, which obscures what defensive violence is.

1.6 VIOLENCE AS A WRONG

As noted, Brennan's version of the commonsense view of violence first assumes that violent killings are wrong but then indicates that defensive violence is an exception and not wrong even if it's a case of killing. The first assumption is a generalization that killing is wrong, which many probably commonly share as an assumption. The second assumption focuses on a particular kind of violence that many likely agree counts as not entirely wrong: defensive violence. However, if a particular kind of violence is not wrong because it is defensive, then the general assumption that killing is wrong seems incorrect. To define violence as a wrong is not to objectively define violence but instead evaluates violence, but commonly, people do consider violence to be wrong. This is why there are paradigm cases of violence.

The point of looking at these claims concerning the wrongness of violence and its relationship to defensive violence is that the paradigm case core conception of violence does not make sense of these relationships. A commonsense view would be limited to the paradigm cases that are unambiguously wrong. But the commonsense views characterized by Greene and Brennan extend the paradigm conception of violence into claims concerning when violence is wrong and when it is not wrong, and when people are normal, despite that they kill a person, and when abnormal. These evaluations extend the paradigm conception of violence.

The core of any commonsense view is that, in paradigm cases, violence is wrong. Theorists who evaluate violence as not wrong are going to face disagreements. Distinctions between when violence is wrong and when it is not wrong can be produced, but these distinctions are not necessarily matters of ordinary agreement. Distinctions between kinds of violence are inevitable because the core notion of violence in the paradigm cases does not itself value kinds of violence as not wrong. It instead defines what counts as violence based on the wrongness of the events and actions that involve an intentional use of physical means for the sake of causing physical or psychological harm or destruction. When the core of the paradigm cases of wrongness is extended into versions of a commonsense view, and also into distinctions between kinds of violence, though all violence is wrong, some is defined in the standard philosophical literature as not wrong, and disagreements emerge from these evaluations of the wrongness of violence that transform that wrongness into a positively valued, not wrong kind of violence.

1.7 DISAGREEMENTS CONCERNING A COMMONSENSE VIEW OF VIOLENCE

There are competing commonsense views of violence, as we have seen. But at the core of these conceptions of violence are paradigm cases that most people agree count as violence. To think of such events as not counting as violence would be odd, and "abnormal," as Greene puts it. Greene's research indicates who is normal and abnormal, neurologically speaking, according to how the brains of subjects respond to situations in which they have a choice to use "prototypical" violence. Prototypically, the automatic antiviolence system defines violence, and a normal, common thing people do is emotionally reject this violence. Brennan, though, begins with the common assumption that killing is wrong in order to show that defensive violence is justifiable, even against government officials and agents. Greene's definition defines violence, in a commonsense way, and Brennan's definition evaluates killing, in a different commonsense way. Brennan and Greene's assumptions concerning what is common sense about violence are embedded within their respective, neuroethical and political projects, which cannot be separated from how they define commonsense views of violence.

On the other hand, disagreements over what the commonsense view is indicate why there is disagreement concerning kinds of violence. Disagreements arise due to how violence itself is valued. Evaluations of kinds of violence distinguish between wrong and not wrong, defensive and nondefensive, legal and illegal, legitimate and illegitimate, emancipatory and oppressive, normal and abnormal, and vengeful and sacrificial violence. This list is incomplete because there are many other ways that kinds of violence could be distinguished. However, what we see is that these evaluations generally follow a formula. A positively evaluated kind of violence is defined as superior in relation to the negatively evaluated kind of violence. The positively evaluated kind of violence (such as defensive violence) is superior because it is defined as that which defeats the inferior kind of violence. Yet an opposed view can define those very same actions and events in an inverted way. What counts as defensive violence, from the perspective of a private citizen, can be defined as illegal and criminal from the perspective of the government agent that the private citizen violently attacks. Even though it may be commonly agreed that the action or event itself is violent, the kind of violence it is depends upon what and how the violence is related to other things. The government agent relates the private citizen's use of violence to a violation of law and the assumption that private citizens cannot use violence against public officials. The private citizen relates their use of violence against the government agent to their own right to defend their life, or that of others, possibly because there is a duty to protect life, or to the claim that it is natural for life to protect itself. These relationships between kinds of violence and other things, evaluated in relationships of superiority and inferiority, produce conditions for disagreement.

In fact, this shows that commonsense views of violence are not neutral. The wrongness of violence is extended so that kinds of violence reflect this wrongness, some of them being entirely wrong, and others not being entirely wrong because they are defined as that which defeats the kind of violence that is entirely wrong. Agreement that violence is an intentional use of physical means to cause physical or psychological harm or destruction does not mean that everyone will always agree in each case that an event or act is violent. Instead, there are divergences within commonsense views of violence.

1.8 THE POLITICIZATION OF THE CONCEPT OF VIOLENCE

Commonsense views arise as reactions to the wrongness of paradigm cases of violence. Without the general recognition of the wrongness of these paradigm cases, there would be no commonsense view. The paradigm cases, such as smashing someone's face for the sake of causing harm, are altogether wrong, but there is agreement that when such actions are instances of self-defense, then they are justified. However, what counts as self-defense is defined in relation to other things, which opens the door for political disagreements concerning whose violence is self-defensive and, therefore, justified. For example, if one prioritizes the role of defense played by police violence, proletarian violence, or anarchistic violence, then it is because one believes these to be superior to other things, particularly those things these kinds of violence are defined as capable of defeating, because these are defined as related to things that need to be defended, such as security or human rights. A commonsense definition for violence may be useful toward garnering agreements in relation to which collectives of individuals form. And it also seems to be the case that whether an act of violence, in a commonsense view of the term, is a particular kind of violence depends upon which collective of individuals, society, or state one belongs to and believes in. It might be that the act or event is evaluated negatively as a kind of violence if it interferes with the goals and vision that a collective of individuals, a society, or a state has of itself, so that for example, if *our* violence achieves *our* freedom it is good, but the violence of *them* is bad, even if they also aim toward freedom. Because a collective of individuals, whether as a community, society, or state, aims toward sustaining their existence as a people, in the name of the good, justice, freedom, rights, religion, or something else, these "group-vision" distinctions between kinds of violence are nonneutrally political.

Brennan explicitly politicizes his justification for defensive violence used against government agents and officials when he reveals his political preference for liberal democratic regimes, despite that he justifies violence against the agents who are representative of those regimes. He explicitly indicates what he is *not* endorsing. He writes, "totalitarian communist regimes do not value individual human life," and then he uses as evidence the assassinations of four US presidents and thirteen US congresspersons, as well as the targeting of these kinds of people to indicate that liberal democratic regimes handle assassinations of government agents and officials much better than "totalitarian communist regimes" who respond to attempted assassinations by terrorizing their citizens, such as when Fanni Kaplan failed to assassinate Lenin in 1918.[38] His point is that defensive violence used against government officials and agents within liberal democratic regimes is more likely to be handled well than in totalitarian communist ones. Anyone who agrees with this may be led to agree that in liberal democratic regimes defensive violence against government officials is not as bad as in totalitarian communism itself. This evaluates defensive violence in liberal democratic regimes as superior to totalitarian communist regimes. Of course, someone who prefers an opposed political ideology could agree with Brennan that private citizens may justifiably kill government agents in self-defense or in the defense of others but disagree with his claim that liberal democratic regimes handle this better. This demonstrates how a definition of a kind of violence is politicized in relation to collectives of individuals who agree with a definition and in opposition to those who do not.

Despite common agreement upon paradigm cases of violence, no commonsense definition of violence or distinction between kinds of violence is politically neutral because even here there are disagreements concerning what counts as a kind of violence. The disagreements within the commonsense views of violence are extended in the philosophical literature and in the writings of political ideologists, as will be addressed later. There are accounts of violence produced by diverse figures situated in historical contexts. For everyone, and not only these figures, the question is, whose account is believable, and therefore legitimate? As a historical matter, legitimacy is contingent on beliefs and beliefs are held within the particular contexts that influence having them.

1.9 DEFINITIONS FOR VIOLENCE AND A LOGIC OF EXCEPTION

Distinctions between kinds of violence, including those within commonsense views of violence, follow a logic of exception. In general, an action or event counts as violence or a kind of violence, *except when* X, where X is anything that the definition does not capture. For example, the paradigm case core of commonsense views of violence identifies violence with an intentional use of physical means for the sake of causing physical or psychological harms or destruction. Commonsense views of violence already extend this conception to allow for exceptions. If an action or an event is an exception to this definition, then that action or event does not count as violence. This means that some unintentional uses of physical means that result in harm or destruction do not count as violence. Likewise, if there is the intentional use of physical means to cause violence but no harm or destruction results, then no violence has occurred. Unless an action or event fits a definition, it is excluded from counting as violence or as a kind of violence.

It is also in the sense of this logic of exception that definitions for violence are not politically neutral, including commonsense views. Distinctions between violence and nonviolence, legitimate and illegitimate violence, legal and criminal violence, prototypical and atypical violence, and defensive and aggressive violence, for example, operate according to this logic of exception. An act or event is a kind of violence, except when it does not fit that kind of violence, and whether it fits that kind of defined violence depends upon whether one or a people relate that act or event to a kind of defined violence. Because another person or people can relate that act or event to an opposed kind of defined violence, the opposition between these people demonstrates that definitions for violence and kinds of violence are not politically neutral.

For example, if legitimate violence is that which law defines as legitimate violence, and the law defines legitimate violence by excluding illegitimate kinds of violence that threaten law's power (its ability to dominate over lives), then no violence is legitimate *except* that violence that defeats the illegitimate violence that threatens law's power. That is, no violence is legitimate, *except* the violence law defines as legitimate in relation to sustaining itself. This logic of exception is the way in which definitions for violence exclude some things, *except* those things that are included, as counting as kinds of violence. By focusing only on what is obviously violent and that most people would agree counts as violence, a commonsense view apparently excludes political evaluations of kinds of violence. Instead, it is a definition that includes the criteria that an act or event is violent only if there is an intentional use of physical means for the sake of causing physical or psychological harm or destruction. People agree with this definition because people generally, immediately and emotionally, reject such actions and events as wrong. When exceptions are considered, as they inevitably are even within a commonsense view, they rest on other considerations.

1.10 TRANSFORMING THE "ABNORMAL" FAILURE TO REJECT PROTOTYPICAL VIOLENCE INTO A "NORMAL" APPROVAL OF KINDS OF PROTOTYPICAL VIOLENCE

A person can begin from the paradigm case core conception of violence and then distinguish violence into kinds so that not all prototypical violence, in Greene's sense of the term, is objectionable. This is exactly what Brennan has done. When individuals act violently against government officials, their violence is not objectionable when it is defensive. Brennan achieves this by defining killing as wrong but then indicates the exceptional cases in which it is not wrong. Police violence, for example, can be assumed to be defined as good in relation to a goal of successful law enforcement, which is itself defined as a good. This violence is not wrong but justified in relation to the goal that is itself evaluated positively. Any use of violence *except* this use is neither justified nor good. Definitions for kinds of violence, in this way, transform the violence that would typically be rejected into something that is approved *for a reason* that is itself defined in relation to a use of a kind of violence. The definition of a kind of violence as good and justified in relation to a goal, such as freedom for example, is that which conceptually transforms violence into something positive, thereby overriding the automatic antiviolence alarm system Greene infers from his research. That is, distinctions between kinds of violence transform the abnormal into the normal. The "normal" emotional rejection of personal uses of violence has to be overridden, and doing so requires a sufficient amount of *positive* meaning defined in relation to a kind of violence.

A simple kind of transformation of abnormal violence into normal violence occurs when some violence is defined as that which defeats violence. The violence that defeats violence is defined in positive value terms of its ability to defeat violence, and the negative evaluation of violence in general is transformed into kinds of violence, namely that which defeats violence and that which does not. The logic of exception, here, is that violence is wrong, except that violence that defeats violence. But when is violence not wrong then? If the answer is when violence defeats violence, then because there is disagreement concerning the violence that defeats violence, a commonsense view of defensive violence (that it is not entirely wrong) is already participating in producing a distinction between kinds of violence that is contestable and no longer commonsensical.

However, it is possible to define more complex relationships between kinds of violence. For example, a kind of intentional use of personal force that is defined as emancipatory, good, and brings about or is a manifestation of freedom, rights, or justice because it causes harms serves to transform the violence that people typically reject into a positively valued means against that which is excluded from counting as that which brings about or is emancipatory, good, freedom, rights, or justice. Defined distinctions between kinds of violence transform the assumed wrongness of violence into something that is sometimes, in particular situations, in the hands of some people, not wrong. However, whether these kinds of violence are what one defines them as, and are related to what one claims them to be related to, is a matter of disagreement and depends upon what political ideology one believes in.

Again, legitimate violence is itself defined in a way that serves to rationally justify uses of violence (those kinds defined by the paradigm case core conception of violence) and thereby override the automatic rejection of the wrongness of uses of personal force as means to goals. This legitimate violence is said to be justified because it is defined in terms of its *relationships* to other things. Power, the state, and a legal order can be valued as superior. If the law defines police violence as that which enforces law, maintains a legal order, and is therefore legitimate, then it is difficult to question the legitimacy of police violence without also simultaneously putting the law itself into question because the legitimacy of police violence and the legal order constitutive of the law that police violence maintains are defined as essentially related.

So in relation to one another, terms like "power," "legitimate," "violence," and other terms like "freedom" and "justice" are defined in terms of their *relationships*, and the definitions follow a logic of exception. For example, the violence that defeats illegitimate violence is not itself illegitimate violence because it is *an exception that proves the rule*, namely that legitimate violence is that which is defined as not being illegitimate violence. Without law being defined as related to power and legitimacy, the law cannot justify uses of legitimate violence. This does not indicate what violence is but only indicates that there are kinds of violence valued in diverse ways, in essential relationships to other things, and thus transforming kinds of violence into normatively negative wrongs and normatively positive not wrong kinds.

1.11 WILLEM SCHINKEL'S REJECTION OF THE CLAIM THAT VIOLENCE IS AN ESSENTIALLY CONTESTED CONCEPT

In the following chapter, it will be argued that, *beyond the paradigm case core conception of violence, violence is an essentially contested concept.* That is, people generally agree that paradigm cases of violence exist, particularly based on their wrongness, but beyond that agreement, there are irreconcilable disagreements concerning what counts as kinds of violence. I am not arguing that violence is altogether an essentially contested concept. I am not meaning to produce a reductive account of violence that would be one that claims that violence is only instrumental, but instead, I mean to address violence nonreductively by inclusively accounting for a variety of kinds of violence. By taking this approach, I don't mean to relativize violence so that too much counts as violence. Violence "makes way" but does so *wrongly*. My point is that the contestedness concerning violence arises only beyond the paradigm case core conception of violence that only focuses on the wrongness of examples of violence.

Willem Schinkel, in his "Regimes of Violence and the *Trias Violentiae*," argues that there are four strategies that social theorists and social scientists utilize when addressing violence, one of which is the strategy of arguing that violence is an essentially contested concept.[39] He also argues against the assumption that a commonsense view of violence is sufficient. Instead of a commonsense view, he argues that there is a "regime of violence," which is "the regime of regulation through which different *forms of violence* become discernible in the first place." A regime of violence controls which forms of violence are acknowledged as violence and which are not. In other words, what counts as violence depends on those who define it.

Schinkel also argues against the strategy of arguing that violence is an essentially contested concept. He writes that "approaches intent on regarding violence as 'essentially contested' . . . lose the ability to contest . . . [the] contingent outcomes [of variously defined kinds of violence] and in practice they will be led to observe violence only where private violence and state violence clash."[40] So Schinkel rejects a commonsense view of violence as insufficient and rejects the view that argues that violence is an essentially contested concept. His main point is that there is a regime of violence that regulates what is recognized as kinds of violence, including the violence of the state and the violence of private individuals. In particular, he argues that recognition of this regime of violence is "*a refusal to reify and ratify state conceptions of violence.*" However, Schinkel's rejection of the view that the concept of violence is essentially contestable is itself reflective of his own political ideological assumption that only his definition of a regime of violence can effectively scrutinize a state's ability to distinguish between kinds of violence. That is, Schinkel's rejection of the view that the concept of violence is essentially contestable is itself contestable, and nonneutrally political. He's simply contributing to the contestedness of the concept of violence. This rejection of the essentially contestable character of violence overlooks the contestedness. Violence is wrong; wrongness could be itself defined in terms of an analysis of an inductive list of examples of violence and how violence violates, harms, disturbs, disrupts, destroys, and causes death, but even if there is general agreement that this is the case, there are justifications given for acts of violence and *there* is where the contestedness occurs. The use of police violence against citizens serves as an obvious example of this contestedness. Sure, their violence is also wrong because police engage in paradigm acts of violence, but whether police violence is legitimate and justified is contestable because collectives of individuals, from their perspectives, are related to that violence in disparate ways. The Black Lives Matter protests and the retorts "Back the Blue" and "All Lives Matter" demonstrate this. Black Lives Matter protests are against police violence unjustly utilized, particularly against unarmed black men. The "Back the Blue" and the "All Lives Matter" retorts support the police and the government that backs the police, arguing that the police officers legitimately utilize violence against those same men. The violence was wrong either way, but whether it was justified depends upon political, ideological questions concerning when, against whom, and in what cases police violence is justified. The same could be said of wars, strikes, riots, revolutions, and so on. Violence is often paired with such things, and whether it is justified is a matter of political, ideological disagreement. If paradigm cases of violence occur, then they are likely to commonly be defined as wrong in the first place, and if they are justified and legitimate, then political, ideological disagreement occurs. This seems to call into question whether violence really is wrong, but this is the incorrect way to look at it. Violence is and will remain wrong. That is where theorists agree. A description or definition of violence focuses on this wrongness. Disagreement arises when, from politically ideological perspectives, people begin to evaluate instances of violence as not entirely wrong. This disagreement and how it occurs must be acknowledged so that the wrongness of violence can be strongly focused upon instead of engaging in politically ideological and contestable attempts to develop justifications for violence. Perhaps then violence can become more effectively addressed, that is, rather than justifying uses of violence against violence, which simply sustains violence as something that occurs, the way to move away from violence is to push the agreement that violence is wrong rather than attempt to develop arguments for ways in which violence can be justified and legitimate.

1.12 CONCLUSION: THE PERSISTENCE OF THE CORE OF THE COMMONSENSE VIEW OF VIOLENCE

Theorists can agree that an event or action is violent, according to the paradigm case core conception of violence, but disagree on the kind of violence it happens to be and on what kind of value the violence bears. One's preferred political ideology is indicated by the way in which one distinguishes between valued and disvalued violence, in relation to other things that are also valued and disvalued. Likewise, sociopolitical and historical context influence the way in which one defines kinds of violence. Kinds of violence exist only insofar as one defines them as such in relation to other things. Yet the paradigm case core of commonsense views of violence persists. At the core of this view is that violence is that which is wrong.

Given the persistence of the general agreement on what paradigmatically counts as violence, the questions are: Why is there less agreement concerning kinds of violence? Why is it that the anarchist's violence is illegitimate according to democratic liberalism, if they both aim for freedom? Why is it that the same action, such as blowing up a building, can count as both terrorism and as emancipation? How can freedom be valued, but when an adversary pursues freedom, their violence is disvalued, while one's own use of violence toward freedom is valued? Perhaps it is because, beyond the paradigm case core, distinctions between kinds of violence are essentially contestable, and this implies that they are not politically neutral. Two opposed political ideologies can agree upon a goal, such as justice or freedom, but consider one another's uses of violent means toward that goal as illegitimate. The following chapter will pursue this line of thought, arguing that violence, beyond the paradigm case core conception of violence that focuses on the wrongness of violence, is an essentially contested concept.

NOTES

1. Ted A. Smith, *Weird John Brown: Divine Violence and the Limits of Ethics* (Stanford: Stanford University Press).
2. Ibid., 8–9.
3. Ibid., 9.

4. Ibid., 10.

5. Joshua Greene, *Moral Tribes: Emotion, Reason, and the Gap between Us and Them* (New York: Penguin Books, 2013), 14, 120. Greene's intention, in this book, is to produce an argument for what he calls "deep pragmatism," which is a kind of utilitarianism that can be used for the sake of globally and domestically serving the greater good, resolving "Us vs. Them" disagreements, and not only for serving the greater good of one's own people ("Us" or "tribe," in Greene's terminology). It is only the moral psychology concerning how people typically respond to violence that is relevant here because it shows how people share a commonsense view of violence.

6. Ibid., 14, 153–54, 289–94.

7. Ibid., 113–16. See Philippa Foot, "Abortion and the Doctrine of the Double Effect," *Oxford Review* 5 (1967): 1–5; and Judith Jarvis Thomson, "Killing, Letting Die, and the Trolley Problem," *The Monist* 59 (1976): 204–17; Thomson, "The Trolley Problem," *Yale Law Journal* 94 (1985): 1395–415; and Thomson, "Turning the Trolley," *Philosophy and Public Affairs* 36 (2008): 359–74.

8. Ibid., 222. Greene and his colleagues utilize numerous variations of these two dilemmas in order to test whether their results are accurate and whether the brain neurologically *causes* people not to want to push the man in front of the trolley. Some of these variations involve the subject being at a distance from the man and some of them involve the subject's touching or not touching when pushing him in front of the trolley. They found that it is not spatial distance but the personal touching that matters. See pp. 214–16.

9. Ibid., 118, 124. Greene argues this because he and others have studied subjects with a damaged VMPFC or amygdala, and the responses of these subjects demonstrate less emotional concern for pushing the man off the footbridge. See especially p. 125, but also 118, 122, and 142.

10. Ibid., 120.

11. Ibid., 119–20. This is neuroscientist Jonathon Cohen's definition of "cognitive control," Greene's colleague.

12. Ibid., 216. Greene used variations of the footbridge and switch dilemmas, in which the subjects are either more closely touching, less closely touching, or not touching the one person who is killed by the actor in order to save five. His results show that the more closely a person must touch the one person to kill him and save five lives, the less the subjects are willing to perform the action. See pp. 215–16.

13. Ibid., 124–26.

14. Ibid., 125.

15. Ibid., 133.

16. Ibid., 134.

17. Ibid., 135.

18. Ibid., 136–37.

19. Ibid., 194; italics added. I return to the significance of Greene's claim that people commonly want to have positive experiences shortly, in relation to how the common view that violence is wrong is transformed by theorists into something good.

20. Ibid., 222. The death of the man wearing the backpack is used instrumentally to stop the trolley to save five, while the man standing on the alternative track, to which the train is switched, dies as a side effect.

21. Ibid.

22. Ibid., 240.

23. Ibid., 241.

24. Ibid., 245.

25. Ibid., 226–27.

26. Ibid., 248.

27. Greene and his colleagues tested people with frontotemporal dementia, Alzheimer's, and damage to their VMPFC. See pp. 121–26.

28. Ibid., 249.

29. Ibid., 247.

30. Ibid., 249–50.

31. Ibid., 251.

32. Jason Brennan, "When May We Kill Government Agents? In Defense of Moral Parity," *Social Philosophy and Policy* 32 (2016): 40–61.

33. Ibid., 49. Brennan argues that this commonsense moral view is common because it is a part of the tradition handed down from English common law, which includes doctrines of defense and self-defense. See p. 44.

34. Ibid., 44.

35. Ibid., 40.

36. Ibid., 34.

37. Ibid., 53.

38. Brennan, "When May We Kill," 60–61.

39. Willem Schinkel, "Regimes of Violence and the *Trias Violentiae*," *European Journal of Social Theory* 16 (2013): 311. The other three strategies include the strategy of not defining violence, the strategy of "enumerating a number of acts among which some form of family resemblance is found to exist that is then called 'violence,'" and the strategy of stipulating a definition that "specifies, usually at an ontic and not an ontological level what counts as violence."

40. Ibid., 323.

Chapter Two

When Violence Is an Essentially Contested Concept

2.1 INTRODUCTION

The paradigm case core of the concept of violence involves cases of the intentional use of physical means for the sake of causing physical or psychological harm or destruction. Most people would agree with this definition, and it would be unusual for someone to disagree with it. Most people consider violence to be wrong. For example, it would be unusual for someone to think that no violence has occurred when a person has intentionally crushed another person's skull with a cinder block. This is an instance of an intentional use of physical means (the body of the person who crushes with the cinder block, the body/skull of the person who is crushed by the cinder block, and the cinder block itself) for the sake of causing harm and destruction (the crushing of the skull and, likely, the death or severe cranial damage of the victim). If most agree that this is a violent act or event, this example serves as a paradigm case of violence. However, as soon as we ask if this action is wrong, or why the action took place, or if it was a justified act, we are confronted with a disagreement because we are *valuing* the kind of violence we *believe* it to be instead of simply describing it as a case of violence. Perhaps the action is justified and perhaps not, but either way, the action will be evaluated by a person in its relation to other things. This indicates that, though there is agreement concerning a core of paradigm cases of violence, as soon as we move away from this core to consider justifications of violence, disagreements emerge.

The political ideologies of liberalism, nationalism, fascism, communism, and anarchism all justify the uses of violence, explicitly or implicitly, as a means toward their goals. The issue is that justifications for uses of violence, such as those given within the purview of these political ideologies, conflict with one another. These political ideologies sometimes compete against one another theoretically, and in actual practice, vying to gain their goals, and to destroy one another. They can fundamentally disagree with one another politically ideologically, and they can disagree with one another's uses of violence toward goals. Each considers its own depiction of human existence, and of relationships between humans, to be the correct or best one. These opposed political ideologies agree on the wrongness of violence in the paradigm cases but disagree upon what kind of violence those actions and events happen to be. Examples of definitions of violence produced by Vittorio Bufacchi, the World Health Organization, Thomas Nagel, and Verena Erlenbusch are outlined in order to show that Walter Bryce Gallie's and Alasdair MacIntyre's characterizations of essentially contested concepts are fulfilled by the concept of violence, but only beyond the wrongness of the paradigm cases of violence.

Here, two points are made concerning distinctions between kinds of violence. First, what counts as kinds of violence is essentially contested beyond the wrongness of the paradigm cases of violence, and second, because there is agreement concerning the wrongness of violence in the paradigm cases, the concept of violence plays a special role within political philosophy. Because there is agreement in relation to wrongness with respect to the paradigm cases, it is rhetorically effective to extend the concept to other kinds of acts that *prima facie* do not appear to be cases of violence.

2.2 VITTORIO BUFACCHI ON WHAT VIOLENCE IS NOT

Vittorio Bufacchi, in his recent (2013) encyclopedia entry "Violence," distinguishes violence from what it is not, namely, power, coercion, harm, and force.[1] He means to zero in on one defining set of characteristics that is unique to violence and that significantly distinguishes violence from power, coercion, harm, and force. On power, for example, he conceives of it as "a dispositional concept, something that people who possess it have the option to use," and violence as "not something we possess or [do] not possess; it is not a capability we either have or [do] not have. Instead, violence is something we do; it is an act." This indicates that there is a difference between a person's ability to act and a person's performance of that act. A person has the power (ability) to be violent, and then when the person is violent, that power is enacted as an act of violence. This means that power precedes violence, and is related to violence, but is not violence itself. Violence is not something that is possessed as a capability but is instead an act.[2]

On the distinction between violence and coercion, Bufacchi explains that "while violence can be used to coerce, in which case violence is a form of coercion, not all acts of violence are necessarily acts of coercion, since it is possible for coercion to occur without violence." This distinction between violence and coercion amounts to the claim that violence and coercion can occur together, but not necessarily. Violence is sometimes coercive, but not always. Bufacchi adds the distinction that "coercion is . . . an act that undermines voluntariness," and violence does not always "undermine voluntariness."

On the distinction between violence and harm, Bufacchi writes that "'harm' is a term we use to describe the consequences of violence, but it is not necessarily what constitutes the act of violence itself. In other words, the experience of harm is a consequence or sign of violence; to define violence in terms of the harm is to mistake the symptom for the disease." Here, Bufacchi distinguishes between actions and what results from them. First there is the power (ability) to be violent, then the violent act itself is performed, and then harm results. Violence produces harm, but we should not refer to the harm itself as violence. So, altogether, violence is sometimes coercive and sometimes "undermine[s] voluntariness," but not always; violence is an act and is not possessed as an ability in the way that power is possessed as an ability; violence is not the harms that result from violent acts.

In addition to indicating what violence is not, Bufacchi adds that "violence is an evaluative concept, perhaps even a normative concept." This means that an action is evaluated as counting as a violent act. As indicated in the previous discussion concerning the paradigm case core conception of violence, an action or event may commonly be evaluated as violent, but beyond the core cases, there are distinctions between kinds of violence. So in addition to this evaluation of an action as counting as a violent one, there are also evaluations of the kind of violence the action happens to be, which Bufacchi does not discuss. Instead, he next focuses on defining violence on the basis of its etymological relationship to the concept of violation.

2.3 NEWTON GARVER'S INFLUENTIAL ARGUMENT CONCERNING THE RELATIONSHIP BETWEEN A VIOLATION AND VIOLENCE

In order to relate the concept of violence to the concept of "to violate," Bufacchi utilizes Newton Garver's influential "What Violence Is" because Garver defines violence in terms of a violation, and notes that "following Garver, many contemporary theorists of violence have converged on the idea of defining violence in terms of a violation, although there seems to be some disagreement about what exactly is being violated when an act of violence takes place."[3] There may be convergence on this etymological relationship, but disagreement persists. Perhaps this disagreement persists because we tend to use the word "violence" in many ways. For example, we might say that a person violently slams on the brakes of their car to avoid a collision. However, whether the braking mechanism, the car itself, or the possibility of a collision are violated is highly debatable. So the etymological relationship between violence and "to violate" may be informative but does not indubitably establish what counts as violence.

2.4 AN ETYMOLOGICAL RELATIONSHIP BETWEEN VIOLENCE AND VIOLATE

The etymological relationship between "violence" and "violate" exists because the terms share the Latin root "*vis*." The term "violent" comes from the Latin *violentus*, which is composed of *vis* and *-olentus*. *Vis* means "strength, force, power, energy, [and] hostile strength."[4] *-olentus* means "having in quantity, full of." So *violentus* means "forcible, violent, vehement, impetuous, [and] boisterous."[5] The Latin word for "violation" is *violātus*, which is the participle of *violo*. *Violo* means "to treat with violence, injure, dishonor, outrage, violate."[6] So there appears to be a strong etymological relationship between the terms "violation" and "violence," but this relationship constitutes only one way of thinking about what violence is. It only tells us that violence and violate have an etymological relationship. It does not tell us what violence is. Also, the Latin root, "*vis*," includes "force" and "power," which disagrees with Bufacchi's distinctions between violence and power. This etymological relationship does not provide a static, agreed upon definition of the concept of violence. All it does is relate the word "violence" to the word "violate" on the vague foundation of their shared root, "*vis*." There is a difference between an etymological relationship between concepts and how those concepts are used.

Additionally, in order to rebut a claim that this etymological relationship indicates a definition for violence only requires finding an instance in which we claim that violence has not occurred, but a violation has, or that a violation has not occurred, but violence has. If such situations are tenable, then the etymological relationship is not a strong one. We can separate the concept of violence from the concept of violation in a way that erodes the claim that the etymological relationship is significant. As long as it is debatable whether every instance of violence involves a violation, and whether every instance of a violation involves violence, this etymological relationship does not serve as a ground for a definition of the concept of violence and does not reveal what violence is. In part, this is why I focus on the wrongness of paradigm cases of violence, which establishes a discernible pattern of how violence "makes way" by doing something evaluated as wrong. A violation may also "make way," but whether it does doesn't matter because what does matter is that paradigm cases of violence are recognized as wrong.

2.5 BUFACCHI ON THREE KINDS OF VIOLENCE

Bufacchi distinguishes between (1) a Minimalist Conception of Violence (MCV), which equates to a deliberate use of physical force for the sake of producing suffering or injury; (2) psychological violence, which does not necessarily involve a use of physical force; and (3) structural or institutional violence, which he refers to as "the Comprehensive Conception of Violence" (CCV).[7] The general distinction between MCV and CCV is that the former entails a "notion of excessive force," while the latter implies "the notion of a violation of rights." One commonsense view of violence, discussed earlier, includes the first two kinds of violence Bufacchi defines. Here, Bufacchi relates "excessive force" to violence, however, he also associates "force" with power on the grounds that force and power are dispositional, in the sense of abilities and potentialities. So he argues that because force "is a dispositional concept, to the extent that it refers to an ability or potentiality," and because "violence is an evaluative concept," these concepts are distinct. It is difficult to see how violence can be defined in a politically neutral way, in that whether there is excessive force is relevant to the goals in question.

Bufacchi also suggests a "third way" to define violence "as a violation of integrity," and "integrity" is "something that has not been broken, or that has not lost its original form."[8] It is "integrity as wholeness or completeness." That is, "violence can be defined as a violation of integrity to the extent that violence damages or destroys a pre-existing unity." The paradigm case core conception does not depend on notions of integrity, unity, wholeness, or completeness. We might ask, why does there have to be a damaged or destroyed integrity in order for it to be said that violence has occurred? If it is the case that *whenever* something is a preexisting unity that has been violated or broken, violence has occurred, then it could be said that there is a lot of this kind of violence that occurs. For example, on this view, there is the violence of disrupting a serene pond, the violence of an airplane flying through a cloud, the violence of eating a sandwich, and so on. Poetically, this makes sense, but it does not agree with paradigm cases of violence, such as when one person purposefully uses a sledgehammer to break the ankles of another person. Surely, the person's ankles were a preexisting unity that was violated and broken, but I think it makes more sense to simply say that the breaking of their ankles is violence because it is commonly evaluated as a wrong kind of "making way" through their ankles.

In relation to CCV, which implies "a violation of rights," again there arises the problem with establishing what rights are. If sociopolitical and historical context matters, and there is no reason to think it does not, then what counts as a violation of rights is going to vary from one place in history to another. Under a kind of slavery, for example, if a slave has no legal rights but is merely considered the subhuman property of an owner, a slave might not count as suffering "structural or institutional violence" because the slave does not even count as a full-fledged right-bearing human in the way that we would say the person does suffer this once slavery is abolished. The point is that, whether there is a violation of rights and an occurrence of "structural or institutional violence" can depend upon historical and geographical context to the point that on one day, a person does not suffer this kind of violence, but the next week the person does suffer it. So whether a person is violated and suffers "comprehensive violence" is not clear, given the various ways that people are and are not considered rights holders within specific places and times.

Historical and geographical context also applies to the second kind of psychological violence Bufacchi distinguishes, because whether a person is psychologically violated depends on the psychology of that person in relation to the historically contextual understanding of psychology and practice of social norms at a particular time and place. Verbal castigations, deception, and coercion may or may not count as psychological violence if the people in the context in which these take place consider them to be more or less "normal" things for one person to say or do to others. In relation to the paradigm case core conception of violence, Bufacchi's distinctions between these three kinds of violence, though useful for critiquing social practices, institutions, and governments, are not likely to be as commonly shared as the paradigm case core conception of violence that focuses on the wrongness of examples of violence. What counts as psychological or comprehensive violence from the perspective of one person, or from the perspective of a collective of people who share a group vision of some good, may not count as these kinds of violence from the perspective of another person or another collective of individuals.

2.6 BUFACCHI'S DEFINITION OF VIOLENCE

Disregarding for now the criticisms that can be raised against Bufacchi's distinctions between kinds of violence, force, excessive force, and power, let's look at how he defines violence itself. Bufacchi writes,

> An act of violence occurs when the integrity or unity of a subject (person or animal) or object (property) is intentionally or unintentionally violated, as a result of an action or omission. The violation may occur at the physical or psychological level, through physical or psychological means. A violation of integrity will usually result in the subject being harmed or injured, or the object being destroyed or damaged.

This definition extends far beyond the paradigm case core conception of violence, given that it includes unintentional violations of an integrity or unity, and omissions. It also specifies that violence can occur against objects. Bufacchi's aim with this definition of violence is to comprehensively cover a variety of kinds of violence so that anything that could qualify as an instance of violence is accounted for.

Additionally, Bufacchi indicates that an act of violence can be psychological, unintentional, and an omission, which means that whether we are aware of this violence is relative to whether it ever even becomes clear to us that this unintentionally missing thing is psychologically affecting us, particularly if there is no harm or injury experienced. That violence can be psychological, unintentional, and an omission opens the door to a variety of possible claims concerning kinds of violence. For example, events, or significant things that happen within the course of history, are significant in relation to someone who thinks of them as significant. If an event is significant because it did not happen, or unintentionally happened, or only happened psychologically, then there are *many* significant things *not* taking place that destroy some kind of possible integrity or unity. This means that, given all the things that are unintentionally not happening, and that are psychologically affecting us because they are not happening, there is a lot of violence taking place in nonphysical ways of which we are unaware. Clearly, this definition of violence makes violence much more complex than a simple list of paradigm cases of violence, which are commonly considered violence because of their wrongness. If something is unintentionally not occurring, then how can we even say that it is wrong in the first place, and how can it even be known what is unintentionally not occurring and only usually produces harms or injuries that might not be acknowledged or known to have occurred? Bufacchi's definition of violence tends to obscure violence more than make it explicit. The paradigm case core conception of violence, which again focuses on an inductive list of examples of violence that are commonly evaluated as wrong, which is why they are considered violence in the first place, avoids this obscurity. Rape, murder, torture, beatings, hits, punches, kicks, shootings, etc. are obvious cases of violence because they are wrong and they are wrong because they make way through their victims, causing them to be something they would not have been had the action not occurred.

Furthermore, one can always point out that something did not occur due to no one's direct intention, and that one suffers "psychological violence" or "comprehensive violence" as a result, but this could result in too many things being described as violence that we might otherwise not count as violence. It's important to hear people out when they claim to have suffered violence, but wrongness needs to be at the core of the "violence" they claim to have suffered. For example, a person might complain that they did not receive a good upbringing, not because the person's parents intentionally neglected that person but because they unintentionally forgot to buy the person the right kind of shoes, which caused psychological issues in relation to the person's friends who have high standards when it comes to the shoes one wears. Are we really going to characterize this as violence and as wrong? I don't see any reason to do so, particularly if the parents were not able to afford the shoes or simply did not know that their child desired them, though perhaps the person could at least receive some empathetic support from a psychologist in relation to their suffering.

2.7 BUFACCHI ON THE IDENTITY AND CONSEQUENTIALIST ARGUMENTS FOR JUSTIFIED VIOLENCE

Bufacchi goes on to argue that "violence is bad and *prima facie* wrong, yet there are times when, at least in principle, violence can and ought to be justified," and this means that we are justifying an "evil" when we justify violence. But he adds that we might think of violence as both good and bad, *depending on how it is used*. In order to indicate what he means, Bufacchi produces an "Identity Argument," which says that "*violence is good if, through an act of violence, the perpetrator is able to reestablish his or her own identity as a person of equal moral value, deserving the respect of others*." But he adds that this Identity Argument "makes it too easy to justify violence" because someone could use it as an excuse. The Identity Argument assumes that violence can be good when it defeats other kinds of violence. According to this argument, violence is justified and good only when it reestablishes a person's identity such that the person is deserving of respect. The person's identity is reestablished when that person is "of equal moral value." Otherwise, the use of violence is bad.

In contrast to the Identity Argument, which assumes violence to be both good and evil, but good only when it reestablishes a person's identity such that the person is deserving of equal moral respect, Bufacchi also produces a "Consequentialist Argument," which considers violence to be evil, and only justifies violence "*when it is a necessary evil, an indispensable means toward preventing an even greater evil and/or promoting a greater good.*" This Consequentialist Argument justifies violence only if violence is necessary toward eliminating something worse. It considers all violence to be evil. It follows from this Consequentialist Argument that violence can only be known to be a necessary evil and not merely evil, retrospectively. It must be shown that the use of violence does not merely make things worse but eliminates something worse, which cannot be known at the time the violence occurs. If the violence eliminates something worse, then this can only be known after the violence has occurred. So the point at which violence becomes a necessary evil and not only evil violence cannot be the point at which the violence is used. A use of violence can be defined as a necessary evil only on the assumption that one knows what will happen when that violence occurs, but this can only be confirmed after the fact. This reflects Brennan's argument addressed in the previous chapter. Again, we see a theorist begin from the assumption that violence is wrong but quickly move to indicate that it's not entirely wrong when it defeats a worse kind of violence. With Brennan's view on defensive violence, and my point that we can't easily establish whose violence truly was defensive, we see with Bufacchi that the use of violence as a necessary evil suffers the same problem insofar as this also is not easily established. Whether a use of violence really did stop some worse violence and its effects cannot be easily established, particularly if the violence that was stopped does not produce the consequences that it would have produced if it was not stopped. If a use of violence does stop another violence, then in some cases it's a matter of speculation whether something worse really was stopped. This is seen with police violence, for example. Is it a necessary evil? Does police violence really stop something worse from happening, particularly if police often show up on the scene after events have already occurred?

Overall, then, Bufacchi's distinctions between violence and other things such as power, force, coercion, and harm, as well as his definitions of kinds of violence extend far beyond the paradigm case core concept of violence and do not only focus on intentional uses of physical means for the sake of causing physical or psychological harms or destruction. The Identity Argument and Consequentialist Argument are each ways in which violence could be justified. Both arguments evaluate violence, defining it as evil, but sometimes as good, or sometimes as a necessary evil. The next section compares Bufacchi's definitions of violence to the World Health Organization's definition, produced in 2014.

2.8 THE WORLD HEALTH ORGANIZATION'S DEFINITION OF VIOLENCE AND THE ROLE OF INTENTIONS

The World Health Organization (WHO) defined violence as "the intentional use of physical force or power, threatened or actual, against oneself, another person, or against a group or community, which either results in or has a high likelihood of resulting in injury, death, psychological harm, maldevelopment, or deprivation."[9] The obvious difference between Bufacchi's definition and this one is that the WHO does not include unintentional violence, violence as an omission, and violence against objects. The WHO only includes the criteria of "the intentional use of physical force, threatened or actual" as that which distinguishes what counts as violence. One significant difference between the definitions produced by the WHO and Bufacchi is that the WHO requires the intention to use violence as a criterion for an action to qualify as an act of violence, while Bufacchi does not. According to the WHO's definition, an unintended threat to cause harm, destruction, or damage does not count as violence. Even though intentions are psychological, and are not always obvious for that reason, the WHO's definition relies on a transparency of intentions. However, the WHO's definition reflects the agreed upon wrongness of paradigm cases of violence.

The WHO, and most versions of commonsense views of violence, reflect an assumption that people are only ever violent when they intend to be. Bufacchi's definition, in contrast, counts unintentional uses of excessive force that result in harm or destruction as kinds of violence. Bufacchi's definition thus has a political implication: it makes it possible to hold individuals and collectives of individuals accountable for the harms and destruction they produce, even if they did not intend to produce those harms and that destruction, and even if they unintentionally omitted something that usually has resulted in harm or injury.

2.9 DIVERSE PERSPECTIVES, IDEOLOGY, AND FUNDAMENTAL DISAGREEMENTS

The point is not that the definition of violence produced by the WHO is worse or better in relation to Bufacchi's. My goal here is not to produce a hierarchy concerning better and worse kinds of definitions of violence but only to indicate that there is a fundamental disagreement concerning what violence is. That is, beyond the paradigm case core conception of violence, distinctions between kinds of violence are essentially contestable. There are similarities between the definitions produced by various individuals, particularly in that violence is typically treated as a means, intentions can but do not necessarily matter, and something is harmed or destroyed, but the differences between definitions abound, and these indicate that the concept of violence is an essentially contested one beyond the paradigm cases, which provides a reason for why, in practice, not all claims concerning violence are taken seriously and not all kinds of violence are addressed. This is particularly the case when theorists refer to systemic and structural violence such as what results from an economic system or an institutional structure. If such things do result in harms or injuries, then whether the economic system or institutional structure is changed in order for those harms and injuries to be avoided, this is a political question and depends on the ideological perspective of individuals and collectives of individuals who could change such things. If someone suffers exploitation and oppression due to capitalist relationships of production, for example, then not many will work to change those relationships and not many will even consider capitalism itself to be that which produces the suffering, particularly if individuals and collectives of individuals benefit from capitalist relationships of production.

The issue is that definitions for violence, beyond the paradigm case core conception of violence, differ. From the perspective of one definition, some act or event can count as a violent one, but not necessarily from the perspective of other definitions. Likewise, from the perspectives of a person, a collective of people, state, or institution, what counts as violence and as a kind of violence is not always what everyone would agree is violence, unless it is a paradigm case of violence. The violence of an individual can also differ from collective violence, state violence, and institutional violence. The four of these do not necessarily correspond to any commonsense view of violence, if the violent acts and events these produce are something other than an intentional use of physical means for the sake of causing physical or psychological harms or destruction. To complicate matters, there are kinds of violence besides those that produce physical or psychological harms or destruction, intentionally or unintentionally. We have already seen, via the Identity Argument and Consequentialist Argument discussed by Bufacchi, that violence can be defined and justified as good even if it is evaluated as evil and wrong. Definitions can be produced for symbolic, linguistic, objective, subjective, creative, destructive, legal, illegal (criminal), legitimate, illegitimate, vengeful, emancipatory, and revolutionary violence. Later, in the fourth chapter, it is also argued that nonviolence itself can count as a kind of violence. Whether an action or event counts as a kind of violence, and possibly as justified, depends on the definition one agrees with. The paradigm case core conception, because it evaluates all cases that fit the paradigm violence as wrong, does not serve to justify any kind of violence, though it could be used in order to indicate what is and is not violence. The paradigm core cases may be useful for establishing an agreement upon what counts as violence, but in relation to other definitions for and distinctions between kinds of violence, one can disagree, arguing that a given definition does not account for other kinds of violence. Given the diversity of possible perspectives pertaining to kinds of violence, it appears that distinctions between kinds of violence are possible, but these distinctions extend the paradigm case core conception of violence as a wrong.

2.10 THE APPLICATION OF GALLIE'S CRITERIA FOR ESSENTIALLY CONTESTED CONCEPTS TO THE CONCEPT OF VIOLENCE

In his seminal article "Essentially Contested Concepts," Walter Bryce Gallie argues that an essentially contested concept is a concept that is used in different ways within arguments produced by theorists such that it is obvious that "there is no one clearly definable general use . . . which can be set up as the correct or standard use."[10] I will apply Gallie's argument to the concept of violence because violence is a concept "the proper use of which inevitably involves endless disputes about [its] proper uses on the part of the users."[11] Despite that there is common agreement concerning paradigm examples of violence, the proper use of the term "violence" beyond the paradigm case core conception of violence is inevitably disputed. From the standpoint of one political ideology, the concept of violence can be defined, evaluated, and justified in a way that is "proper" according to that political ideology but "improper" according to a different political ideology. So because a proper use of the concept of violence is contestable, the actions and events that are claimed to be instances of kinds of violence, and therefore as justified or not, are not necessarily agreed upon as being instances of those kinds of violence.

In order to qualify as an essentially contested concept, the concept of violence must meet seven conditions, outlined by Gallie, and these reveal that violence is an essentially contested concept and not merely a concept about which theorists are radically confused.[12] In short, an essentially contested concept is one that is "an appraisive term [that] signif[ies] an achievement that is internally complex, variously describable and 'open' . . . [and is] used both 'aggressively' and 'defensively.'"[13] It is Gallie's sixth and seventh conditions that indicate that the concept is not merely "radically confused" but actually is an essentially contested one. I will first discuss these two conditions to show that we are not dealing with a radical confusion. Then, I return to the first five conditions because these are the conditions that, without exception, arise within the political, ideological assumptions of theorists who write on violence, defining and evaluating it in ways that extend beyond the paradigm cases of violence.

Condition six indicates that a concept is contested, and not radically confused, because there is some exemplar upon which all agree that the concept is applicable.[14] In contemporary society, the events of 9/11 and the nuclear bombing of noncombatants in Hiroshima and Nagasaki both serve as exemplars that are variously described as violence. The paradigm case core conception of violence defines these as violent events, just as it defines someone's intentionally smashing another person's kneecap with a hammer as violence. Such examples serve as exemplars, that is, paradigm cases. The events of September 11, 2001, often serve as a primary exemplar in contemporary literature, though the actions of ISIS/ISIL (The Islamic State in Syria/The Islamic State in Libya), mass shootings in the United States by US citizens, the killing of unarmed citizens by police, and wars in general are discussed as well. Ideologues, such as Thomas Nagel and Verena Erlenbusch, who are discussed shortly, produce criteria, according to which such exemplars qualify as violence, and as kinds of violence. In short, though the paradigm case core conception of violence that pertains to actions and events that most everyone agrees count as instances of violence provides exemplars, and this means that disputes concerning the meaning of the concept of violence are not due to radical confusions.

Condition six only shows that disagreement occurs not because of a radical confusion. Instead, the meaning of the concept of violence is contested. However, condition six is not alone sufficient for the concept to be an *essentially* contested one. Together with condition seven, a concept fulfills the conditions set out by Gallie for qualifying as an essentially contested concept: "The probability or plausibility, in appropriate senses of these terms, of the claim that the continuous competition for acknowledgement as between the contestant users of the concept, enables the original exemplar's achievement to be sustained and/or developed in optimum fashion."[15] All could agree that an exemplar for a concept exists, but not *continuously* compete with one another. In this case, the concept would not be *essentially* contested. Without continuous competition for recognition of the ways ideologies define and distinguish kinds of violence, the concept of violence would not be essentially contested. Historic tradition in the philosophical literature demonstrates an ongoing competition between rival political philosophies concerned with kinds of violence. Their claims and definitions are in competition. If competition were to cease, this is no indication of an agreement but is instead only a temporary period in which no novel definitions and distinctions are produced.

The concept of violence satisfies conditions six and seven. There is an ongoing contest between political ideologies that describe and define why and how the concept of violence applies to exemplars, but this typically occurs beyond the paradigm cases, which are usually not contested, which is why they are paradigm cases and serve as exemplars. The disagreement between the WHO's definition and Bufacchi's definitions is only one among many. They might not explicitly acknowledge one another's definitions, but the fact that they define violence in ways that conflict demonstrates that they acknowledge that violence must be defined. That is, if there were an agreed upon definition for violence, then it would be superfluous that either of them tries to define violence. If there were an agreed upon definition of violence, then it could be assumed. Indeed, this is precisely why the paradigm case core conception of violence is useful. It focuses on the wrongness of examples of violence about which there is little debate. This paradigm case core conception of violence is not essentially contested, but *when theorists extend beyond it, defining kinds of violence, that's when the contest begins without end.*

Furthermore, the other five conditions required for the concept of violence to be essentially contested are fulfilled. That is, the concept of violence fulfills the first condition, which requires that it is appraisive, insofar as it is applied in relation to some achievement that is itself assessed as violence, no matter whether the achievement is a use of means or an achieved goal.[16] Means used toward goals and goals themselves can be appraised as violent. Likewise, in accordance with the second condition, the achievement explained using a concept of violence is itself "internally complex" because the assumptions, descriptions, evaluations, and argumentation produced on the basis of political, ideological assumptions contribute to the whole of the evaluation of an achievement as an instance of violence.[17] For example, political ideological assumptions, such as those concerning how human freedom, laws, a state, police, and a military relate to one another altogether contribute to the evaluation of a use of violence, and to the evaluation of that which the violence achieves. If we are to understand why and how a political ideology justifies a use of violence, then these internal complexities must be fully considered.

The third condition pertains to violence insofar as that which is achieved, and declared to be violence, is not only "internally complex" but is also "variously describable."[18] This means that what is referred to as violence is dependent upon whether achievements, in the forms of means and goals, fit within the political ideological assumptions of a theorist who is concerned with defining what violence is. Multiple political ideologies, for example, each concerned with freedom, justice, the rule of law, and the role of violence, can describe these in various ways that rival one another.

Additionally, because there is a variety of ways that theorists can construct their political, ideological perspectives, and there is a variety of ways that they can evaluate the means and goals that they define as violent, there is no way to predict which future use of means and gain of goals will count as violent, and this satisfies the fourth condition.[19] A use of violence today may be considered good, right, and legal, but in the future, this same use of violence may later be valued as evil, wrong, and illegal. The concept of violence, in this sense, is "open." *One cannot always indubitably know now that a use of violence is what one defines it as, and one cannot declare that a use of violence will achieve what is expected in the way that one expects.*

Nevertheless, because the concept of violence is essentially contested, it is possible to depict violence as capable of achieving and as having successfully achieved a goal, even if the means used are not considered to be violent by everyone. Political ideologies aggressively and defensively use the concept of violence, each in their own way, in opposition to one another, and this satisfies the fifth condition.[20] Therefore, violence qualifies as an essentially contested concept, given the seven requirements produced by Gallie.

However, again, note that I am not referring to the paradigm case core conception of violence here. I don't think that it is essentially contested because it's unusual for someone to say that murder, rape, torture, etc. are not cases of violence. People generally agree that the paradigm cases are examples of violence, particularly because of their wrongness. It is when this is extended to other things, such as the violence of a particular person or government is addressed, that the essential contestedness emerges. This is particularly important to acknowledge because there is a lot of disagreement about what should and should not have occurred in the past and what should and should not occur now and into the future. The events of January 6 in Washington, DC, at the Capitol serve as an ongoing example of a disagreement. Unless someone denies what can be seen, as some do, there is likely general agreement that some violent acts occurred. However, that's the end of the agreement, and in relation to political ideologies, such as "Stop the Steal" or those who consider the election of President Joe Biden to have been legitimately free and fair, the disagreement begins in an essentially contested way. Russia's current war with Ukraine is another example. It would be highly unusual for someone to be committed to a claim that there is no violence taking place in this war. However, how the violence of these two countries and of their citizens and soldiers is evaluated is essentially contested.

2.11 MACINTYRE ON ESSENTIALLY CONTESTED SOCIAL CONCEPTS: THE CONTINUOUSLY DEVELOPING DEBATE CONCERNING THE CONCEPT OF VIOLENCE

Alasdair MacIntyre, in his article "The Essential Contestability of Some Social Concepts," points out that some concepts, particularly within the social sciences, are essentially contested in ways that do not occur in the natural sciences.[21] In the natural sciences, "decisive and effective answers which are inseparable from the formulation of certain key generalizations" are produced, if even temporarily, in ways that the social sciences do not produce key generalizations.[22] MacIntyre refers to Friedrich Waismann's notion of "the open texture of concepts," which, MacIntyre argues, "depends upon a contrast between the application of criteria (i) in what have been up to now normal circumstances, (ii) as a result of experience in standard conditions . . . and their application in abnormal or radically new situations."[23] MacIntyre considers this distinction to be similar to one made by Hilary Putnam, who "shows that to convey the normal use of a word involves certain sets of what [Putnam] calls 'core facts.'"[24] Overall, MacIntyre's reason for referring to Putnam and Waismann is that together they demonstrate that even though "there is not a finite and determinate set of necessary and sufficient conditions which determine the application of a concept . . . or a word . . . [we] in normal circumstances and in standard conditions . . . behave *as if* there were such a finite and determinate set."[25] He means that we use some concepts, even though we lack a full-fledged understanding of the conditions that qualify uses of the concepts, because it would otherwise be impractical to use those concepts. Such concepts are "indefinitely debatable" because they are essentially contested. To argue that these concepts, such as violence, are not "indefinitely debatable" is to prove that they are "indefinitely debatable" and essentially contested. The paradigm case core conception of violence serves as the definition with which people typically and commonly refer to particular actions and events as violent ones. Many can point to the same action or event and say that it is "violent," but this is the initial moment from which emerges the question, "why and how is it violent?" and there begin the disagreements.

MacIntyre adds that essentially contested concepts are "indefinitely debatable" because, unlike concepts used within the natural sciences, in the social sciences "beliefs are partially constitutive of at least some central social institutions and practices, and such beliefs always involve some version of a concept of the institution or practice in question."[26] These beliefs are ideological insofar as they correspond to and "are partially constitutive of at least some social institutions and practices . . . [and] affect their relationships to those institutions and practices, and . . . consequently affect the character of such institutions and practices," particularly in the case of political parties.[27] This means that, within a political party, for example, certain beliefs and behaviors constitute the "character" of the party, but there can be disagreement concerning what these beliefs and behaviors are, and there can be disagreement concerning what exactly is the topic of disagreement.[28] These disagreements occur not only verbally but also in practice. Political parties may agree that something is violent but disagree on the kind of violence it happens to be.

So though we can refer to political collectives of individuals by name, their uses of terms such as “violence” that relate to their shared beliefs, but that they disagree upon, leads to their actions not being in agreement. People act in relation to those things they define in relation to their beliefs. If there is agreement that an action is violent but disagreement concerning the kind of violence it happens to be, then how people act in relation to this action differs. Even though a political party may seem to have one motive and shared belief, this belief is articulated and enacted in various ways. So whether something is violent, and what kind of violence it happens to be, depends upon the beliefs, ideological and political, of the person, institution, or state that applies the word “violence” to some event or action. Even if two or more agree on some things, they will disagree on other things, and there is no guarantee that when they utter the word “violence” in relation to the same thing that they agree on anything other than that the word “violence” applies in the sense of the paradigm case core conception of violence.

MacIntyre also argues that disagreement arises because the actions and ideas that pertain to the social sciences are ones that may be identified, but their identity is not something that can be indicated in reference to some “law-governed” example.[29] Actions and ideas are identifiable because there is a “continuity of institutionalized argument, debate, and conflict,” but this identification is not possible because of some agreed upon way in which these actions and ideas are identified.[30] That is, there is no one, law-like way, for example, in which 9/11 can qualify as having involved a kind of violence, even though most people would likely say that 9/11 involved paradigmatic violence. For these reasons, every instance of someone’s declaration or definition of what a concept is amounts to an instance that makes it clear that there is disagreement concerning the concept. A person who declares, “violence is X” or that “X is violence” does not define violence and settle the debate but instead contributes to a continuous debate concerning the concept of violence.

Disagreement, in this way, sustains the existence of the relevance of the contested concept. Disagreement does not continue in the same particular way forever but transforms into new kinds of disagreements in relation to discontinuous breaks that are introduced when individuals produce novel arguments and ways of thinking of some social concepts. The meaning of such concepts is not settled, and if it seems as if the concept’s meaning has been settled, then this is only a period during which there is a lack of a production of discontinuous breaks and novel arguments. Disagreement will arise again, though, even if it seems as though the matter concerning some concept, such as violence, is settled.

Furthermore, MacIntyre argues that “innovations help to define new sets of alternatives which create new occasions for decision and for conflict over decisions," and none of these innovations could have been predicted according to some agreed upon concept.[31] It follows that "normative debate is ineliminable from the question of how the concept . . . is to be applied. [So it is] essentially contestable."[32] The point to take from MacIntyre is not that theorists are getting better at conceptualizing violence but that they are merely engage in an ongoing debate concerning the concept of violence, innovating ways in which violence is defined. It should be noted that the same is the case for other terms as well. Freedom, democracy, rights, legitimacy, and justice, for example, are concepts for which there is agreement in some ways, in relation to particular exemplars, but beyond the common agreement, there is disagreement concerning *what* should be evaluated as freedom, democracy, rights, legitimacy, and justice, and there is disagreement *how* these should be evaluated. Any attempt to "operationalize" such concepts (including violence) so that they are "amenable to scientific procedure" would be trivial, ad hoc, and only serve to contribute to an ongoing debate, not to ending it, because any one way of declaring that a social concept should be used would be an operationalization of the concept only for the sake of operationalizing it.[33]

For example, one might declare that a concept should be used restrictively, but this would be a restriction that is made simply for there being a restricted use of the concept and to maintain that only this one use of the concept qualifies as a use of the concept is trivial and ad hoc. Any restriction that is ad hoc in this way is unwarranted because it trivializes the concept. So strict definitions for social and political concepts are not desirable.[34] From this perspective, it follows that the definitions produced by the WHO and Bufacchi are ad hoc and trivial. They participate in an ongoing debate by producing such definitions. I should note that the paradigm case core conception is not a definition of violence. It's an inductive list of examples that most people typically consider to be wrong. It's only useful because it provides a ground for agreement (we all have experienced violence in various ways and are familiar with what we have experienced) that shows how the wrongness of violence is politically, ideologically transformed when kinds of violence are distinguished.

2.12 WILLEM DE HAAN ON VIOLENCE AS AN ESSENTIALLY CONTESTED CONCEPT

Professor of criminology Willem de Haan argues that violence is an essentially contested concept. In his "Violence as an Essentially Contested Concept," de Haan argues that criminologists should move beyond "one of the most common ways of defining violence[, which is] to argue that violence is the use of force that has been prohibited by law" because

> for a criminologist it is more fruitful, both theoretically and methodologically, to consider definitions of violence to be essentially contested, to accept that, depending on the specific contexts of discovery and contexts of justification, valid arguments are feasible for either inclusive or restrictive definitions of violence, and that a proper definition of "violence" should not a priori be seen as a starting point for empirical research but as a temporary outcome, which may or may not prove to be useful in future research. Exploring a diversity of definitions is fruitful because by means of adjusting concepts scientific progress can [be] made [*sic*].[35]

De Haan's aim is to convince criminologists to avoid approaching violence from the restrictive view of what the law prohibits. Legally defined kinds of criminal violence are insufficient for addressing what counts as violence.

Though de Haan does not explicitly state this, there is a political motivation for criminologists to approach the concept of violence more inclusively. The legitimacy of the law's definition of criminal violence can be questioned, and this is not a politically neutral point for de Haan to make. He writes,

> Occupational groups like the police . . . have a vested interest in ensuring that "violence" is an issue for which they can claim professional competence and which they can use to preserve the image of their jobs as dramatic and dangerous. . . . [They] evinced interest in defining actions so that they fall either inside or outside "violence."[36]

The police want to appear to be authorities on violence, but because the police consider things to be violence that others might not consider violence, the police reveal the need to avoid defining violence only in relation to uses of force that are prohibited by law. De Haan points out, as an example, that while the police claim violence to have occurred when an elderly person slaps a nurse, nursing home workers refuse to call this action violent. If criminologists only account for criminal violence as defined by law, and only when the police claim it to have occurred, then this is a nonneutral, political restriction within the state's political, ideological assumptions concerning its justification for its legal order, namely the assumption that the imposition and enforcement of laws is not itself productive of kinds of violence.

De Haan's concern reflects a political, ideological one because people who commonly agree on a definition of violence, or on distinctions between kinds of violence may overlook other kinds of violence, or may claim kinds of actions to be violent, while other collectives of individuals would not. In relation to other collectives, these disagreements concerning what violence is and the distinctions between kinds of violence are essential. This suggests that there is no neutral definition of violence, nor are there neutral distinctions between kinds of violence. Not even commonsense views of violence are politically neutral because they only define those kinds of actions and events that people commonly agree count as violent ones: the philosophical theories discussed here are critiques of the commonsense view. Not even the paradigm case core conception of violence is politically neutral because how a person conceives of violence based on paradigm cases depends upon what instances of violence the person has experienced and how they experienced them in relation to others. In the following section, I utilize Thomas Nagel and Verena Erlenbusch's arguments concerning the concept of "terrorism" because terroristic violence is itself an exemplary case of a kind of violence that is nonneutrally, politically defined.

2.13 THOMAS NAGEL ON THE CONCEPT OF TERRORISM

Soon after September 11, 2001, Thomas Nagel authored the article "What Is Wrong with Terrorism?"[37] Here, he asks, "what makes *terrorist* killings any more worthy of condemnation than other forms of murder?" He rejects appraising the concept of terrorism and condemning terrorists in relation to the goals they seek. Instead, Nagel focuses on the means used because it is not the goals of terrorists that are condemned but the way in which they utilize means. The goals of terrorists do not help to define terrorism because they are goals that are sometimes the same ones that nonterrorists also pursue, such as freedom or justice. So when terrorism is condemned, it is not the goals themselves that are condemned but the means used.

Terroristic means, though, must be of a particular kind so that they are distinguishable from other nonterroristic uses of means that may *prima facie* appear to be the same. Nagel commits to the distinction that portrays terrorists as those who intentionally kill noncombatants. Nonterrorists do not intentionally kill noncombatants. This distinction enables Nagel to sustain the view that "collateral damage" (the killing of noncombatants) is justifiable when states use violence, particularly when doing so is "unavoidable—and morally permissible." Terrorism's abhorrent character exists, in other words, because it directly aims to kill noncombatants and does not accidentally produce collateral damage. This raises the issue concerning why it is considered morally permissible for noncombatants to be killed as "collateral damage" but not morally permissible for the use of terroristic means to kill noncombatants. This is particularly problematic, if there are no noncombatants, given that indirectly, citizens can contribute to the development and strengthening of combatants, which might mean that they are also combatants, at least in an indirect sense. Last, it is also problematic because Nagel denies that a terrorist could accidentally, unintentionally produce collateral damage.

In order to explain why it is wrong for terrorists to kill noncombatants and acceptable for states to kill noncombatants in the sense of "collateral damage," Nagel refers to the exemplary case of the bombing of Hiroshima. The intentional killing of noncombatants, in this case, is contestable as a case of terrorism. The United States, some might argue, did not intend to kill noncombatants, despite that President Harry S. Truman knew that noncombatants would be harmed as a result of bombing Hiroshima.[38] In this case, the killing of noncombatants is accidental. The use of the atomic bomb, in this case, is not considered terrorism because the United States did not directly intend to kill these noncombatants. That they were harmed, or killed, was not the intended result but an unfortunate consequence. Thus, their victimization is defined as "collateral damage." The United States is not morally condemnable, some could say, because the victimization of noncombatants was not what the United States meant to do.

The paradigm case core conception of violence and the WHO's definitions are relevant here because the US political leadership claimed its intentions. Almost everyone will agree that the use of an atomic bomb to attack, harm, kill, and destroy people and property is an instance of violence. However, not everyone will agree that this action-event counts as one that produces collateral damage, particularly because the United States knew that noncombatants would be harmed and killed.

Nonetheless, Nagel then adds that the difference between intentional and nonintentional uses of violence against noncombatants rests upon an assumption that each individual deserves "minimal basic respect," in the sense that, unless an individual is "a danger to others," each individual may not be killed "just because it would be useful to do so." Any violation of this "minimal basic respect" is wrong. So the question concerning the use of the atomic bomb centers on whether the United States thought it to be useful to use violence against harmless noncombatants. If the United States knew that the harmless noncombative residents of Hiroshima were not a "danger to others," then did the United States violate Nagel's "minimal basic respect" requirement? If so, then the bombing was an act of terrorism, and wrong.

The issue is that, during warfare, noncombatants are injured and killed, but this is not necessarily considered terrorism because a state never declares its intention to kill them and can deny it intended to do so. The state can always declare that it never intended to harm noncombatants, and if it does so, then these deaths are "collateral damage." In the case of terrorism, though, the killing of noncombatants is the explicit, intended aim. So the issue concerns whether there is an intention to use violence against noncombatants. The significance of the role played by intentions makes it possible for Nagel to define the term "terrorist" such that a terrorist is one who intentionally aims to use violence against noncombatants.

Nagel's definition of the concept of terrorism sets out three conditions. First, an act of terrorism is one that is intentionally directed toward innocent, noncombatants. Second, terrorism does not aim to minimize civilian casualties. And third, terrorism does not demonstrate a minimal basic respect for (human) life.[39] So Nagel's characterization of the conditions for violence counting as terrorism portrays the bombing of Hiroshima, which the US leadership knew would harm noncombatants, as not being an instance of terrorism, and the events of 9/11 as an instance of terrorism. When the United States bombed Hiroshima, it did not intend to kill noncombatants but instead aimed to minimize civilian casualties, which indicates its minimal basic respect for human life, despite the fact that the United States knew that it would kill noncombatants and that the use of the atom bomb completely destroys, or at least significantly disfigures and poisons, life.

At this point, it appears that Nagel's distinction concerning what counts as terrorism is controversial. The paradigm case core conception of violence would define the dropping of an atomic bomb on humans as a violent act or event. Whether or not it is justified is not something that the paradigm conception of violence can argue. Instead, beyond the commonsense view of violence, whether this action-event counts as terroristic is disputable, given that the United States knew that noncombatants would be killed or harmed. To define these killings and harms as collateral damage is to relate these to the concept of an unintended consequence, which itself is contestable.

In the following, Verena Erlenbusch's argument concerning the ability of a state to define who counts as a terrorist is discussed because this contests Nagel's definition for terroristic violence. Not only does Erlenbusch argue that terrorism is an essentially contested concept, but she also indicates how the ability to wield greater violence enables an entity, such as a state, to act as an authority on what counts as kinds of violence. This indicates that terrorism is an essentially contested concept because violence is an essentially contested concept. As a result, neither Nagel nor Erlenbusch define what violence is, though they discuss terroristic violence at length and agree that actions and events like 9/11 are paradigm cases of violence.

2.14 VERENA ERLENBUSCH ON THE CONCEPT OF TERRORISM

In her "Notes on Violence: Walter Benjamin's Relevance for the Study of Terrorism," Erlenbusch argues that "if the theorist uncritically adopts the state's account of terrorism, [then the theorist] occludes an important dimension of the phenomenon that allows for a rethinking of the state's claim to a monopoly on legitimate violence," which is that a state can declare any threat to its own "legitimate" use of violence, or to its legal order, to be an act of terrorism.[40] Erlenbusch means that states have the ability to define uses of violence against them as terrorism, despite that a state's own use of violence can be a similar use of violence to that which the state declares to be terrorism. For example, a building can be blown up by a person and people harmed and killed, but if it is a state that performs this action, rather than nonstate actors, then it is legitimate violence, from the perspective of that state. If it were nonstate actors who produced this violence, then states could define it as terroristic violence. The use of drones by the United States in other countries, for example, which sometimes kill noncombatants rather than the intended targets, is not considered to be terroristic by the United States, though if others were to use drones on US territory in this way, odds are that the United States would define this as an act of terroristic violence. The actions themselves are defined as violence by the paradigm case core conception of violence, but how they are evaluated as kinds of violence depends on the entity that distinguishes between kinds of violence. The state's distinctions mean that a state would never define its own uses of violence as terroristic but only as legitimate. However, rather than posit intentions as a criterion, as Nagel does, Erlenbusch's point is that a state that has a monopoly on legitimate violence, and this monopoly makes it possible for a state to distinguish between kinds of violence, defending its own uses as legitimate ones.

Erlenbusch refers to Walter Benjamin's 1921 influential essay "Critique of Violence" in order to ground her conception of terrorism and its relationship to a state's monopoly on legitimate violence.[41] Her aim is "to examine the discursive portrayal of terrorism by governments and mainstream media as an illustration of Benjamin's analysis of state power."[42] She utilizes Gallie's phrase "essentially contested concept" but does not mention Gallie's argument, nor the conditions that qualify a concept as an essentially contested one. Erlenbusch also utilizes Max Weber's definition of a modern state as that which has a monopoly on legitimate violence within a territory, though she does not mention this.[43] Nonetheless, we can ask on what basis Erlenbusch claims that terrorism is an essentially contested concept in relation to a state's monopoly on legitimate violence.

2.15 TERRORISM AS AN ESSENTIALLY CONTESTED CONCEPT

In order to test whether terrorism counts as an essentially contested concept, we have to ask whether Erlenbusch qualifies "terrorism" as a concept that is "an appraisive term [that] signif[ies] an achievement that is internally complex, variously describable and 'open' . . . [and is] used both 'aggressively' and 'defensively,'" as Gallie puts it.[44] Erlenbusch indicates that "the state has to impose a certain understanding of terrorism against other contesting interpretations . . . [and] has to successfully portray a particular form of violence as terrorism," but she also warns that to simply adopt the perspective of the state on what constitutes terrorism is to be "uncritical."[45] This assertion can be directed against Nagel.

Nagel argues that the state's production of "collateral damage," which is the unintentional killing of noncombatants, is not an instance of terrorism. To agree with Nagel, from Erlenbusch's point of view, is to uncritically side with the state. In order to understand the concept of terrorism, and how it is essentially contested, how terrorists and states utilize violent means must be addressed, but we should also take into account how the use of particular means is itself usurped by a state such that the state authorizes itself as the only authority capable of making the distinction between what counts as terrorism and what does not. Terrorism is warfare not conducted by, or recognized as, a legitimate state entity. Terrorists intend to kill noncombatants, while states do not. However, states can claim that they do not intend to kill noncombatants because they possess a monopoly on legitimate violence.

Here, we see relationships between the essentially contested concept of terrorism and the essentially contested concept of violence emerge. States enter into the continuously developing debate concerning what counts as terroristic violence by claiming that only their own definition of terrorism is the correct one. A state rejects the claim that its own use of violence is terroristic and rejects the claim that the violence that the state defines as terroristic is not terroristic. So this is a foundation for a fundamental disagreement, particularly when states use violence when they know that noncombatants will be harmed or killed.

Both Nagel and Erlenbusch are concerned with the same events that occurred on 9/11. This exemplar serves as the foundation for a disagreement. How they explain these events as acts of terrorism differs. That they agree upon this exemplar indicates that their disagreement concerning the concept of terrorism is not due to radical confusion. Erlenbusch states that "the years following the events we call 9/11 have cemented a public understanding of terrorism as political violence against states that is exercised by groups or individuals who do not belong to recognized states and thus lacks [*sic*] legitimacy."[46] The issue, in her view, is that "the concept [of terrorism] has undergone a process of fragmentation that resulted in the potential applicability of terrorism to all sorts of actions that are perceived as threats to the so-called 'Western' way of life."[47] Because a state can define threats and can define threats as terrorism, the result is an "obscurity that underpins and troubles any effort that seeks to establish a once-and-for-all definition of terrorism." There is a fundamental disagreement concerning the concept of terroristic violence. Because states define, decide, and apply the concept of terrorism, a static, agreed upon definition of violence is impossible. What one state or collective of people define as an act of terrorism, another state or collective of people can define as an act of war, or as revolutionary violence, for example.

The consequence of this, according to Erlenbusch, is that "states tend to outlaw as criminal those acts that are interpreted as terrorist . . . [and] rely on emergency decrees that allow for the restriction of civil liberties and preemptive action." Once terrorism or a potential for terrorism is defined, civil liberties are curtailed for the sake of gaining an upper hand on the state-defined means of potential terrorism. For example, if organizations defined as terroristic utilize internet platforms and telephones, then states may curtail privacy rights for the sake of tracking the communication that takes place within these terrorist organizations. The result of states defining what counts as terrorism is twofold: (1) terroristic violence is rendered illegal and illegitimate, in relation to the state's use of violence; and (2) states thereby endorse their own "excessive and extraordinary measures to be taken against those designated terrorists; measures that would normally lack both legality and legitimacy." Erlenbusch's view significantly disagrees with a view like that of Nagel in that she takes into account that states authorize themselves as the authorities that distinguish between terroristic violence and nonterroristic violence. Nagel's distinction between terroristic violence that intentionally harms noncombatants and state violence that produces collateral damage is a view produced from the state's perspective, and it is this kind of view that Erlenbusch's argument criticizes as an uncritical view of how violent actions are defined as terrorism by states.

Erlenbusch's point can be put in these terms: It is only because the state has a monopoly on legitimate violence that a state can declare the harms it produces upon noncombatants to be collateral damage. If nonstate actors had this monopoly on legitimate violence, they too could define their own uses of violence as legitimate and productive of collateral damage. Yet because they do not possess this monopoly, nonstate actors can always be defined as terrorists by a state. This does not occur due to a state's animosity toward the nonstate actors themselves, she argues, but because the nonstate actors produce an exception to the state's authority, threatening that authority and the state's existence. A state utilizes this threat to its authority and existence as the reason for defining these threats as terroristic and as a justification for its own uses of violence against the nonstate actors. Even if a state's use of violence is greater and more destructive than the terrorist's use of violence, this is for the sake of sustaining the state's authority and existence against the threat produced by terrorists, and therefore, from the state's perspective, the state's violence is legitimate.

Also, Erlenbusch argues that intentions only play a role because states are able to openly define their intentions. Nagel's restriction to intentional uses of violent means supports a state's definition of its own uses of violence against noncombatants as collateral damage and ignores the state's ability to openly define its own uses of violence. Anyone who produces violence against a state, which might be defined as terroristic violence, is already demonized by the state and is not necessarily afforded an opportunity to openly declare intentions.[48] So states can distinguish between what is terroristic violence and its own uses of violence as legitimate because of the greater monopoly on legitimate violence that secures the states' authority to make these distinctions. Erlenbusch can restrict a definition of terroristic violence to Nagel's definition and, at the same time, show that Nagel's definition ignores the significance of a state's monopoly on legitimate violence. Both of their claims can be aggressively defended against one another, even if they agree and use the word "terrorism" in reference to the same kinds of actions and events defined by the paradigm case core conception of violence. So because terroristic violence evaluates kinds of violence, terroristic violence is an essentially contested concept. Disagreement with the claim that terroristic violence is an essentially contested concept only demonstrates that it is an essentially contested concept.

2.16 CONCLUSION

This chapter has outlined various definitions for violence produced by Bufacchi and the WHO. The WHO's definition is akin to a commonsense view concerned with paradigm cases of violence, and Bufacchi's distinction between kinds of violence extends beyond these. It was also shown that, though there is an etymological relationship between the concept of violence and the concept of "to violate," this relationship does not define violence. Instead, at bottom, there are paradigm cases of violence that are immediately understood to be wrong. In general, violence makes way by cutting through, disrupting, destroying, harming, and killing. Distinctions between kinds of violence are evaluations of kinds of violence that extend beyond the paradigm cases view. These evaluations, such as the distinction between terroristic and legitimate violence, positively and negatively value kinds of violence. These evaluations appraise actions and events as complex achievements that count as kinds of violence, but these actions and events are variously describable, as shown by the outline of Nagel and Erlenbusch's definitions and discussions concerning terroristic violence in relation to the state. These actions and events are also "open" in that they can be defined, described, and evaluated in novel ways in the future. Furthermore, how and why actions and events, such as 9/11, count as kinds of violence is debatable, and both Nagel and Erlenbusch's views can be aggressively and defensively used against one another. In other words, beyond the paradigm case core conception of violence, which theorists and the general population usually agree upon, particularly upon their wrongness, distinctions between kinds of violence are essentially contestable in the way that Gallie requires a concept to count as an essentially contested one. So violence is an essentially contestable concept *when such distinctions are produced.*

The positive and negative evaluations of kinds of violence each arise from an assumed political ideology. Political ideologies oppose one another, as seen between Nagel's view that supports a state's claim that it produces collateral damage when the state's violence harms or kills noncombatants, and Erlenbusch's critique of a state's ability to make this claim only because it possesses a monopoly on legitimate violence. Nagel's supportive view reflects his political ideology, and Erlenbusch's critical view reflects hers. Their arguments fundamentally disagree with one another. Their definitions of and distinctions between kinds of violence are not politically neutral. So beyond the paradigm cases of violence, distinctions between kinds of violence are essentially contestable and nonneutrally political.

In the following chapter, various political ideologies are outlined from the perspectives of influential theorists concerned with the existence of modern states. Their distinctions between kinds of violence are shown to disagree with one another, demonstrating the continuously developing debate and the nonneutral political character of their distinctions. These disagreements reveal that, beyond the paradigm case core conception of violence, not only is the concept of violence an essentially contested one but these disagreements are nonneutrally political, which means that definitions for violence and for kinds of violence are *essentially* nonneutrally political. Agreement with any of them likely reflects one's own political, ideological beliefs, and if one believes in the correctness of a definition or distinction between kinds of violence, then one authorizes that definition and distinction as legitimate. The result is that what counts as legitimate is itself, therefore, contestable. Because kinds of violence distinguished beyond the paradigm case core conception of violence are essentially contested, we cannot know for certain that uses of violence are what we believe them to be because others can disagree with us.

NOTES

1. Vittorio Bufacchi, "Violence," in *International Encyclopedia of Ethics*, ed. H. Lafollette (Hoboken: Wiley-Blackwell, 2013), https://doi.org/10.1002/9781444367072.wbiee146.

2. Bufacchi also provides reasons for thinking of violence as distinct from "excessive force," which are the same as the reasons he gives for thinking that violence is distinct from power. He writes, "force (as with power) is a dispositional concept, to the extent that it refers to an ability or potentiality."

3. Newton Garver, "What Violence Is," in *Violence: A Philosophical Anthology*, ed. Vittorio Bufacchi (New York: Palgrave Macmillan, 2009), 5338. Here is Garver on the relationship between the concept of violence and the concept of violation. He writes, "Violence in human affairs is much more closely connected with the idea of violation than with the idea of force. What is fundamental about violence is that a person is violated . . . because a person has certain rights which are undeniably, indissolubly, connected with being a person. One of these is a right to one's body. . . . Apart from a body, what is essential to one's being a person is dignity . . . [and] autonomy is essential to being human." A violation of a body, of dignity, or of autonomy counts as violence.

4. Charlton Thomas Lewis, *An Elementary Latin Dictionary* (New York: American Book Company, 1890), 924.

5. Ibid., 922.

6. Ibid.

7. Bufacchi, "Violence," 5339. Garver characterizes four kinds of violence: "Violence in human affairs amounts to violating persons. It occurs in several markedly different forms, and can usefully be classified into four different kinds based on two criteria, whether the violence is personal or institutionalized, and whether the violence is overt or covert and quiet."

8. Ibid., 5340.

9. WHO Global Consultation on Violence and Health, Violence: A Public Health Priority, WHO/EHA/SPI.POA.2 (Geneva: WHO, 1996).

10. Walter Bryce Gallie, "Essentially Contested Concepts," in *Proceedings of the Aristotelian Society* 56 (1955–1956): 168.

11. Ibid., 169.

12. Ibid., 171–72, 180.

13. Ibid., 180–81.

14. Ibid., 180.

15. Ibid.

16. Ibid., 171.

17. Ibid., 171–72.

18. Ibid., 172.

19. Ibid.

20. Ibid.

21. Alasdair MacIntyre, "The Essential Contestability of Some Social Concepts," *Ethics* 84 (1973): 1.

22. A triangle is a three-sided figure, for example, and nothing more is necessary for understanding what counts as a triangle.

23. Ibid., 1–2. See also Friedrich Waismann, D. M. McKinnon, and W. C. Kneal, "Symposium: Verifiability," *Proceedings of the Aristotelian Society, Supplementary Volumes* 19 (1945): 101–64. Here, Waismann argues that "open texture is a very

fundamental characteristic of most, though not all, empirical concepts, and it is this texture which prevents us from verifying conclusively most of our empirical statements." In relation to the concept of violence, when it is used to refer to some experienced thing, the only way in which one can avoid vagueness is by more stringently defining the rules that indicate why the concept of violence applies, though this does not eliminate the fact that it has an "open texture," in that there are other ways those rules could be defined. Again, therefore the paradigm case core conception of violence is useful. It doesn't eliminate the possibility for disagreement but at least provides a generally common way to think of violence. See especially p. 23.

24. MacIntyre refers to Hilary Putnam, "Is Semantics Possible?" *Metaphilosophy* 1 (1970): 187–201.

25. MacIntyre, "The Essential Contestability," 2.

26. Ibid., 3.

27. Ibid.

28. Ibid., 4.

29. Ibid., 4–5.

30. Ibid., 5.

31. Ibid.

32. Ibid., 7.

33. Ibid., 8.

34. Ibid.

35. Willem de Haan, "Violence as an Essentially Contested Concept," in *Violence in Europe: Historical and Contemporary Perspectives*, ed. Sophie Body-Gendrot and Pieter Spierenburg (New York: Springer-Verlag, 2008), 27, 38.

36. Ibid., 38. De Haan is also referencing how workers at nursing homes differentiate between their patients being violent when they slap someone, and when they are not violent when they slap someone. He argues that police "dramatize" by referring to all slaps as violence, in a way that nursing home staff do not.

37. Thomas Nagel, "What Is Wrong with Terrorism?," *Project Syndicate*, November 19, 2002, accessed January 12, 2023, https://www.project-syndicate.org/commentary/what-is-wrong-with-terrorism.

38. Three days after Hiroshima was bombed by the United States of America, on August 6, 1945, and on the day that Nagasaki was bombed, on August 9, 1945, President Truman gave a speech from the White House at 10:00 p.m., in which he states that "the world will note that the first atomic bomb was dropped on Hiroshima, a military base. That was because we wished in this first attack to avoid, insofar as possible, the killing of civilians. But that attack is only a warning of things to come. If Japan does not surrender, bombs will have to be dropped on her war industries and, unfortunately, thousands of civilian lives will be lost. I urge Japanese civilians to leave industrial cities immediately and save themselves from destruction." Obviously, President Truman was thoroughly aware that the atomic bomb would destroy the lives of civilian noncombatants because he publicly admits that the military aimed to avoid civilian casualties. See "Radio Report to the American People on the Potsdam Conference," *Harry S. Truman Library & Museum*, accessed January 13, 2023, https://www.trumanlibrary.gov/soundrecording-records/sr61-37-radio-report-american-people

-potsdam-conference. It is on this assumption that because Hiroshima was a military base, which Truman targeted first, fewer civilians would be there that leads Nagel to reference this event rather than Nagasaki. It appears to be a case of Truman's intention to avoid killing and injuring noncombatants.

39. "Human" is placed in parentheses here because Nagel's description of the moral condition, "minimal basic respect for life," is intended to only apply to humans here. In relation to wilderness, contemporary human society could, on Nagel's terms, be depicted as terrorists, should one wish to point out the intentional destruction of the environment, and the purposeful production of animals for the sake of their later destruction, which violates the condition of "minimal basic respect for life." I don't think that Nagel intends to extend this "minimal basic respect for life" to nonhuman life. Furthermore, Nagel is implicitly utilizing the Doctrine of Double Effect. The intention to respect life and to avoid harming noncombatants is defined. This makes it possible for states to define the deaths and harms of noncombatants as "collateral damage." Violence intentionally used to harm and kill noncombatants is terroristic.

40. Verena Erlenbusch, "Notes on Violence: Benjamin's Relevance for the Study of Terrorism," *Journal of Global Ethics* 6 (2010): 167. State leaders declaring their own uses of violence as not counting as terror has not always been the case. For example, Maximilien Robespierre, the leader of the Committee of Public Safety that governed France, urged uses of terror as a virtue of democracy and freedom. In his speech, *On the Moral and Political Principles of Domestic Policy*, given on February 5, 1794, Robespierre states, "If the spring of popular government in time of peace is virtue, the springs of popular government in revolution are at once *virtue and terror:* virtue, without which terror is fatal; terror, without which virtue is powerless. Terror is nothing other than justice, prompt, severe, inflexible; it is therefore an emanation of virtue; it is not so much a special principle as it is a consequence of the general principle of democracy applied to our country's most urgent needs. . . . Subdue by terror the enemies of liberty, and you will be right, as founders of the Republic. The government of the revolution is liberty's despotism against tyranny." See Maximilien Robespierre, "Robespierre February 1794: Justification of the Use of Terror," accessed January 13, 2023, https://www.marxists.org/history/france/revolution/robespierre/1794/terror.htm.

41. Walter Benjamin, "Critique of Violence," in *Reflections: Essays, Aphorisms, Autobiographical Writings*, trans. Edmund Jephcott (New York: Shocken, 1986), 277–300. I more thoroughly address Benjamin's argument later.

42. Erlenbusch, "Notes on Violence," 167.

43. Max Weber, "The Profession and Vocation of Politics," in *Weber: Political Writings*, ed. Peter Lassman and Ronald Speirs (New York: Cambridge University Press, 1994), 310–11.

44. Gallie, "Essentially Contested Concepts," 180–81.

45. Erlenbusch, "Notes on Violence," 167.

46. Ibid., 173.

47. Ibid., 174.

48. This point is complicated by the fact that some organizations, such as ISIS/ISIL, do openly declare their intentions and take ownership of uses of violence

directed against innocent noncombatants. In these cases, when these organizations define themselves as using terroristic violence, it is difficult to disagree with them, though this does not eliminate the fact that these organizations are unable to define their uses of violence as legitimate in relation to the monopoly on legitimate violence possessed by a state.

Chapter Three

Disagreement Concerning Political Violence

A Legitimacy Issue

3.1 INTRODUCTION

As we have seen, beyond the paradigm case core conception of violence, there is a fundamental disagreement concerning what counts as violence, what counts as kinds of violence, what kinds of violence are legitimate, and to what violence is essentially related. In this chapter, it will be argued that this disagreement is essentially nonneutrally political and that defined kinds of violence are essentially nonneutrally political. Much of this has to do with the fact that philosophers, historians, and scholars are concerned with the existence of the modern state and its relationship to violence, power, and the political formation of collectives of individuals in relation to visions of what they aim to be, such as freedom, justice, legitimate, lawful, and other things. Each individual person concerned with these kinds of things in their relation to the modern state produces moral equivalence claims, relating these things in relationships to one another in evaluative ways that fundamentally disagree with how others relate them. Each of their views conflict with the views of others in ways that are politically ideological and, therefore, are nonneutrally political. The result, it is argued, is that, beyond the paradigm case core conception of violence, violence is an essentially contested concept for which no definition in the standard philosophical literature is politically neutral. Choosing one definition or distinction between kinds of violence reflects one's belief in a political ideology, even if one chooses a presumably commonsense view. This is because choosing how to define and value kinds of violence means believing in the legitimacy of that definition or distinction between kinds of violence.

Hannah Arendt, for example, in her *On Violence*, argues that violence is not essential to a state's political power because "power always stands in need of numbers, whereas violence up to a point can manage without them because it relies on implements."[1] She disagrees with traditional political philosophy's definition of violence, particularly in the form of war, as essential to state political power and intends to demonstrate the superior legitimacy of nonviolent political power. By treating violence as essentially related to uses of implements, Arendt aims to demonstrate that violence is not essential to state political power because state political power can be construed as not necessarily requiring uses of implements. She argues, "power is indeed of the essence of all government, but violence is not. Violence is by nature instrumental; like all means, it always stands in need of guidance and justification through the end it pursues. And what needs justification by something else cannot be the essence of anything."[2]

In response to the view that violence is not essential to state political power, it will here be argued that whether violence is essential to state political power cannot be settled because there is a disagreement concerning what counts as kinds of violence. That is, there is a tradition of disagreement concerning those things to which violence is essentially related. Furthermore, in response to the traditional liberal assumption that a state's uses of violence are legitimate, it will be argued that what counts as legitimate uses of violence is also a matter of disagreement, given that how a theorist defines kinds of "good" and "bad" uses of violence mobilizes collectives of individuals who believe in a merely theoretical distinction between kinds of violence. The liberal state's definition of its own uses of violence as defensive is not politically nonneutral because the liberal state's definitions contribute to this continuously developing debate. Belief in the legitimacy of a liberal state's use of violence, on the ground that the liberal state claims its own uses of violence to be justified in relation to things like freedom and justice, does not eliminate the disagreement but instead politically and nonneutrally reproduces it.

3.2 VIOLENCE AND THE POLITICAL: ESSENTIALLY RELATED?

In the preface to his work *Disagreement: Politics and Philosophy*, Jacques Rancière describes how disagreements occur, even when two or more people use the same word in reference to the same thing:

> We should take disagreement to mean a determined kind of speech situation: one in which one of the interlocutors at once understands and does not understand what the other is saying. Disagreement . . . is the conflict between one

> who says white [for example] and another who also says white but does not understand the same thing by it or does not understand that the other is saying the same thing in the name of whiteness.[3]

We can substitute the concept "violence" for "white" in the previous sentence. Two persons can both apply the word "violence" to something and understand that they both utter the same word in relation to that thing but can fail to understand what one another means to say because each has their own reasons for speaking the word "violence" in relation to that thing. There are paradigm cases of violence, but the kind of violence people consider them to be within the context in which they occur is a ground for disagreement. Each person agrees that the action or event is violent, enabling them both to apply the word "violence," but their appraisals of the action or event as a kind of violence disagree.

Arendt, for example, detaches violence from the "essence" of state political power so that violence is essentially the instrumental use of implements or instruments as means to goals, regardless of the various ends that are thought to justify their use. She does this in order to elevate the legitimacy of the power of people acting in concert without uses of violence. She thus separates "power" from the instruments of violence: "The extreme form of power is All against One, the extreme form of violence is One against All. And this latter is never possible without instruments."[4] One individual can dominate the "All" only through uses of instruments of violence. It is questionable whether "the All" is a politically meaningful concept. It implies that no one rejects or deviates from this "power." The power of a "people" is not of "All," if it defeats some minority or the way of life preferred by some collective of individuals. It is a form of domination, which could itself be interpreted as violence.

Likewise, whether violence is essentially a use of instruments as means is disputable, particularly because theorists such as Walter Benjamin and Slavoj Žižek describe kinds of violence, which are not in any way uses of implements and instruments, as is discussed toward the end of this chapter. Still, Arendt's claim that violence is essentially the instrumental use of implements as means does not settle the question concerning what violence is, particularly because what counts as an instrument of violence is itself disputable because the power of a people acting in concert could itself be interpreted as the use of themselves as means toward some goal and from the perspective of those who oppose them, this acting in concert can itself be interpreted as a kind of violence.

The concept of violence can commonly be applied to the same action or event, but people can disagree upon why it applies. Authors relate the concept of violence to other things, legitimating some uses rather than others, in relation to those things. An analysis of an author's claims concerning what violence is related to demonstrates what an author believes to be legitimate. Arendt's emphasis on the superiority of the extreme case of a collective of individuals acting entirely in concert is that which she believes to be superior, and so she defines it as such. Likewise, the disagreement between Arendt's definition of violence as a use of implements or instruments by "one," and Nicholas Machiavelli's affirmation of Livy's claim to Lorenzo de' Medici that "*Iustum enim est bellum quibus necessarium, et pia arma ubi nulla nisi in armis spes est*," which translates as "because a necessary war is a just war and where there is hope only in arms, those arms are holy," reveals that Machiavelli means to show to Lorenzo de Medici what counts as a superior kind of violence.[5] The relationships defined by Livy entail that, if war is a kind of violence, and it is necessary, then the violence is necessary and also "just." However, this tells us nothing of when violence becomes necessary and ignores other possible disagreements concerning the concept of "justice." Justice itself can count as an essentially contested concept, given various ways the term can and has been defined throughout history.

The addition that the holiness of war lies in the "hope . . . in arms" reflects a belief in the ability of the "necessary" arms of warfare, that is, violence, to successfully defeat some threat against which violence is the only option. The superiority indicated of a necessary, just war is elevated above other kinds of wars by this "hope," which is a kind of belief in legitimacy, insofar as the "legitimacy" of violence lies in the belief that the violence is what people believe it to be, namely that which is believed to be capable of achieving the goals of those who believe in it. Livy's quote indicates that this hope is related to the holiness of necessitated uses of violent means of warfare. Machiavelli would never suggest to Lorenzo de Medici, his intended audience of *The Prince*, that a prince can rely on the "power of his people acting in concert" because it is this itself that constitutes a rebellious threat and the possible overthrow or demise of the prince's limited power. The power defined by Arendt, because it is the people acting in concert, limits the power of the prince and is, perhaps, the reason why Machiavelli implies that Lorenzo should believe in the holiness of necessary, just wars, that is, uses of violence.[6]

Of course, Machiavelli is thinking in terms of principalities and not modern states or a republic in his book *The Prince*, and Arendt is thinking in terms of modern, liberal democratic republics, but the point on which they disagree holds. There is no agreement concerning their definitions of violence in its relation to power. Their disagreement arises because, for Arendt, the power of the All is legitimately superior to the violence of an individual's uses of violent instruments, while for Machiavelli, the limited power of the prince is secured by his placing all hope in necessitated uses of violent means of war, and certainly not in the people.[7] Their disagreement lies in that, while Arendt places power in the theoretical possibility of a people's united actions, which makes state power redundant, Machiavelli places power in the rule of the prince, which is secured through uses of violence and cruelty. Legitimacy plays the primary distinguishing factor in their disagreement. We do not gain a definition of violence, beyond the paradigm case core conception of violence, but an indication of what they each believe to be legitimate and superior in relation to illegitimate and inferior things. Were they to directly engage with one another, Machiavelli and Arendt could both say that an action is violent, but because they disagree on other things in relation to violence, they disagree on why and how the action is violent.

Additionally, Rancière also explains that disagreements are "not misconstruction[s]" because this would imply that an interlocutor "does not know what [they are] . . . saying. Or what the other is saying." A disagreement does not imply that someone is ignorant, deluded, or misunderstood and does not result from a lack of knowledge. Disagreements do not arise because someone is not "getting things correct." Instead, disagreements arise "wherever contention over what speaking means constitutes the very rationality of the speech situation."[8] In terms of the concept of violence, two people can disagree because they disagree about "what speaking [the word 'violence'] means" such that what each says only makes sense on the basis of there being a fundamental, entrenched disagreement. None of the interlocutors are confused or misunderstood because there is a set of paradigm cases of violence that ground the disagreement. Were they able to speak to one another, both Machiavelli and Arendt could agree that uses of weapons for the sake of causing harm and destruction are instances of violence, but their disagreement would concern the relationship between violence and power.

In contrast to Machiavelli and anyone else who defines violence as related to something that has to do with a state, Arendt argues that violence can no longer be essential to politics, particularly because, with the introduction of nuclear weapons, if violence were essentially related to politics, then the result would be "universal suicide."[9] Her definition of violence reflects her concern with advanced technological weaponry. She urges for the separation of violence from politics because she fears a devastating outcome, which she evaluates negatively, and this leads her to evaluate positively a kind of political power that lies in the people, and not in the uses of violent means. Her argument is that, essentially, violence is not essential to a state because state political power is essential to the concerted actions of a collective of individuals, and she believes in the superiority of "the All" over the violence of one.

Arendt also adds another distinction between rational uses of violence as a last resort for the sake of self-preservation and irrational uses of violence, which are not instances of rational uses of self-defensive violence.[10] However, this is still a definition concerning violence used as a last resort. Violence used as a last resort is defined as an act of self-defense. The issue here again concerns what counts as self-defense. If a use of violence is rational because it is self-defensive, but at some point it is no longer rational because it is no longer self-defensive, then disagreements are possible, particularly concerning the point at which a rational, self-defensive use of violence becomes irrational because it is no longer self-defensive. Everyone could agree that an action is violent, but whether it is self-defensive depends upon how that violent action is evaluated, and it is not necessary that everyone will agree that it is self-defensive. For Machiavelli, waiting to use violence as a last resort and only in self-defense would possibly lead to the failure of a prince to secure his limited power.

3.3 RANCIÈRE ON THE LOGIC OF DISAGREEMENT

The general logical structure of disagreements can be formulated, as Rancière notes, in the following way: "Disagreement is where X cannot see the common object Y is presenting because X cannot comprehend that the sounds uttered by Y form words and chains of words similar to X's own."[11] Rancière describes this as an "extreme" kind of disagreement because there are incommensurable assumptions held on the part of the interlocutors. They fail to communicate with one another, even though they utilize similar words in relation to the same things. What appears as an agreement may be an agreement to disagree, but such an agreement is merely an avoidance of a more fundamental disagreement. As shown via the disagreement between Arendt and Machiavelli concerning the relationship between violence and power, we can say that they use the same words, but because they disagree in relation to other things, they do not agree on this relationship between violence and power. These disagreements are political, which the next section addresses.

3.4 THE POLITICAL AS AN ESSENTIALLY CONTESTED CONCEPT

In contrast to Arendt, Carl Schmitt (who sided with the Nazis in 1933), in his *The Concept of the Political*, defines "the political" as the condition for the state.[12] But the political itself is distinct in that it is defined according to criteria specific to the political, and not in relation to other things, such as "the moral, aesthetic, and economic."[13] The criteria for this "specific political distinction" is the "friend and enemy" distinction. The distinction between friends and enemies is the condition for the existence of the political, which is itself the condition for the existence of a state such that the enemy is "existentially something different and alien, so that in the extreme case conflicts with him are possible."[14] Schmitt defines the other as enemy and only conceives of the political as an antagonistic relationship between friends and enemies. Assuming Schmitt's definition of the political, violence is a political concept, but this is only one way of defining the political. The other need not be defined by the friends as enemy, and the collective interest of a group of individuals need not be unified by a common enemy. The political, as the collective interests of a group of individuals, or as an agreed upon "good" that a collective of individuals pursues need not be defined in any one way. For this reason, the political itself is an essentially contested concept, as is violence, and other related concepts, such as freedom, justice, power, and legitimacy, which cannot all be addressed here.

In the following, I continue to address various political philosophies produced by influential theorists who are directly concerned with the violence of a state and with violence directed against a state. In contrast to Arendt, many theorists define violence as essential to a state or to some aspect of the state, such as to a state's military, power, greatness, law, morality, or to the systemic-symbolic structures that frame the ongoing unfolding of a state's existence. Machiavelli and Schmitt both consider violence to be essential to the state, but both produce anti- or nonliberal arguments that favor this violence and reject any notion of the equality of peoples. In Machiavelli's view, there is no one equal to the prince, and in Schmitt's view, the unequal enemy defines the equality of a collective of individuals. The use of violence against those who are unequal is given a favorable and positive description by both because it dominates and eliminates those who are unequal.

3.5 THE POLITICAL, IDEOLOGICAL DISAGREEMENT BETWEEN HOBBES AND KANT ON THE LEGITIMACY OF THE LIBERAL STATE

Thomas Hobbes and Immanuel Kant's agreement that the state secures individuals from the violence of others presents a useful way toward seeing how there is a disagreement concerning what kinds of violence are superior in relation to other things that are themselves defined as superior. Though both assume from the start a hypothetical assumption of a naturally violent situation of anarchy, their agreement ends here. On the one hand, Hobbes, in chapter 13 of his *Leviathan*, defines the state of nature as a condition in which "man is enemy to every man . . . [such that there is] continual fear and danger of violent death, and the life of man, solitary, poor, nasty, brutish, and short."[15] However, in accordance with the "fundamental law of nature . . . to endeavour peace, as far as he has hope of obtaining it," an individual will "be willing, when others are so too, as far-forth as for peace and defence of himself he shall think it necessary, to lay down this right to all things, and be contented with so much liberty against other men, as he would allow other men against himself."[16] In the state of nature, each individual has a "right to all things," but in the interest of peace, in the form of protection from the threats that other individuals pose, each individual agrees to submit to a sovereign, and forfeits this "right to all things."[17]

Kant, on the other hand, in his *Foundations for the Metaphysical of Morals*, writes that

> before a public lawful condition is established individual human beings, peoples and states can never be secure against violence from one another, since each has its own right to do *what seems right and good to it* and not to be dependent upon another's opinion about this. So, unless it wants to renounce any concepts of right, the first thing it has to resolve upon is the principle that it must leave the state of nature, in which each follows its own judgment, unite itself with all others (with which it cannot avoid interacting), subject itself to a public lawful external coercion, and so enter into a condition in which what is to be recognized as belonging to it is determined *by law* and is allotted to it by adequate *power* (not its own but an external power); that is, it ought above all else to enter a civil condition.[18]

In relation to the violent insecurity of the state of nature that exists before a "public lawful condition" is achieved, once this "civil condition" is achieved between a united collective of individuals, they choose to subject themselves individually to the law's coercive power. This civil condition is

> the original contract [which] is only the idea of this act [the formation of a state via a social contract], in terms of which alone we can think of the legitimacy of a state. In accordance with the original contract, everyone (*omnes et singuli*) within a *people* gives up his external freedom in order to take it up again immediately as a member of a commonwealth, that is, of a people considered as a state (*universi*).[19]

So Kant conceives of the formation of a state in political liberal terms, like Hobbes. A kind of freedom is secured through the existence of the state, and the state is that which is legitimate because people believe in the state's ability to protect them from the violence of the state of nature. They both assume that the state of nature is violent and that exiting from the state of nature is a means to defeating this violence. The common liberal assumption is that a social contract, civil condition, or state is that which secures an individual against this violence and is, therefore, legitimate.

However, beyond this agreement, Hobbes and Kant disagree, as Howard Williams argues in his *Kant's Critique of Hobbes: Sovereignty and Cosmopolitanism*. In particular, Hobbes's liberalism tends toward "an absolutist form" such that the state is "unitary, [but] non-representative and anti-republican," while Kant's republicanism rejects Hobbes's absolutist liberalism as "insufficiently liberal and progressive."[20] For the sake of what he defines as liberal, Kant explicitly rejects Hobbes's work as insufficient. For example, in Kant's article "On the Common Saying: That May Be Correct in Theory, but It Is of No Use in Practice," Kant presents "his own republican approach to political obligation . . . in stark contrast with Hobbes's absolutism.[21]" Kant begins with the assumption that there is a need for a civil constitution, that is, social contract, but for goals and reasons that oppose those of Hobbes.

For example, Williams points out that "for Hobbes moral and political truth are one and the same," producing and applying political justice universally *within* the boundaries of *each* state, while Kant is concerned with universally produced and applied political justice not only within each state but also *between* states, *internationally*.[22] Kant utilizes Hobbes's universalization of moral and legal norms *within a state* as a catalyst toward universalizing moral and legal norms *between states*. Thus, Kant "enters Hobbes's absolutist world [in order to] . . . make his own republican ideas logically follow from [his] reading of Hobbes," Williams argues.[23] The disagreement is that, though both legitimate the existence of a civil state on the basis of the state's securing its members from violence, Kant aims for security between states, and not only within a state. This means that their definitions for a liberal state disagree with one another because they relate the existence of the liberal state to the violence of the state of nature in different ways.

This disagreement arises because Kant takes issue with Hobbes's view expressed in chapter 13 of the *Leviathan*, where Hobbes states that

> in the nature of man we find three principal causes of quarrel: first, competition; secondly, diffidence; thirdly, glory. The first maketh men invade for gain; the second, for safety; and the third for reputation. The first uses violence to make themselves masters of other men's persons, wives, children, and cattle; the second, to defend them; the third, for trifles, as a word, a smile, a different opinion, and any other sign of undervalue, either direct in their persons, or by reflection in their kindred, their friends, their nation, their profession, or their name.[24]

Opposed to this, Kant, as Williams argues, aims to "supersede" Hobbes's claims by distinguishing two aspects of the human individual: "The human individual is part of two realms: one where we regard ourselves from the standpoint of reason, where we can be guided by moral laws; and, secondly, one where we regard ourselves from the standpoint of sense-experience, where we are moved by instinct, inclination, and desire."[25] The disagreement between Hobbes and Kant lies in that Hobbes only addresses the second, "animal" aspect of the human individual and not the first because a human's desires, inclinations, and instincts leads that human to submit to a sovereign in exchange for freedom from violence. However, they also disagree in that, though they agree that there is some kind of social contract; for Hobbes the social contract is a means to "happiness or felicity of the individual subjects," while for Kant, the social contract establishes a "civic constitution," which is "an end in itself."[26] Happiness is not the goal, in Kant's view.

Furthermore, for Hobbes, the social contract achieves "self-preservation and self-protection," which requires limits placed on freedom, which is transferred to the sovereign body.[27] Kant agrees that freedom must be limited, except that the freedom of an individual is not limited and transferred to the sovereign body for the sake of protection in exchange for obedience but is instead transferred to "the impersonal power of the law" itself. This raises the issue of the legitimacy of coercion as an effective violent means toward sustaining the legitimacy of public power, particularly when that coercion is exercised by a public authority.

Kant defines coercion as "any limitation of freedom through another's choice."[28] In Hobbes's *Leviathan*, the freedom of individuals living in the state of nature is absolute in the sense that there is an "absence of external impediments," but under a social contract, this freedom is transferred to the sovereign state.[29] Individuals, in Hobbes view, agree to limit their freedom in exchange for protection, but once they enter the social contract, they continue to be coerced, insofar as they are "tie[d] by fear of punishment to the performance of their covenants."[30] So as Williams points out, Kant disagrees with Hobbes's rationale concerning why an individual would enter into a relationship with a covenant, particularly because the reasons Hobbes gives for a person's entering a social contract are "expediency and prudence," while for Kant, an individual enters due to "the supreme or transcendent requirements of reason."[31] In Kant's view, freedom is restricted, and this restriction is coercion, but insofar as it is the law that restricts freedom, and a rational individual sees this restriction as a rational thing to choose, this coercion is legitimate. For Hobbes, though, an individual escapes the state of nature due to the "danger of violent death," while for Kant, an individual escapes the state of nature in order to enter into a civic constitution because it is rational to enter into legal relationships produced by "the law-making capacities of pure reason."[32] This means that, for Hobbes, entering a social contract is a means to an end, but for Kant, entering into a civic constitution is an end in itself because it is rational to enter into rational (legal) relationships with other rational beings. The reasonableness of morality is the motive for individuals acknowledging the need for political obligations and coercion, for Kant, while Hobbes conceives of legal obligations as only possible if there is a power that enforces law.[33] For Hobbes, the force of law is the ability of power to coerce individuals to act as obligated to act, and this coercion works as a threat of violent punishment or as the threat of exiling an individual to the violence of the state of nature; for Kant, the force of law is reason itself. However, this does not mean that Kant dismisses violence as something that is never needed.

For example, Kant argues in the "Doctrine of Right," the first part of his *Metaphysics of Morals*, that laws produce freedom by hindering obstacles to freedom.[34] In this way, actions in accordance with law do not themselves violate freedom, but are freedom, in the juridical and moral sense. Kant states, "If . . . my action or my condition generally can coexist with the freedom of everyone in accordance with a universal law, whoever hinders me in it does me wrong; for this hindrance (resistance) cannot coexist with freedom in accordance with a universal law."[35] In other words, as long as a person's freedom does not infringe upon or restrict another's freedom, then those free actions are right, lawful actions.

It would seem that violence is wrong because it is a kind of obstacle to freedom, but Kant defines at least one instance in which violence is acceptable. In particular, if a person violently restrains or hinders the freedom of another for the sake of defending himself, then this is justifiable, violent coercion, even if the person who uses violence is not suffering violence.[36] Kant states, "the deed of saving one's life by violence is not to be judged *inculpable* . . . but only *unpunishable*." Kant does not define violence but gives commonsense examples, such as a person's pushing someone out of the way in order to save themself. Such an action is blameworthy, but they cannot be punished for saving their own life through a use of a violent push. In this sense, violence is only punishable when it does not occur for the sake of preserving one's own life, that is, in self-defense.

However, as with Arendt's view that violence is only rational when it is self-defensive, we can again ask what counts as self-defense and when violence ceases being self-defense, and various, opposed explanations could be given. Self-defense might be justifiable in general, but the specifics of a situation would have to be assessed and this is where disagreements can emerge given the possibility of opposed interpretations of what happened. Furthermore, to claim that an act of violence, in a commonsense view's definition of the term, is self-defensive is to extend the paradigm case core conception of violence. A violent action, which would typically be considered wrong by most people, is evaluated as self-defensive, and such an evaluation is not necessarily going to be universally agreed upon without dispute. This indicates that, if the coercive enforcement of law rights wrongs, and self-defense is a justified use of violence, then insofar as the law and freedom are themselves violently defended, violence is sometimes justifiable, in Kant's view. The legitimacy of law, of violent coercions, and of self-defensive violence lies in that these are rational, universalizable, and uphold the freedom of individuals. Coercion, the interference with freedom, is legitimate as a kind of violence, so long as it occurs for the sake of freedom, despite the fact that it restricts freedom.

The point is that the liberal state is conceived of as that which legitimates its own uses of violence, but theorists of the liberal state disagree with one another concerning the legitimacy of a state's use of violence, in terms of what that violence is related to. The disagreement here is that while Kant believes reason leads individuals into rational, universalizable relationships because it is rational to avoid violence within and between states (though violence as self-defense is legitimate because it is rational for freedom to defend itself), Hobbes believes in the sovereign's ability to secure the individual from violent threats such that happiness is attained only within a state. Both consider obedience to be that which is achieved in exchange for the belief in the ability of a liberal state to achieve security from violence, and this constitutes their agreed upon legitimation of the modern state's uses of violence, though they disagree upon the reasons why this legitimacy exists. Their political ideologies disagree, so their distinctions between how the violence of the state of nature is avoided disagree, and the legitimacy of the states they describe is disputable. For both, security is achieved through the exchanges between protection and obedience, but in Hobbes's view, the violence of a liberal state that secures freedom is prudent, and in Kant's view, it is rational self-defense. In what follows, Treitschke's focus on the liberal state's destined power and greatness is discussed next because this demonstrates that there is not only this one way that disagreement arises in relation to violence and the liberal state. Hobbes, Kant, and Treitschke are each concerned with the existence of a liberal state, but how the liberal state relates to violence is a ground for their fundamental disagreement, even though they all implicitly agree upon paradigm cases of violence.

3.6 TREITSCHKE ON MILITARY VIOLENCE AS THE CONDITION FOR THE POWER AND GREATNESS OF THE STATE

In agreement with Hobbes and Kant that the liberal state secures and protects obedient citizens through uses of coercion and violence, Heinrich von Treitschke (who favors an authoritarian monarchy and military state rather than individual rights and liberalism), in his *Politik* lectures, argues that "the state would no longer be what it has been and is, did it not visibly girt about with armed might."[37] For Treitschke, if a state is "incapable of drawing the sword when it sees fit," then the sustainability of that state's existence is uncertain.[38] The use of "armed might" and "the sword" amounts to uses of military violence. His claim is that it is necessary for a state to use this kind of violence: "without war no state could be," he says.[39] So the use of armed violence is an essential condition for the existence of a state.

The existence of a state requires military and legal violence, in Treitschke's view, to the extent that any "blind worshiper of an eternal peace falls into the error of isolating the state, or dreams of one which is universal, which [is] . . . at variance with reason." This rejection of the possibility of "eternal peace" disagrees with Kant's view. Kant, in his *Perpetual Peace,* outlines six preliminary articles that are meant to lessen the likelihood of the conditions for the possibility of war, the third of which is that "standing armies shall in time be totally abolished."[40] However, Kant adds that armies may be used for the sake of peace, until peace is achieved, but these armies must be used only for the sake of achieving peace and not for the sake of punishing enemies.[41] In Kant's view, reason itself, "the supreme moral legislating authority," condemns war as a means to making law and dictates peace as a duty.[42] So Treitschke disagrees in that he considers a belief in the possibility of peace to be "at variance with reason" in such a way that there is nothing commensurable between his and Kant's view concerning uses of military violence and the possibility of peace. Treitschke considers war to be necessary for a state's existence and peace to be a utopian dream, while Kant considers war to be needed only until peace is established, assuming that it actually could be.

Treitschke also argues that the state is power and greatness, which are both achieved and upheld by the state's use of kinds of violence, in the forms of legal compulsion and military force. On state power, he writes,

> Since the state is power, it can obviously draw all human action within its scope, so long as that action arises from the will which regulates the outer lives of men, and belongs to their visible common existence. Historical experience . . . teaches that the state can overshadow practically the whole of a people's life. It will dominate it to the precise extent in which it is in a position to do so.[43]

The state's power lies in its ability to dominate the lives of citizens through legal compulsion, which is the will of the state that regulates the "outer lives" of citizens. In this sense, a state's ability to dominate the lives of its citizens is unlimited in its "attempt to dominate the outer life of its members as far as it is able to do so."[44] Treitschke considers this power, that is, ability to dominate, as a derivative of "its first duty," which is "the double one of maintaining power without, and law within, its primary obligations must be the care of its Army and its Jurisprudence, in order to protect and to restrain the community of its citizens."[45] The care of the army and maintenance of its law are conditions for a state's remaining a state and require violence. The state only directly interferes with individual citizens, though, "in the domain of criminal law," to the extent that "the principles of common law are . . . absolutely binding," and "public servants have no option in the extent to which they exercise their functions," which means that they have no choice other than to fulfill their duty as defined by the laws of the state, particularly when it comes to violently punishing criminals.[46]

Treitschke then argues that war is "the next essential function of the state" because "the protection of their members by armed force remains [a state's] primary and essential task," and this means that "war . . . will endure to the end of history, as long as there is a multiplicity of states."[47] However, given "the economic ravages of war," civilized nations seek wars that are "rarer and shorter," but this is no indication that "wars can ever cease." "They neither can nor should," he adds.[48] The point is that, as with other theorists discussed thus far, Treitschke defines kinds of violence as essential to the existence of a state. Without violence, a state cannot achieve its destined power.

On the greatness of a state, Treitschke writes that

> the greatness of the state [as that which] lies precisely in its power of uniting the present and the future; and consequently no individual has the right to regard the state as the servant of his own aims but is bound by moral duty and physical necessity to subordinate himself to it, while the state lies under the obligation to concern itself with the life of its citizens by extending to them its help and protection.[49]

Military violence in the present is not only a condition for but essential to achieving the existence of a state now and into the future, and when military violence occurs, the greatness of a state is achieved through the unity of all of its uses of violence. Treitschke disagrees that any peace could be achieved because the state only exists on the condition of its uses of violence for the sake of protecting its people and maintaining their existence from one generation to the next. Treitschke's point is that wars fought in the past and in the present bring about "national honour," which each generation inherits from former ones such that, within a state the sacrifice of individuals for the state is considered "positively sacred."[50] All of this increases the "greatness" of the state. Uses of violence for the sake of the state, and the protection of its people, is positively evaluated because it achieves "greatness."

Treitschke adds that

> most undoubtedly war is the one remedy for an ailing nation. Social selfishness and party hatreds must be dumb before the call of the state when its existence is at stake. Forgetting himself, the individual must only remember that he is a part of the whole, and realize the unimportance of his own life compared with the common weal.[51]

Through war, individuals sacrifice themselves, heroes emerge, and "the chaff is winnowed from the wheat," as "puny" citizens are "annihilated."[52] The "whole" of a state exists not only in the present but as the unity of past, present, and future. Citizens must realize the superiority of the state's entire existence. Weak citizens must willingly be sacrificed for the sake of the greatness of the state. So in Treitschke's view, the state's uses of military violence and willingness to engage in war, through which "puny" citizens are sacrificed and heroes arise, is that which achieves the state's power and greatness, which the people of the state believe in, because they have faith in the state's ability to protect their legally bound existence, in exchange for their obedience.

This true belief in the state's power, secured through uses of violence, is that which legitimates the state's uses of violence. If there were no such *belief* in the state's power, that is, its ability to protect its citizens in exchange for submissive obedience and to sustain its existence into the future, then the state's uses of violence would be illegitimate. Insofar as the people are protected, the state's uses of violence are legitimate because the people correctly believe that such uses of violence are those that secure their protection. Without the state's uses of violence, the people would lack security from internal and external threats, and the state's existence would lack power and greatness.

Considering the arguments outlined earlier produced by the others addressed thus far, it is evident that legitimacy is at the heart of the disagreements that result from opposed political ideologies, particularly because various theorists disagree on how, when, and why violence is to be believed in. Treitschke, Kant, Hobbes, Machiavelli, and Arendt each describe violence as related to kinds of thing(s). For Treitschke, violence is essential to the power, greatness, and existence of the state; for Kant, there is the violence of the state of nature, of self-defense of the freedom of an individual secured by universal laws, and of coercion; for Hobbes, there is the violence of the state of nature and of the violent punishments utilized for the sake of enforcing a social contract that secures individuals from the violent state of nature; for Machiavelli, there is the rebellious violence that threatens a prince's rule and the necessitated, justified, and holy violence required for the security of the prince's limited power; for Arendt, violence is essentially uses of instruments as means to goals, which means that state political power is not essentially violent. These kinds of violence, for the person who defines them, are defined as legitimate or not to the extent that the violence is related to the thing defined. Without the paradigm case core conception of violence as the intentional use of physical means for the sake of causing physical or psychological harm or destruction, these disagreements would not make sense. Only with the paradigm cases of the violence of the state of nature, the violence of self-defense, and the violent uses of implements can these disagreements arise because these paradigm cases, captured by commonsense views of violence, serve as a fulcrum upon which distinctions between kinds of violence, positively or negatively evaluated, are defined by theorists. Despite these definitions of violence as related and not related to other things, no agreed upon distinction between kinds of violence is produced by theorists. Instead, various kinds of violence are defined in relation to diversely defined things. Yet *they all agree that something must be secured by a collective of people against the threat of violence.*

However, a commitment to one distinction or definition rather than another does not mean that there is any one way to distinguish between kinds of violence, other than the definition of the paradigm case core conception of violence. In the following, Max Weber's characterization of legitimacy as a kind of belief is discussed to develop the point that definitions of the concept of violence and distinctions between kinds of violence constitute a legitimacy issue.

3.7 WEBER ON THE STATE AND ITS RELATIONSHIP TO VIOLENCE

Max Weber argues in his "The Profession and Vocation of Politics" that legitimacy is merely a belief and nothing more. Weber defines a modern state in terms of the means "specific to it," such that "a state is that human community which (successfully) lays claim to the *monopoly of legitimate physical violence* within a certain territory."[53] In other words, the state is that which possesses a monopoly on uses of violent means that count, for the relevant collective of followers, as "legitimate" uses of violence: "The state is a relationship of *rule* (*Herrschaft*) by human beings over human beings, and one that rests on the legitimate use of violence. For the state to remain in existence, those who are ruled must *submit* to the authority claimed by whoever rules at any given time."[54] The ruled must obey, however, they choose their obedience on the basis of their belief in the state's possessing a monopoly on legitimate violence. So, like Arendt, Weber exclusively defines violence *only as a means*, and not in relation to goals, which contrasts with other authors discussed. But unlike Arendt, Weber does not separate state political power from violence. Weber writes, "the decisive means of politics is the use of violence," and politics is the "striv[ing] for a share of power or for influence on the distribution of power."[55] "Politics operates with a quite specific means, namely power, backed up by the use of *violence*."[56] Altogether, Weber defines politics as that which uses violence, as the struggle for power, and power as that which is backed up by uses of violence. Politics, power, and violence are defined in these relationships and not in relation to goals, though violent means are a condition for politics and power.

On legitimacy, Weber distinguishes between three sources: the authority of tradition and custom, the authority of charisma, and the authority of legality.[57] In each case, citizens are obedient because they *believe* in tradition and custom, or in the charismatically presented goals promised by a leader, or in the legal-normative realm established by the rule of law. These three kinds of legitimacy constitute three kinds of rule. Given these three kinds of legitimacy, legitimacy itself is contestable. For example, someone who believes in the authority of charisma disagrees with someone who rejects the authority of charisma in favor of the authority of tradition and custom. However, all three center on the role of belief. Legitimacy, in general, is the belief in a political leader's use of violent means as legitimate.

So there is a fundamental disagreement concerning extended definitions of violence and how these extended definitions extend to disputed things. Next, it will be demonstrated that this disagreement reappears in relation to antistate political ideologies. For example, a legitimate use of violence by the state in the name of freedom is an "oppressive" or "bad" use of violence from the perspective of revolutionaries who legitimate their own uses of violence against the state in the name of freedom. Given this disagreement, liberal state theorists and antistate revolutionaries are, for one another, "enemies of freedom." For each, there should be "no freedom for the enemy of freedom." However, their definitions of freedom disagree in the first place, which means that though they utter the same word, "freedom," there is only a fundamental disagreement, particularly in relation to whose freedom counts as violence and whose violence counts as a means to freedom.

3.8 BAKUNIN AND SOREL ON THE VIOLENCE OF THE STATE

Mikhail Bakunin and Georges Sorel agree that states are violent, but as revolutionaries who desire the complete destruction of modern states, and not merely their reform, they consider a state's uses of violence to be illegitimate in relation to revolutionary violence. For example, in contrast to the liberal conception of the state's legitimate uses of its own violence for the sake of defeating uses of violence that the state considers to be a threat, Bakunin inverts the view that "all that is instrumental in conserving, exalting, and consolidating the power of the State is good . . . and vice versa, whatever militates against the interests of the State is bad, even if it be in other respects the most holy and humanely just thing."[58] In other words, from the perspective of the state, its own uses of violence serve its interests, particularly its ability to secure the protection of its people of whom it demands sacrifices. But this is merely the state's perspective and its justification for its own uses of violence. From the perspective of an anarchist, such as Bakunin, the state's uses of violence are bad, and illegitimate, particularly because the state's uses of violence violate natural freedom. This is a direct inversion of liberal political ideology concerned with what a state does and why it exists. Bakunin argues on the assumption that natural freedom exists external to the state and defines the state as that which destroys natural freedom.

For example, in contrast to a claim that a state makes freedom possible, Bakunin argues that the natural liberty (freedom) of individuals is immediately threatened by the existence of a state. He defines the liberty of an individual human being such that "so long as men remain isolated in their absolute individuality, enjoying all their natural liberty, recognizing no limits to this liberty but those imposed by fact and not by right, they follow only one law—the law of natural egoism."[59] This definition of liberty as existing "naturally," and independent from any state, enables Bakunin to criticize the typical "theoretical premise of the State," which claims that this natural liberty of individuals leads individuals to "insult, maltreat, rob, murder, and devour one another," which means that natural liberty "produces not good but evil, man being *bad* by nature."[60] In this sense, Bakunin's view disagrees with Kant and Hobbes, who consider the state of nature to be terrible. Kant and Hobbes portray the state as that which, via a freely entered social contract, leads people to be good. However, Bakunin rejects this view, asserting that "the state . . . is not the product of liberty, but, on the contrary, the product of the voluntary negation and sacrifice of liberty." Furthermore, this "voluntary negation and sacrifice of liberty" results in individuals becoming "*slaves of the State*." So Bakunin infers that, because "from the point of view of the State the good *arises not from liberty, but, on the contrary, from the negation of liberty*," this negation of liberty constitutes the immorality of the state.[61] The state is immoral because its existence is a negation and sacrifice of natural liberty. On the assumption that "morality presupposes freedom," because a state negates and sacrifices freedom, it destroys the possibility for morality and is itself immoral.[62]

Bakunin's disagreement with the liberal conception of the state is scrupulous. The immorality of the state is its negation of liberty, which is a kind of violence, and provokes the violence of individuals against the state. He argues,

> Even when the State enjoins something good, it undoes and spoils it precisely because the latter comes in the form of a command, and because every command provokes and arouses the legitimate revolt of freedom; and also because, from the point of view of true morality, of human and not divine morality, the

> good which is done by command from above ceases to be good and thereby becomes evil. Liberty, morality, and the humane dignity of man consist precisely in that man does good not because he is ordered to do so, but because he conceives it, wants it, and loves it.[63]

This is an inversion of the commands of a state such that what is good from the perspective of the state is evil from the perspective of a person because the person is capable of understanding what is good and evil independent from the state's commands. This inversion disorients the legitimacy claims concerning a state's uses of violence, defines the state as illegitimate, and the revolutionary violence that state commands and state violence provoke as legitimate in its defined relation to natural liberty. Like others, Bakunin does not explicitly define violence but instead distinguishes kinds of violence that are then valued in relation to other things.

The anarcho-syndicalist Georges Sorel, in his *Reflections on Violence*, agrees with Bakunin that the state's existence does violence to freedom but disagrees insofar as Sorel focuses on the violence of calculated, rationalistic laws of capitalism oppressively forced upon an individual's internal freedom of creative consciousness. Sorel utilizes Henri Bergson's dualistic presentation of human existence, discussed in Bergson's *Time and Free Will*, in order to emphasize the distinction between the internal and external selves that are constitutive of an individual human's existence.[64] Sorel's point is that a person can freely reflect internally, for the sake of making a free decision to create a new individuality, which is an inward, emotional decision that becomes an outward enacted movement.[65] The emotional, inner decision moves into the world through action.

In terms of an enacted movement, he writes, "to say that we are acting, implies that we are creating an imaginary world placed ahead of the present world and composed of movements which depend entirely on us. In this way our freedom becomes perfectly intelligible." That which is imagined as a potential future is that which is acted toward, and this constitutes the "movement" Sorel refers to. State-imposed laws and capitalistic relationships constitutive of relations of production violently oppress and destroy this internal, emotional, creative freedom, forcing a person's actions to conform to these laws and capitalistic relations despite a person's decision. The decision to enact a revolutionary movement is decisive, therefore, in that it is a condition for the revolutionary movement such that, without this internal, emotional, free, and creative decision, no such movement would be enacted.

Additionally, according to Sorel, the decision to act is motivated by indescribable myths of a proletarian general strike, which "are not descriptions of things, but expressions of a determination to act."[66] The myth of a proletarian general strike is indescribable because the emotions that lead a person to imagine it are irrational and cannot be formulated or defined by reason. For this reason, the revolutionary strike that destroys the capitalistic state cannot be predicted or known by reason with any certainty. So the myth of a proletarian general strike is irrational, insofar as it is not subject to rationalistic calculations, but arises from an emotional decision to act toward the total destruction of the state.

Violence is an issue, for Sorel, because violence is required for the total destruction of a state's violence. The "myth of the 'general strike' . . . implies an absolute revolution," he writes.[67] His aim is to explain "the function of the *violence of the working classes* in contemporary Socialism."[68] However, in consideration of how violence functions, Sorel is not concerned with the immediate effects of violence but with "its distant consequences," particularly in the class relationship between workers and employers.[69] The destruction and harm that immediately result from uses of violence are irrelevant in relation to the imagined future. These "distant consequences" are imagined by anyone who violently acts upon the desire for the transformation of the state and capitalism in an ineffable myth of a proletarian general strike. "*The general strike must be taken as a whole and undivided, and the passage from capitalism to Socialism conceived as a catastrophe, the development of which baffles description.*"[70] Any prediction or calculation of how the state would be overthrown is impossible. At best, there is only a description of the complete destruction of the state and its violence. However, violence plays an important, particular role in the present, insofar as "working class violence" produces fear: "doubtless fear is an excellent weapon," Sorel says, but it must be used with reservation so that it does not "provoke obstinate resistance" against the revolutionary movement.[71]

Sorel also equates "working class violence" to "proletarian violence" and "strike violence," all three of which are conditions for "keep[ing] the revolutionary spirit alive."[72] As such, this violence is a "*clear and brutal expression of the class war*."[73] If these kinds of violence did not occur, then the "revolutionary spirit" would, presumably, cease to exist. However, it is because these kinds of violence occur that Sorel considers it to be a fact that a class war exists.

Proletarian violence also reveals the inevitability of class war due to the exploitative and oppressive relationships between workers and employers under capitalistic relations of production. Without proletarian violence, redemption from capitalistic relationships cannot be achieved, and capitalistic relationships ensure that proletarian violence occurs. Additionally, proletarian/working-class violence is related to "the experience of this great epoch [that] shows quite clearly that in this warlike excitement which accompanies this *will-to-deliverance* the courageous man finds a satisfaction which is sufficient to keep up his ardour."[74] As long as this epoch exists, the conditions for proletarian violence exist in the form of a revolutionary movement that aims to emancipate itself from the capitalistic relationships of oppression sustained by modern states.

Sorel also characterizes proletarian violence such that

> proletarian violence, carried on as a pure and simple manifestation of the sentiment of the class war, appears . . . as a very fine and very heroic thing; it is at the service of the immemorial interests of civilization; it is not perhaps the most appropriate method of obtaining immediate material advantages, but it may *save the world from barbarism*.[75]

Because Sorel describes proletarian violence as that which "saves the world from barbarism," he elevates it to a superior position, as a legitimate kind of violence. He frames proletarian violence as that which should be believed in. The most superior use of violence is that violence deployed by the working class because it transforms and destroys the state and capitalist relations of production. He equates proletarian violence to an army of worker-warriors intent on destroying the state, and not on merely reforming it. So in this sense, Sorel is opposed to liberal state theorists who legitimate state violence.

Sorel also explicitly defines violence in relation to other things, and in kinds. He writes, "the term *violence* should be employed only for acts of revolt; we should say . . . that the object of force is to impose a certain social order in which the minority governs, while violence tends to the destruction of that order."[76] Here, Sorel indicates the distinction between the force of capitalistic relations of production and state laws imposed upon workers and the superior violence that is the inevitable ability of the workers to destroy that force. The force of capitalism and laws destroys the inner, free, and creative consciousness of workers, whose own violence can defeat this force. There is, in this sense, a hierarchy of kinds of violence defined by Sorel based on which kind defeats another kind. Sorel aims to usurp the concept of violence as superior to the concept of force, embellishing his own political ideology with the superiority of violence.

In this sense, there is what Sorel defines as "a regime of violence":

> (a) On the lowest level, we find a scattered kind of violence, which resembles the struggle for life, which acts through economic conditions, and which carries out a slow but sure expropriation; violence of this character works especially with the aid of fiscal arrangements; (b) Next comes the concentrated and organized force of the state, which acts directly on labor, "*to regulate wages*," *i.e.*, force them within the limits suitable to surplus value making, to lengthen the working day, and to maintain the laborer himself in the normal degree of dependence; this is an essential element of the so-called primitive accumulation; (c) We have, finally, violence properly so called, which occupies so great a place

> in history of primitive accumulation, and which constitutes the principle subject of history.[77]

Sorel's definitions for these three kinds of violence are hierarchical. There is the lowest kind of violence that is unorganized, "scattered," and a "struggle for life"; and then the "force of the state" that organizes labor; and finally "violence properly so called" that is "the principle subject of history." The superior kind of violence is the "subject of history," that is, proletarian violence, insofar as "it represents the highest moral ideal ever conceived by man . . . [and is the] *birth of a virtue* . . . which has the power to save civilization," transforming history.[78] This embellishment of proletarian violence extends far beyond the paradigm case core conception of violence. In fact, Sorel writes that "it is to violence that Socialism owes those high ethical values by means of which it brings *salvation* to the modern world."[79] So though in agreement with Bakunin that the state must be destroyed, and that its existence and uses of force and violence are illegitimate, Sorel disagrees with Bakunin in that it is not only the state's immoral destruction of natural liberty that provokes the need for its destruction but also capitalism's oppressive forces imposed upon workers as rational calculations of bare life, which exploit but also guarantee proletarian violence as a response to state capitalism. Proletarian violence, in short, is defined by Sorel as the means to salvation from the barbaric imposition of state laws and capitalistic relations of production.

3.9 VIOLENCE AND A LOGIC OF DOMINATION

At this point, we've seen the logic at work, formulated by Rancière, namely that there are disagreements that arise, not because there is a failure of theorists to agree on anything but because they agree only to the extent that the word "violence" is commonly used by most people in relation to what counts as actions and events defined by the paradigm case core conception of violence. Distinctions between kinds of violence are evaluations of kinds of violence and extend the definition of violence to include or exclude acts as wrong. There is violence itself, and then there are kinds of violence positively and negatively evaluated in relationships of superiority and inferiority.

Except for Arendt, state theorists and antistatists agree that a state's existence is related to violence but disagree on why there is this relation, on what a state's violence achieves, and on how it is valued. However, the liberal state theorists who agree on some things disagree on other things, and antistatists who agree on some things disagree on other things. It is not that these theorists would be unable to acknowledge that one another speaks of or writes the term "violence" but that they disagree with what one another means when each uses the word "violence" in relation to other things. The term "violence" in these cases only makes sense in terms of that person's political ideology. Without the paradigm case core conception of violence, this disagreement would constitute a radical confusion, but with paradigm cases, this disagreement continuously develops in novel ways. Furthermore, each of the discussed authors distinguish between kinds of violence according to a logic of domination.

Karen Warren, in her "The Power and Promise of Ecological Feminism," formulates a "logic of domination" such that "for any X and Y, if X is morally superior to Y, then X is morally justified in subordinating Y."[80] Though Warren's concern is to demonstrate that the oppression and subordination of women and of the environment logically imply one another because a patriarchal oppressive framework commonly utilizes this logic against them both, this "logic of domination" is also useful for analyzing definitions of violence that characterize violence as related to other things. Kinds of violence are defined in relationships of superiority and inferiority, and the superior is then believed to be justified in its subordination of the inferior, based on a person's politically ideological definitions. The previous discussion demonstrates that political ideological distinctions between kinds of violence are defined as superior and inferior in relation to other things. Then the defined superior kinds of violence are defined by theorists as something to believe in because they are defined as superior and justified toward destroying the inferior kinds. Arendt's definitions, though they sever the relationship between violence and state political power, still work within this logic of domination. She defines violent uses of instruments as inferior to the nonviolent power of people acting in concert, thereby justifying this power's subordination of the violence that can be produced by one.

Now, in the following, the issue for Arendt's definition of the power of people acting in concert as essentially not requiring violence is addressed, namely because, according to Slavoj Žižek, nonviolent actions like this can count as a kind of violence. Like others, Žižek defines violence as related to the state's existence by defining kinds of violence, and one kind of violence he defines is the nonviolence that defeats the violence that is systemic, structural, and linguistic. This systemic, structural, and linguistic violence is not only consistent with the agreement of the All, but is typically a condition of collective agreement itself.

3.10 ŽIŽEK ON THE LEGITIMACY OF NONVIOLENCE

Žižek's definition of nonviolence as a kind of violence hangs on his interpretation of the kinds of violence defined by Walter Benjamin. In Benjamin's

Critique of Violence, three kinds of violence are defined in their relationships to one another such that a value hierarchy is produced, establishing the superiority of divine violence, which is by definition superior to the merely human "All," over law-making and law-preserving violence. Benjamin assumes that "all violence as a means is either law-making or law-preserving."[81] That is, when violence is a means, it is law making or law preserving. If violence is not a means, then it is neither law making nor law preserving. He also distinguishes between how natural law and positive law regard violence.

Against positive law's distinctions between legitimate, legal violence, and illegitimate, illegal violence, Benjamin characterizes a kind of "divine violence," which is defined as "law-destroying" because it expiates by destroying the instrumentalist, means-ends positive laws produced and sustained by law-making and law-preserving violence.[82] Divine violence is *not a means* and, thus, is neither law making nor law preserving. Divine violence arises from a position external to the means-ends, instrumentalist, legal relationships sustained by law-making and law-preserving violence. Because it destroys law, divine violence eliminates state power, and because state violence can only establish legal power, it does not attain justice. Instead, divine violence, which destroys law, "is the principle of all divine end making" and attains justice, Benjamin says.[83] From the perspective of a state, its power is attained through its legitimate uses of violence against illegal violence, but the legitimacy of this violence is that which is defeated by the justice of divine violence.[84] Benjamin depicts divine violence as something capable of transcending and destroying the violence of a state and its laws. So though Benjamin agrees that violence is a condition for a state's existence, Benjamin's disagreement concerns the superiority of legitimacy.

Legitimacy only exists insofar as there is the belief in the superior ability of a kind of violence to defeat other kinds of violence. Benjamin, though, defines the superiority of the justice of divine violence above the legitimacy of a state's law-creating and law-preserving violence. Divine justice, in this sense, overrides, dominates, and transcends legitimacy. Divine violence is justice, which the inferior, legitimate violence of law does not attain because violence that makes or preserves law is not divine violence. If legitimacy is a kind of belief, as has been argued here, then divine violence is that which no one can believe in because they cannot believe in it as a means to anything, because divine violence is not a means but simply happens.

Slavoj Žižek also distinguishes between kinds of violence in such a way that his distinctions agree with others discussed earlier, namely in the sense that violence is a condition for the existence of a state. In his book *Violence: Six Sideways Reflections*, Žižek distinguishes between subjective violence and objective violence, which splits into systemic and symbolic violence.[85]

He also produces an interpretation of Benjamin's conception of divine violence, but one that disagrees with Benjamin, particularly in the sense of the violence of nonviolence. If nonviolence is a kind of violence, then we have come a long way from the paradigm case core conception of violence.

On objective and subjective violence, Žižek argues that objective violence (the symbolic and systemic) is the condition for the possibility of subjective violence.[86] He defines subjective violence as "directly visible" and "performed by a clearly identifiable agent."[87] Subjective violence includes all those actions and events that we would typically refer to as instances of violence, particularly because they are visible.

In contrast to subjective violence, objective violence is "invisible" and is that which sustains the "normal" as a "zero-level standard against which we perceive something as subjectively violent." That is, subjective violence is that which is "experienced . . . against the background of a non-violent zero level" and disturbs the "normal," or what is *considered* to be a "peaceful" situation.[88] This "normal" is produced and reproduced by the repetitive actions of individuals, which sustain the sociopolitical and economic framework that constitutes the hidden, objective violence. Objective violence is invisible and is not typically thought to be a kind of violence, but Žižek disagrees and argues that it is a kind of violence. That is, this presumed "nonviolent" "normal" of everyday life involves a kind of objective violence, from which subjective violence erupts as an "abnormal" disruption. The "normal" sustains a kind of violence, though its appearance as "normal" veils its violence, which results in violence directed against this "normal" appearing as "abnormal." In this sense, objective violence is the transcendental condition for the possibility of the abnormality of abnormal, subjective violence.

On the two kinds of objective violence, that is, the symbolic and systemic, the symbolic side of objective violence is violence "embodied in language and its forms."[89] That is, language is a kind of violence. Things that create and sustain a symbolic realm of meaning, "essenc[ing]" a "universe of meaning" that imposes a division upon the world insofar as what is said of things divides things into what they are and what they are not, what they should be and what they should not be, in terms of superiority and inferiority.[90] The things people say and the ways that people speak of things produces what seems to be a nonviolent linguistic realm constitutive of a nonviolent normalcy, but this is only because this violence is invisible.

The systemic side of objective violence is the "often catastrophic consequences of the smooth functioning of our economic and political systems."[91] Political and economic orders appear to be productive of "a comfortable life," but such orders involve "subtle forms of coercion that sustain relations of domination and exploitation, including the threat of violence."[92] Not everyone enjoys the "comfortable life" produced by a political or economic order.

This is particularly the case in capitalist societies, where class conflicts are symptomatic. So systemically and symbolically, an objective framework of invisible violence is structurally sustained through everyday practices and the linguistic expressions of individuals, which reproduce this framework that is typically overlooked because it is accepted as "normal." It is from and due to this objective violence that subjective violence emerges as "abnormal" violence.

So in agreement with those discussed earlier, Žižek depicts violence as a condition for the state and relies on the paradigm case core conception of violence, but this is the limit of his agreement. Žižek is not exclusively focused on military violence against other states, nor is he exclusively concerned with coercive or legal violence against criminals. Instead, the very structures constitutive of a state's existence are kinds of violence. Because objective violence is invisible, there is the potential that anything counts as a kind of violence because anything could be the condition for the possibility of someone's being subjectively violent in a way that disrupts a "normal" state of affairs.

Žižek interprets Benjaminian divine violence as a refusal that interrupts objective violence, and the subjective violence it brings about, by means of a violent refusal to act. Indeed, Benjamin describes revolutionary violence as that which serves as one possible example of divine violence, but divine violence could occur in other forms, such as an earthquake or volcanic explosion that destroys the laws of a state by literally destroying the state.[93] Revolutionary violence can count as divine violence, in Benjamin's terms, but only if it is not a means to some goal and instead is suddenly a kind of eruption. Žižek, though, simply runs with revolutionary violence as that which counts as divine violence, and conceives of the ideal revolutionary violent action as one in which the agent intentionally does *nothing* for the sake of *passionately refusing* one's participation in the systemic, linguistic, and symbolic structures that constitute and uphold the existence of invisible, objective violence. Refusal defeats objective violence and appears as something "abnormal" against the "normal" of the symbolic and systemic components of objective violence, but the refusal that is one's doing nothing when otherwise expected to act is a kind of violent nonviolence.

Žižek writes that the "domain of pure divine violence . . . is the domain of sovereignty."[94] Divine violence is not pathological, not a crime, not a sacrifice, not aesthetic, not ethical, and not religious, in his view. Instead, divine violence is like the "bio-political disposal of *Homini sacer*: in both cases, killing is neither a crime nor a sacrifice," and it makes no distinctions between good and evil. Divine violence does not simply occur for the sake of producing a spectacle and is not subordinate to law; it transcends these as that which commands simply because divine violence commands by freeing individuals from the guilt imposed upon them by law. In this sense, divine violence is, at the same time, a refusal to submit and a refusal to accept sacrifices.

However, Žižek adds that "those annihilated by divine violence are fully and completely guilty: they are not sacrificed, since they are not worthy of being sacrificed to and accepted by God—they are annihilated without being made a sacrifice." They are guilty of merely living a natural life: "divine violence purifies the guilty not of guilt but of law, because law is limited to the living." Divine violence simply commands and its commands are sovereign in the sense that they are free from any possible subordination of divine violence to anything at all. Divine violence is not any other kind of violence. It is not a means; it is violence that has no goal. Divine violence is completely sovereign, independent, free, beyond good and evil, and expects nothing in return. It is an end in itself that has no further end. Divine violence is freedom and frees the living from the guilt of living. Divine violence brings to an end, but for no purpose.

So divine violence is sovereign, but not in the sense of state sovereignty because divine violence does not produce a foundation for law. Instead, according to Žižek, divine violence should be conceived in the sense of the old Latin motto: "*vox populi, vox dei* . . . as the heroic assumption of the solitude of sovereign decision. It is a decision (to kill, to risk or lose one's own life) made in absolute solitude, with no cover in the big Other."[95] Divine violence cannot be used as a means because it is not a means. It is instead unconditional freedom from the imposition of any universal norm that strikes "'blindly,' demanding and enacting immediate justice/vengeance . . . strik[ing] out of nowhere, a means without end." It is, so to speak, "a leap of faith," irrational, but as such, it works toward expiating individuals from their guilt under law to their freedom from law.

Žižek also defines divine violence in relationships to a variety of things, particularly to what various significant figures have claimed throughout history. For example, divine violence, in relation to the words of Robespierre, strikes as "lightning," immediately, passionately, and with love. And in relation to the words of Che Guevara, divine violence strikes with hatred, but because it loves.[96] And in relation to the words of Kierkegaard, on the Christian demand to "*love one's enemy*," it is "the demand to *hate the beloved* out of love and in love." So given these various characterizations of divine violence, it is beyond the domain of law and legal power, and it arises from the domain of love, which law and legal power cannot control or force into submission.

However, divine violence is also a revolutionary refusal to act. This love that strikes with hatred is *nothing* in relation to law and legal power because *there is nothing* about a loving refusal to act that law and legal power can respond to without resorting to a kind of violence related to law and legal power. However, as a nonviolent, nonaction, doing nothing refuses law and legal power and actively destroys law because the violence of law is not allowed to dominate. In this way, the most effective action, "the first gesture to provoke a change in [a] system is to withdraw activity, to do nothing."[97] Žižek concludes, stating that "sometimes doing nothing is the most violent thing to do."[98] So Žižek defines kinds of violence and defines nonviolence and doing nothing as kinds of violence, evaluating these in relation to one another, while assuming that subjective violence ought not to occur and thwarting the possibility of subjective violence requires refusing the conditions that constitute objective violence by doing nothing when otherwise expected to act. Whether anyone agrees with him is a matter of belief in the legitimacy of the distinctions he defines from the position of his political ideology. Given other ways to define and evaluate kinds of violence, Žižek's definitions for divine violence and objective violence, both symbolic and systemic, reveal kinds of violence that extend the paradigm cases of violence, which are grounds for political disagreement.

3.11 CONCLUSION

Recall Walter Bryce Gallie's brief description of essentially contested concepts. An essentially contested concept is "an appraisive term [that] signif[ies] an achievement that is internally complex, variously describable and 'open' . . . [and is] used both 'aggressively' and 'defensively.'"[99] Rancière logic of disagreement was added to Gallie's definition: "Disagreement is where X cannot see the common object Y is presenting because X cannot comprehend that the sounds uttered by Y form words and chains of words similar to X's own."[100] Now that the political ideologies pertaining to violence and the existence of kinds of states has been discussed, it should be obvious that each person outlined earlier evaluates kinds of violence defining kinds of violence in relation to other things that are themselves evaluated positively and negatively in accordance with a logic of domination that serves to justify superior kinds of violence dominating inferior kinds of violence. Machiavelli, Arendt, Hobbes, Kant, Treitschke, Schmitt, Weber, Bakunin, Sorel, Benjamin, and Žižek each utilize a commonsense view of violence, explicitly or implicitly, in such a way that the definition of what is commonly considered to be a violent act or event is appraised in relation to other things, such as power, greatness, the state itself, the political, law, justice, capitalism, freedom, the divine, and other things. In the end, there are distinctions between kinds of violence that disagree with one another. One person's distinctions between kinds of violence in relation to other things can be inverted by another person so that what the first person defines as superior is defined by the second person as inferior, even in relation to the same things, such as freedom. Nonviolence, which commonsensically speaking does not count as violence, is definable as a kind of violence.

Altogether then, there are numerous definitions of kinds of violence. The definitions I have discussed here, which are representative but not exhaustive of the philosophical literature and include all the major examples, follow the same pattern. One person's evaluation fundamentally disagrees with another. Each person's evaluation of kinds of violence reflects that person's political ideologies. Political ideologies disagree with each other. Except for the paradigm cases of violence, distinctions between kinds of violence are essentially contestable. Any attempt to stop this debate by defining kinds of violence is to reproduce the debate. To attempt to stop the debate by only affirming a commonsense view of violence is also to reproduce the debate. Doing so would introduce another political ideology and political ideologies are in competition. Finally, for these reasons, these distinctions between kinds of violence are nonneutrally political and fundamentally disagree with one another, except for the paradigm acts that most people define as wrong, and as violence. Belief in any one way of defining violence or in one way of distinguishing kinds of violence is merely a belief.

In the following chapter, I will consider what might on the surface appear to be an alternative approach: starting not from the concept of violence but from the concept of nonviolence. But given Žižek's claim that nonviolence can count as a kind of violence, it appears that even this starting point is contestable: nonviolence can count as a kind of violence. If there is a logic of domination at work in the distinctions between kinds of violence, then this argument can be generalized: if nonviolence is evaluated as superior to other kinds of violence and justified in its attempt to defeat them, then nonviolence must count as a kind of violence.

NOTES

1. Hanna Arendt, *On Violence* (New York: Harcourt, Inc., 1970), 42.

2. Ibid., 51.

3. Jacques Rancière, *Disagreement: Politics and Philosophy*, trans. Julie Rose (Minneapolis: University of Minnesota Press, 1999), x.

4. Arendt, *On Violence*, 42.

5. Niccolò Machiavelli, *The Prince* (New York: Penguin Books, 2005), 110.

6. Machiavelli, a former diplomat who served the Signoria of Florence when it was a republic, is also trying to return to Florence, which had become a principality. He dedicates *The Prince* to Lorenzo de Medici for this reason.

7. For example, in Chapter XVII of *The Prince*, Machiavelli argues that it is far better for a prince to be feared by his people rather than loved because it is easier to control those who fear a prince than for a prince to gain their loving commitment to obediently following his commands. See pp. 70–73. His point is that it would be folly for a prince to think he can depend on his people's commitment to act in concert for the sake of the rule of a prince.

8. Rancière, *Disagreement*, xi.

9. Arendt, *On Violence*, 10.

10. Ibid., 61.

11. Rancière, *Disagreement*, xii.

12. Carl Schmitt, *The Concept of the Political*, trans. George Schwab (Chicago: The University of Chicago Press, 2007), 19.

13. Ibid., 26.

14. Ibid., 27.

15. Thomas Hobbes, *Leviathan: With Selected Variants from the Latin Edition of 1668*, ed. Edwin Curley (Indianapolis: Hackett Publishing Company, 1994), 76.

16. Ibid., 80.

17. Ibid., 80–82.

18. Immanuel Kant, "The Metaphysics of Morals," in *Practical Philosophy*, ed. Paul Guyer and Allen W. Wood (New York: Cambridge University Press, 1999), 456.

19. Ibid., 459.

20. Howard Williams, *Kant's Critique of Hobbes: Sovereignty and Cosmopolitanism* (Cardiff: University Wales Press, 2003), 1–4.

21. Immanuel Kant, "On the Common Saying: That May Be Correct in Theory, but It Is of No Use in Practice," in *Practical Philosophy*, ed. Paul Guyer and Allen W. Wood, trans. Mary J. Gregor (New York: Cambridge University Press, 1999), 302. [Hereafter, "Theory and Practice."] Quoted from Williams, *Kant's Critique of Hobbes*, 4.

22. Williams, *Kant's Critique of Hobbes*, 13.

23. Ibid., 14.

24. Hobbes, *Leviathan*, 76.

25. Williams, *Kant's Critique of Hobbes*, 15.

26. Ibid., 15–16.

27. Ibid., 17.

28. Kant, "Theory and Practice," 290.

29. Hobbes, *Leviathan*, 79–80.

30. Ibid., 106.

31. Williams, *Kant's Critique of Hobbes*, 17.

32. Ibid., 18. See also Hobbes, *Leviathan*, Chapter 13, p. 76.

33. Ibid., 19.

34. Kant, "Metaphysics of Morals," 388.

35. Ibid., 387.

36. Ibid., 392.

37. Heinrich von Treitschke, *Politics*, trans. Arthur James Balfour (New York: The MacMillan Company, 1916), 18.

38. Ibid., 30.
39. Ibid., 65.
40. Immanuel Kant, *Perpetual Peace*, ed. Lewis White Beck (New York: Macmillan Publishing Company, 1957), 5.
41. Ibid., 8
42. Ibid., 18.
43. Treitschke, *Politics*, 62.
44. Ibid., 63.
45. Ibid.
46. Ibid., 64.
47. Ibid., 64–65.
48. Ibid., 70.
49. Ibid., 61.
50. Ibid., 15.
51. Ibid., 66.
52. Ibid., 67.
53. Max Weber, "The Profession and Vocation of Politics," in *Weber: Political Writings*, ed. Peter Lassman and Ronald Speirs (New York: Cambridge University Press, 1994), 310–11.
54. Ibid., 311.
55. Ibid., 360 and 311, respectively.
56. Ibid., 357.
57. Ibid., 311–12.
58. Mikhail Bakunin, *The Political Philosophy of Bakunin: Scientific Anarchism*, ed. G. P. Maximoff (New York: The Free Press, 1953), 137.
59. Ibid., 143.
60. Ibid.
61. Ibid.
62. Ibid. 145.
63. Ibid.
64. Georges Sorel, *Reflections on Violence*, trans. T. E. Hulme and J. Roth (New York: Collier Books, 1974), 47. Bergson, it should be noted, discusses "violent emotions," such as "acute desire, uncontrolled anger, passionate love, and violent hatred," noting that these always involve a kind of "muscular contraction" that grows in "intensity" the "deeper and deeper" there is a "disturbance of the organism," that is, the human body. Bergson adds that "there is . . . no essential difference from the point of view of intensity between . . . deep-seated feelings . . . and the acute or violent emotions which we have just passed in review. To say that love, hatred, desire, increase in violence is to assert that they are projected outwards, that they radiate to the surface, that peripheral sensations are substituted for inner states: but superficial or deep-seated, violent or reflective, the intensity of these feelings always consists in the multiplicity of simple states which consciousness dimly discerns in them." See pp. 28–31 of Bergson's *Time and Free Will: An Essay on the Immediate Data of Consciousness*, trans. F. L. Pogson (London: George Allen & Unwin Limited, 1950).

Bergson treats violence as a kind of muscular tension that projects outward, as a kind of emotion. It is these violent emotions that Sorel aims to mobilize.

65. Sorel, *Reflections on Violence*, 48.

66. Ibid., 50.

67. Ibid., 27.

68. Ibid., 58–59.

69. Ibid., 60.

70. Ibid., 148.

71. Ibid., 68, 81.

72. Ibid., 90.

73. Ibid., 91.

74. Ibid., 37.

75. Ibid., 98.

76. Ibid., 171.

77. Ibid., 172–73.

78. Ibid., 228.

79. Ibid., 249.

80. Karen, Warren, "The Power and Promise of Ecological Feminism," in *Environmental Ethics: Readings in Theory and Application*, sixth edition, ed. Louis P. Pojman and Paul Pojman (Boston: Wadsworth, 212), 591.

81. Walter Benjamin, "Critique of Violence," in *Reflections: Essays, Aphorisms, Autobiographical Writings*, trans. Edmund Jephcott (New York: Shocken, 1986), 287.

82. Ibid., 297–300.

83. Ibid., 295.

84. Jacques Derrida, in his lecture on Benjamin's *Critique of Violence*, makes it clear that the relationship between law and justice is such that justice is not law, law does not achieve justice, and justice cannot be defined by law because whatever law defines as just is measured by law, therefore, it is simply a rationally calculated extension of law. Ultimately, any attempt to define "justice" leads to an aporia, in Derrida's view. Jacques Derrida, "Force de Loi: le 'Fondement Mystique de l'Autorité'" (Force of Law: The "Mystical Foundation of Authority"), *Cardoza Law Review*, trans. Mary Quaintance 11 (1990): 919–1045.

85. Slavoj Žižek, *Violence: Six Sideways Reflections* (New York: Picador, 2008).

86. Ibid., 1.

87. Žižek's conception of subjective violence is akin to the paradigm case core conception of violence because subjective violence is that which people commonly refer to as violence.

88. Ibid., 2.

89. Ibid., 1.

90. Ibid., 67–68.

91. Ibid., 2.

92. Ibid., 9, 12–13.

93. Benjamin, "Critique of Violence," 282, 300.

94. Žižek, *Violence*, 198.

95. Ibid., 202. "*Vox populi, vox dei*" translates as "The voice of the people is the voice of God."

96. Ibid., 204.

97. Ibid., 214.

98. Ibid., 217.

99. Walter Bryce Gallie, "Essentially Contested Concepts." *Proceedings of the Aristotelian Society* 56 (1955–1956): 180–81.

100. Rancière, *Disagreement*, xii.

Chapter Four

On the Violence of Nonviolence

4.1 INTRODUCTION

As indicated in the previous chapters, there is a paradigm case core conception of violence, and various extensions of this conception that hierarchically distinguish between kinds of violence, indicating wrong kinds and not wrong (or not entirely wrong) kinds. The core cases involve the intentional use of physical means for the sake of causing physical or psychological harm or destruction. These core cases provide ground for commonsense views. This implies that a commonsense view of nonviolence defines an action as nonviolent when it does not involve an intent to use physical means for the sake of causing physical or psychological harm or destruction. A paradigm example of violence is a person's intentional slamming of another person's head between two bricks for the sake of causing harm and destruction. Similarly, there are paradigm examples that most people would agree count as involving no violence, such as when a forest hiker who intentionally leaves no trash behind and aims to avoid disturbing wildlife and plants, for the sake of not disturbing nature to the greatest extent possible. It would be unusual for someone to think that a tidy, conscientious hiker like this one walking through the forest is being violent.

However, as shown in previous chapters, there are many extended concepts of violence, based on claimed equivalence to paradigmatic violence, which define violence on the basis of the wrongness of paradigmatic actions and events. Likewise, as will be shown in this chapter, extended definitions for kinds of nonviolence can also be produced. Distinctions between kinds of nonviolence evaluate those kinds of nonviolence, unlike a commonsense view of nonviolence that only describes paradigm cases of nonviolent actions and events. Also argued in previous chapters, distinctions between kinds of violence are essentially contestable, and there is a fundamental disagreement concerning what counts as kinds of violence. Definitions for kinds of violence are typically nonneutrally political. Kinds of violence are defined by theorists, for example, by Heinrich von Treitschke, Mikhail Bakunin, Walter Benjamin, and others, as conditions for the goals of the state, its power, greatness, its immorality, and the preservation of its law. The same occurs with distinctions between and definitions of kinds of nonviolence, beyond a commonsense definition of nonviolence that is based on paradigm cases. That is, given that kinds of nonviolence can be defined by theorists in relation to other things, and opposed political ideologies do not necessarily agree, we should expect a political, ideological disagreement concerning what nonviolence is beyond the paradigm cases of nonviolence.

Unlike the forest hiker, those who engage in nonviolent *political* actions are actors who aim for their actions to be legitimate means used in relation to the state, laws, justice, dignity, equality, freedom, or other things so that they can successful achieve a transformation through a defeat or an undermining of something "normal" or status quo within a society, and these nonviolent means may perhaps be defined as working in the way that violence is thought to work as a legitimate means, often used toward very similar goals. Like violence, nonviolent political actions *make way* but in ways that result in less physical and psychological harm and destruction. However, if these nonviolent means are definable as kinds of violence, then nonviolence counts as a kind of violence. Because nonviolence is simply that which is not violence but is also construed as something that can be used as a means to a goal, it is worth asking if nonviolence works in a way that is not clearly distinct from how violence works, and if it is impossible to guarantee that one's own actions are nonviolent in relation to other things, then is nonviolence another kind of violence? Because we are not referencing actions that just happen to be nonviolent, like the forest hiker, but ones that are used by protesters as means to political ends, we are concerned with nonviolence used as a means and the effects it produces in relation to other things that may themselves count as kinds of violence. This distinguishes nonviolent action from the paradigm case of the forest hiker.

We should ask whether it is possible for nonviolence really to be not violent when used as a means particularly because there is a variety of diverse and opposed views that might not agree upon the goals toward which the so-called nonviolent means should be used. Disagreement concerning goals may indicate that the means used toward them can be valued in opposed ways, particularly as violent or nonviolent means. A kind of purely nonviolent political action is likely impossible, given perspectives; scales of relationships between actors, institutions, and states; and the contingency of the future that may turn what were nonviolent actions into some kind of violence. But if pure nonviolence is impossible as a political action, particularly because there is disagreement concerning whether it works as a means to goals, such as justice, freedom, and equality, and whether it works toward such goals as a *nonviolent* means, then nonviolence is another kind of violence that aims to eliminate other kinds of violence in the same way that kinds of violence are thought to work as a means toward defeating other kinds of violence.

In the following, it is shown how some believe that nonviolence cannot exist without violence that makes nonviolence possible. Maurice Merleau-Ponty and René Girard both define, each according to his own political ideology, a kind of violence that is a condition for human existence. However, their definitions of this violence disagree.

4.2 MERLEAU-PONTY AND VIOLENCE AS A BASIC FACT OF HUMAN EXISTENCE

In his *Humanism and Terror: An Essay on the Communist Problem*, Merleau-Ponty argues that "we do not have a choice between purity [that is, nonviolence] and violence but between different kinds of violence . . . [and adds that] inasmuch as we are incarnate beings, violence is our lot. . . . Violence is the common origin of all regimes. Life, discussion, and political choice occur only against a background of violence. [So] what matters . . . is not violence but its sense or its future."[1] In other words, Merleau-Ponty defines violence as a condition for human existence, in the sense of "regimes." No regime exists without violence; no regime is nonviolent. In particular, he means to distinguish between the violence of liberalism and communism because both political ideologies claim to be equivalent to freedom. Their claims that their own uses of violence are equivalent to freedom only make sense against the background situation from which Merleau-Ponty writes. Given the Cold War, the French were in a position of having to choose to take sides with the Soviet Union or the United States.

Even though both communism and liberalism value freedom, how they utilize violence as a means toward freedom differentiates liberalism from communism. Merleau-Ponty writes,

> Violence is the basic fact on which we have to build freedom. We are not accusing liberalism of being a system of violence; we reproach it with not seeing its own face in violence, with veiling the pact upon which it rests while rejecting as barbarous that other source of freedom—revolutionary freedom—which is the origin of all social pacts. With the assumptions of impersonal Reason and rational Man, and by regarding itself as a natural rather than an historical fact, liberalism assumes universality as a datum whereas the problem is its realization through the dialectic of concrete intersubjectivity.[2]

The main point is that, according to Merleau-Ponty, without violence, liberalism's freedom is impossible. "Violence is the basic fact." Liberalism hides its violent foundation and claims that it only violently protects the freedom that liberalism produces, when it only defends an idea of freedom. Liberalism's assumptions of "impersonal Reason and rational Man" are merely "universality as a datum," a claim, and liberalism fails to produce actual freedom in concrete, intersubjective relationships between actually existing humans.

Merleau-Ponty assumes that this actually existing intersubjective freedom is possible and agrees with Trotsky, Bukharin, and Stalin, who "are all opposed to the liberal ethics because it presupposes a given humanity, whereas they aim at making humanity."[3] The point is that liberalism hides its violence, merely defending its idea of humanity, while it simultaneously violently upholds bourgeois, capitalistic conceptions of freedom, and not actually existing freedom between humans. In this sense, "Bourgeois justice adopts the past as its precedent; revolutionary justice adopts the future. [Revolutionary justice] judges in the name of the Truth that the Revolution is about to make [historically] true."[4] So the key difference is that, on the one hand, liberalism conceives of its existence as something "*well and truly made*." Liberalism utilizes violence for the sake of defending its existence, imposing itself upon individuals who cannot refuse liberalism for the sake of freedom, while communism uses violence for the sake of a future of humanism and actual, free, human relationships, particularly because liberalism has not succeeded at achieving freedom.

The difference between communistic, revolutionary justice and the bourgeois justice of liberalism lies in the temporal direction each emphasizes, the future and the past, respectively. Both justify their own violence in relation to freedom, aiming to preserve the past or to create a future, and because they are political ideologies enacted in the post–World War II world, each person is already on one side or the other, at least indirectly allied with the violence of the state that protects them. Both liberalism and communism utilize violent means toward a nonviolent goal of freedom, but whether this freedom exists now or a different kind is possible in the future is a matter of disagreement, and therefore, whether the violent means each use are justified and can be believed in as legitimate is a matter of disagreement.

Nonviolence might be assumed as a choice against this dichotomy but cannot work against violence because the violence of the violent will dominate the nonviolent, in any kind of political system, because "violence is the basic fact," according to Merleau-Ponty. In such a world, no one who seeks freedom can be nonviolent because it is violence that is defined as equivalent to that which produces freedom, not nonviolence. One is always already involved in some kind of violence. Freedom cannot be achieved nonviolently, and the violent defense of an idea of freedom, no matter how impartial and rational it may be, is not any more justifiable than the violent defense of actually existing freedom. There is only disagreement between these two political ideologies concerning whether freedom exists, and its relationship to justified kinds of violence. Nonviolence would either allow liberalism to dominate with its violence or would fail to achieve freedom in "the dialectic of concrete intersubjectivity." Merleau-Ponty sums up his point, stating that "all we know is different kinds of violence and we ought to prefer revolutionary violence because it has a future of humanism."[5]

So Merleau-Ponty's distinction between the violence of communism and of liberalism should be taken as pointing to the inability of an individual to avoid at least being complicit, even in a minimal and indirect way, in relation to a kind of violence. This puts into question whether nonviolence is possible, and whether it could work toward goals, such as freedom or justice, without some kind of violence.

4.3 POLITICAL CONFLICT, MEANS TO JUSTICE, AND THE IRRELEVANCE OF NONVIOLENCE: BUSH AND BIN LADEN'S FUNDAMENTAL DISAGREEMENT AND JUSTIFICATIONS FOR VIOLENCE AGAINST VIOLENCE

A more recent example than the conflict between liberalism and communism in relation to freedom and justice is reflected in the words of two adversaries: George Walker Bush and Osama bin Laden. Both are concerned with sustaining freedom, defending it against the injustices caused by the other. There is no question of a nonviolent use of means toward their goals because both conceive of the other as someone to be destroyed. For example, in his September 20, 2001 speech, "Address to a Joint Session of Congress and the American People," US president George Walker Bush denies the justice that the enemies of the United States seek and urges violence against them.[6] Here I indicate main points from Bush's speech that highlight what Bush had to say about freedom, justice, and the violence necessary for these to be upheld:

> Tonight we are a country awakened to danger and called to defend freedom. Our grief has turned to anger, and anger to resolution. Whether we bring our enemies to justice, or bring justice to our enemies, justice will be done. . . . On September the 11th, enemies of freedom committed an act of war against our country . . . freedom itself is under attack. . . . Every nation, in every region, now has a decision to make. Either you are with us, or you are with the terrorists. . . . The advance of human freedom . . . now depends on us. Our nation . . . will lift a dark threat of violence from our people and our future. . . . I will not relent in waging this struggle for freedom and security for the American people.

> . . . Freedom and fear, justice and cruelty, have always been at war, and we know that God is not neutral between them. . . . Fellow citizens, we'll meet violence with patient justice—assured of the rightness of our cause, and confident of the victories to come.

Bush does not outright say that the United States and those who join it in its fight against terrorism will use violence but instead repetitively uses the word "justice," rhetorically implying violence, such as when he states that "we'll meet violence with patient justice." That is, Bush is not referring to using nonviolence against terroristic violence.

In opposition, Al-Qaeda founder Osama bin Laden had argued in his August 23, 1996, letter, "Declaration of War Against the Americans Occupying the Land of the Two Holy Places: Expel the Polytheists from the Arabian Peninsula," that the West and "America" in particular are enemies who should suffer violence because they deny justice.[7] Both claim the other denies justice (bin Laden's view is indicated shortly), and both portray the other as an enemy against whom violence must be used because there is no other path to take. They nominally have the same goal, but despite this, they justify the use of violent means against one another, and this demonstrates their fundamental disagreement. Their arguments do not allow for any reconciliation because they both define the other as equivalent to an enemy against justice, which they both define as that which they themselves, with their "people," achieve. What they really aim for is the elimination of the threat of the other's violence, and only violence is conceived as capable of defeating that threat.

In the following, bin Laden clearly blames America, accusing it of deception and of being the cause of injustices for the people of Islam:

> The people of Islam have been struck by oppression, hostility and injustice. . . . All this happened before the eyes of the world, but the clear imperial arrogance of America, under the cover of the immoral United Nations, has prevented the dispossessed from arming themselves . . . we work to do away with the injustice that has befallen our Umma at the hands of the Judeo-Crusader alliance. . . . We pray to God that He might bless us with victory.

Osama bin Laden defines the injustice experienced by "the people of Islam" as being a result of the "imperial arrogance of America" that pretends to be moral by appealing to the United Nations. Nonviolence is not even an option for "the dispossessed." Bin Laden aims to delegitimize America's uses of violent means by defining them as unjust and immoral, and thereby legitimizes the violence of "the people of Islam" by defining it as just and moral.

For both Bush and bin Laden, the "other" is defined as an enemy and as an obstacle to each of their own goals in a way similar to how Merleau-Ponty distinguishes liberalism and communism in relation to freedom. Bush states, "They stand against us because we stand in their way," which accords with liberalism standing in the way of communism. When Bush says, "either [Nations] are with us or . . . are with the terrorists," this describes America as that which all must recognize as the promoter and defender of "freedom" and "justice." Anyone who does not side with the United States, or who remains passive or pacific in this situation, is complicit with the enemy. There is no other choice than to engage in some form of punishment of terrorists: "Terror unanswered can not only bring down buildings, it can threaten the stability of legitimate governments," Bush says. The implication is that anyone who sides with someone like bin Laden does not believe in the US government Bush leads. Anyone who is not with Bush is against him and is implicitly an enemy. If the aim is to defeat the violence that threatens one's own people and way of life, then nonviolence is not the means political leaders choose because they suspect the violence of their enemy. Again, nonviolence as a means is in question because, in relation to Islamophobia and ISIS (ISIL), nonviolently confronting those who are willing to utilize violence seems ineffective because then there is no defensive violence used by the state to defend one's own way of life and people. If nonviolence is in principle opposed to violence, including defensive violence, and the enemy's violence occurs nonetheless, then to be nonviolent would seem to be a case of granting the enemy victory.

Furthermore, when Bush declares, "whether we bring our enemies to justice or bring justice to our enemies, justice will be done," he engages in a fundamental disagreement. The American occupation of the Middle East is "justice delivered," from the liberal state's perspective, and an "invasion of evil," from bin Laden's theological one. Bin Laden calls for "jihad against the enemies of God, your enemies the Israelis and Americans," adding later that "you know that your coming-together and co-operation [*sic*] in order to liberate the holy places of Islam is the right step towards unification of the world of the Umma under the banner of God's unity." Unlike Bush's liberal ideological conception of political justice, bin Laden's eschatological ideology concerns a kind of divine justice.

There is no question for these leaders that if there is an enemy who impedes upon their own ability to achieve justice, then in practice it is violence that is the means to defeating the enemy, and not nonviolence. Both agree that violence is justified against enemies, but they politically disagree on who counts as enemy. Their definitions utilize the same terms, such as justice, but their definitions politically and ideologically disagree. So whether nonviolence can succeed against enemies is in question, particularly when those enemies wield violence. Not to use violence against an enemy's violence is defined as allowing the enemy's violence to succeed. That is, nonviolence cannot be justified against an enemy's violence because, by definition, this would grant victory to the enemy's violence.

Merleau-Ponty's claim is relevant here: "He who condemns all violence puts himself outside the domain to which justice and injustice belong."[8] The point that he makes, and that is reflected by the opposed definitions implied by George W. Bush and Osama bin Laden, is that anyone who works toward some political goal is already on the side of some kind of violence that the goal itself justifies, *even if one is not oneself engaged in violent* actions that pertain to the paradigm cases. To condemn violence and to commit to non-violence is to give up on pursuing goals of justice and freedom, particularly in a world in which one has enemies.

If one is protected so that one can enjoy living in relation to a defined kind of justice and freedom, then one is living a life that sides with a kind of violence, even if one is intentionally nonviolent. Even if nonviolent means are intentionally utilized, as Merleau-Ponty argues, the ability to be intentionally nonviolent is protected by other kinds of violence. Also, it is possible that one's intention to be nonviolent now may later become a kind of violence in the future because the future is contingent and we cannot know now what our nonviolence will mean in the future. One's intention to be nonviolent can be violent because, as indicated earlier and shortly, some kinds of violence are defined as invisible, systemic, and symbolic. If one avoids engaging in paradigm acts of violence, this is no guarantee that one is not violent in some other way. The political disagreements concerning what counts as violence mean that one's nonviolence can count as violence.

In his reflections on liberalism and communism, Merleau-Ponty argues that "once humanism attempts to fulfill itself with any consistency it becomes transformed into its opposite, namely, into violence."[9] That is, the pursuit for the goal of humanism will inevitably result in some kind of violence, such as that of a humanism's oppressive imposition against those who threaten the goal that is that "humanism." So nonviolence cannot work as a means to these goals because some kind of violence can always be implicated by a pursuit of this kind.

4.4 GIRARD ON MIMETIC RIVALRY AND THE MODERN LEGAL SYSTEM AS A SCAPEGOATING MECHANISM

Merleau-Ponty's criticism of liberalism's masking its own violence with conceptions of justice and freedom that are meant to serve as justifications for liberalism's violence as instances of defensive violence is reflected in Girard's anthropological work on violence, though Girard does not discuss

Merleau-Ponty's arguments. In Girard's view, the modern state, including the liberal state, veils its own uses of violence by pretending as though its use of violence were for the sake of achieving nonviolent harmony within a community, when anthropologically, evidence indicates that states merely engage in violence, violently protecting themselves, and scapegoating "victims," that is, "criminals," who threaten that nonviolent harmony that states only claim to achieve, but do not actually achieve. In other words, without violence, nonviolence is not possible. The violence of modern states is merely a secularized version of an ancient, primitive logic of sacrificial violence.

In his *Violence and the Sacred*, through anthropological analyses of primitive and ancient cultural practices and texts, Girard argues that in both primitive and modern cultures, only kinds of violence defeat violence and temporarily establish nonviolent social harmony, and that this is an inherently religious aspect of human existence. The relationship between ancient, primitive forms of violence that are thought to be capable of defeating violence and the juridical violence of modern states lies in their need for collectives of individuals to believe in these kinds of violence as legitimate and effective toward defeating violence. On religion, Girard writes,

> Religion invariably strives to subdue violence, to keep it from running wild. Paradoxically, the religious and moral authorities in a community attempt to instill nonviolence, as an active force into daily life and as a mediating force into ritual life, through the application of violence. Sacrificial rites serve to connect the moral and religious aspects of daily life, but only by means of a lengthy and hazardous detour. Moreover, it must be kept in mind that the efficacy of the rites depends on their being performed in the spirit of pietas, which marks all aspects of religious life. . . . Primitive religion tames, trains, arms, and directs violent impulses as a defensive force against those forms of violence that society regards as inadmissible. It postulates a strange mixture of violence and nonviolence. The same can perhaps be said of our own judicial system of control.[10]

Girard indicates how the cultural role of traditional, ritually performed violent sacrifices works in a way that includes nonviolence, but only in relation to violence, "mixed" with it. The purely nonviolent is not a means to cultural harmony because a kind of violence is needed for defeating the violence that "society regards as inadmissible." For this reason, it is paradoxical that religion and moral authorities try to instill nonviolence because they do so through uses of kinds of violence. Inadmissible violence is that which threatens the existence of a society. Religion adopts nonviolent sacrificial rites as a means of keeping violent impulses outside of a community, but nonviolent sacrificial rites only work to the extent that they mimic an original, violent sacrifice.

Additionally, modern culture reflects religion in that it uses violence as a means to defeat violence. In modern cultures, the guilty party is directly punished "because [the judicial system] possesses a monopoly on the means of revenge."[11] Due to this monopoly, revenge against the law is less likely. Though the judicial system directly punishes the guilty, few are willing to try to exact revenge on the judicial system. The judicial system's "control" of violence via its greater ability to be violent is assumed to keep violence in check. Modern society's belief in judicial systems lessens fears of vengeful violence that arise from people pursuing revenge against those who had pursued revenge against them.[12] Like the violent sacrifices utilized in primitive cultures for various goals, such as gaining a deity's favor or for the atonement of sins, the legal system of punishment depends on its uses of violence, without which it would no longer work. Religion tends to mask its dependency on violence, while judicial systems do not because they have a practical monopoly on the means of revenge.

The role of religious, violent sacrifices, in Girard's anthropological analysis, is that they serve to defeat the desire for vengeance against others that leads to reciprocating, vengeful violence. Without violent sacrifices, the nonviolent harmony of a community would not be possible. Without the almost universal agreement that violent sacrifices are wrong, in the sense of paradigm cases of violence, there would be no nonviolently unified communities. It may appear that the modern judicial system does not engage in pursuits for violent vengeance, but this is merely an appearance because, in the end, as "the most efficient of all curative procedures," the judicial system pursues violent vengeance against criminals and outlaws.[13] Nonviolent harmony in juridically policed communities that do not allow their members to seek vengeance against other members is secured through the direct use of violence. Nonviolence is only a consequence of the use of violent means.

In order to see why only violence is a means to nonviolence, note that Girard argues that the anthropological cause of violence is mimetic, triangular desire, which produces rivalry.[14] He explicitly disagrees with a "traditional view" of mimetic desire, which claims that violent conflict results from two or more humans competing for an "object [that] comes first, followed by human desires that converge independently on this object," followed by their violent confrontation when they attempt to possess the object.[15] It is not the case, according to Girard, that conflict results from two or more competing desires for an object. That is, "it is [not] . . . the intrinsic value of the object that inspires . . . [violent] struggle; rather, it is . . . violence itself that bestows value on the objects."[16] The object itself is only a "pretext" for violent conflict in the sense that, without the object, one would not see another individual manifest that the object is desirable through that other individual's being a violent obstacle to that object.

In this sense, mimetic, triangular rivalry involves three factors: a subject, an object, and a rival, who "desires the same object as the subject."[17] Two different subjects compete against one another in pursuit of being the one who exhibits the desirability of being the one who demonstrates the desirability of possessing the object. That is, because "the rival alerts the subject to the desirability of the object . . . the rival . . . serves as a model for the subject . . . in regard to desires."[18] This rival-model shows a "disciple" that an object is desirable, which means that we desire objects only because others demonstrate to us what is desirable.[19] For example, it is not that a person first desires owning natural resources and then the person competes with a rival for those natural resources but that the other person who owns the natural resources demonstrates that it is desirable to be the one who owns these. One is shown what one lacks, in particular, the desirability of being the one who possesses the object.[20] The disciple does not want to be the one who has the object but to be the one who manifests the desirability of being the one who possesses the object.

Girard also explains that this mimetic, triangular rivalry produces a "double bind," which is "a contradictory double imperative . . . [that] is so common that it might be said to form the basis of all human relationships."[21] The contradictory imperatives are "Imitate me!" and "Don't imitate me!"[22] A model demonstrates the desirability of being able to be an obstacle to expressing the desirability of having an object. As an obstacle to being the model, this model is a kind of violence that "commands" others to become the model. The model-obstacle commands "Imitate me!" However, when the disciple imitates the model-obstacle, they are violent threats in relation to one another. At this point, there is a double bind, the irreconcilable commands that the disciple should and should not be the model. This mimetic rivalry occurs such that the disciple-rival aims to imitate being a violent obstacle "by means of a mimetic counterviolence" that aims to overcome the model's being the violent model-obstacle.[23] When the disciple succeeds, their roles are inverted. The disciple becomes the model-obstacle, and the model-obstacle becomes the disciple. Thereafter, this inversion repeats reciprocally, oscillating back and forth as they each aim to outdo one another's being the violent model-obstacle.

The worst of possibilities that may result from this mimetic rivalry occurs when there is a steady growth of violence that "oscillates between the combatants, without either managing to lay final claim" to being the model-obstacle.[24] This growth of violence continues to escalate toward greater and greater kinds of violence in a mimetic, reciprocating process that occurs because "each person prepares himself for the probable aggression of his neighbors and interprets his neighbor's preparations as confirmation of the latter's aggressiveness."[25] The difficulty of attaining nonviolence internationally is relevant here. In terms of the security dilemma, this mimetic growth threatens at a global level, given that the increased security of one state can lead to other states increasing their own security. The other appears as a threat, and this leads to the building up of defenses, which results in one's increased defenses appearing as a threat to the other, which results in the other building up defenses and appearing as a threat, and so on. This continues to spiral as a vengeful reciprocation of aims to mimic the violence of the other recurs.

Anthropologically speaking, though, Girard describes how cultures have rescued themselves from this threat of the reciprocating, vengeful violence that arises from mimetic rivalry. This is the scapegoating mechanism. His assumption is that, due to mimetic rivalry and the double bind, people "make a duty of vengeance."[26] The model-obstacle's violence serves as a reason and justification for violent revenge against it. At a certain point, the event reaches an epiphany when everyone involved in the oscillation of violence must altogether redirect their reciprocating, vengeful violence away from one another and toward some single thing so that their desire for vengeance can be extinguished. At this point "only an act of collective expulsion can bring this oscillation to a halt and cast violence outside the community."[27] This requires the collectively produced sacrifice of a surrogate-scapegoat victim.

When a mimetic rivalry has become violent to the intense degree Girard describes, differences quickly shift back and forth between individuals intent on overcoming one another's violence. Then the situation simplifies, as participants increase their being violent and thereby lose their differences in relation to one another because each is engaged in violence.[28] As manifestations of violence, they become the same, and at this point a sacrificial crisis exists.[29] One can imagine a community in which everyone is engaged in violence to the point that what would otherwise distinguish each person from every other is erased. The differences required for cultural harmony are erased. At the point when a sacrificial crisis is reached, the "epiphany" occurs, and "violence . . . generate[s] unanimity, either in its favor or against it."[30] Either all continue to spontaneously reciprocate vengeful violence until they destroy themselves, or they collectively and spontaneously turn their violence onto a surrogate victim who serves as a scapegoat.[31] Anthropologically speaking, Girard shows that "violence is both the disease and the cure."[32] Nonviolent means are not the means to nonviolent consequences. Nonviolence is not defined as the cure to violence. Only violence can defeat violence, and though in modern states violent sacrifices of surrogate-scapegoats do not explicitly occur, this scapegoating mechanism that unifies a community against violence by way of a kind of sacrificial violence is retained in the juridical structure.

Girard defines the ancient, primitive situation in this way:

> Everything suggests a crowd whose intentions were initially pacific; a disorganized mob that for unknown reasons . . . came to a high pitch of mass hysteria. The crowd finally hurl[s] itself on one individual; even though he had no particular qualifications for this role, he served to polarize all the fears, anxieties, and hostilities of the crowd. His violent death provided the necessary outlet for the mass anguish, and restored peace.[33]

Given Girard's arguments, every society has this kind of violence at its origin, and their nonviolent existence as societies is only made possible by uses of violence. To claim that nonviolence is possible without violence or to claim that there is a society that does not have violence at its origin is to disagree with Girard's anthropological studies concerning the role violence plays in societies and with his analysis of the meaning of the kinds of action he interprets as responses to original violence, such as sacrifice.

Girard's point is that violence brings people together, either in terms of their unification or in terms of their self-destruction. Religion "hides" the violence it uses for the sake of maintaining nonviolent social harmony, but Girard suggests that the religious hiddenness of the role of the scapegoating mechanism is revealed by the judicial system. He argues,

> As the focal point of the system shifts away from religion and the preventive approach is translated into judicial retribution, the aura of misunderstanding that has always formed a protective veil around the institution of sacrifice shifts as well, and becomes associated in turn with the machinery of the law. . . . As soon as the judicial system gains supremacy, its machinery disappears from sight. Like sacrifice, it conceals—even as it also reveals—its resemblance to vengeance, differing only in that it is not self-perpetuating and its decisions discourage reprisals. In the case of sacrifice, the designated victim does not become the object of vengeance because he is a replacement, is not the "right" victim. In the judicial system the violence does indeed fall on the "right" victim; but it falls with such force, such resounding authority, that no retort is possible.[34]

Law, by definition, is a means to the preservation of nonviolence, but it can only do so by using violence, which law itself justifies, for the sake of defeating the desire for vengeance that leads to acts of violence. Without violent acts directed against the "right" victim, violence cannot be defeated. The "machinery of law" eliminates the religious veil, making the function of its violence explicitly obvious, though it would shroud its uses of violence as that which achieves nonviolence. But the judicial system cannot escape the fact that, when legal norms are violated, violent actions are the means used to punish criminals directly. Judicially, the violent actions justified by a modern state appear to be legal and secular, but they retain this religious character because the violent actions justified by the state bind a community together in nonviolent harmony. In short, Girard's point is that "vengeance, sacrifice, and legal punishment . . . are essentially the same [because] they tend to adopt the same types of violent response in times of crisis."[35] So again, but anthropologically (and juridically) speaking, nonviolence can only be gained as a goal through some kinds of uses of violent means, and not nonviolent ones.

4.5 CAN NONVIOLENCE BE ACHIEVED IN PRACTICE?

Merleau-Ponty's criticism of liberalism demonstrates that no one can seriously claim to be nonviolently seeking freedom. A person can experience means used toward sustaining or creating freedom as an imposition and as violence. Whether such impositions are violent is a matter of political and ideological disagreement. Girard shows that only by way of kinds of violence, sacrificial and judicial, can peaceful, nonviolent harmonies be achieved.

A person who argues in favor of nonviolence needs to show that nonviolent means are capable of achieving nonviolent goals (in the social-political and economic sense), and that those nonviolent means actually are nonviolent. In the following, we turn to arguments concerned with nonviolent resistance, nonviolent direct action, nonviolent civil disobedience, pacifism, forgiveness, and prayer. These arguments, produced by Todd May, John Rawls, Slavoj Žižek, Martin Luther King Jr., Gil Bailie, and Hannah Arendt, disagree with one another politically and ideologically. The kinds of nonviolence they define either demonstrate that nonviolence counts as a kind of violence or show that whether nonviolence is attained in practice is a matter of political and ideological disagreement.

4.6 THE VIOLENCE OF NONVIOLENCE: RESISTANCE, DISOBEDIENCE, AND REFUSAL

4.6.1 Todd May, Neoliberal Violence, and Nonviolent Resistance

With a focus on the United States and Europe, instead of the entire global population, Todd May argues that, since the Great Depression, there has been "a decline of the welfare state . . . and a turn to . . . *neoliberalism*," that is, "Chicago School economics," which argues for less government intervention and contrasts the Keynesian economics that influenced Franklin Roosevelt's creation of social welfare programs that intervene and invest in the public by providing public welfare in various ways.[36] With Ronald Reagan and Margaret Thatcher's elections, neoliberalism arrived in full force.

May cites David Harvey's definition of neoliberalism as "a theory of political economic practices that proposes that human wellbeing can best be advanced by liberating individual entrepreneurial freedoms and skills within an institutional framework characterized by strong private property rights, free markets, and free trade."[37] Neoliberalism privatizes, deregulates, and eliminates public services but intervenes in national and sometimes international markets, via the World Bank and International Monetary Fund. The main goal of neoliberalism is to "liberat[e] individual entrepreneurial freedoms and skills," but in Harvey's view, neoliberalism shifts wealth back to economic elites. This shift in the distribution of wealth and lack of investment in the public means that "where once it was considered an important social duty to assist one's fellow citizens, now they are left more nearly to their own devices," May says.[38] As a result, more people are forced into situations where they are afraid and alone to the extent that neoliberalism "erodes social solidarity; it contributes to an increasing individualization."[39] The government's use of money is distrusted, so neoliberalism privatizes and deregulates, and private companies do what they want without government interference. It follows, in May's view, that "neoliberalism leads to more neoliberalism in a cycle of isolated individualism creating more isolated individualism."[40] May's intention is to argue that nonviolent political action (that is, nonviolent resistance) can confront neoliberalism because such actions bring about "cooperation, trust, and solidarity."[41]

May characterizes neoliberalism as a kind of violence that extends beyond the commonsense view that is based on paradigm cases of violence. Neoliberalism's violence is "generally more structural than physical or psychological," which means that uses of violence against particular persons whose actions reproduce neoliberalism are uses of violence against victims of that same structural violence.[42] Also, using violence against those individuals whose actions defend neoliberalism, including the police and military, is likely to result in the police and military using their greater ability to wield violence to stop the violence directed against those who defend neoliberalism.[43] So May looks at nonviolence as the only way collectives of individuals acting in solidarity can work against the structural violence of neoliberalism. He argues that neoliberalism does not need to be "*overthrow[n]*," which could result in greater uses of violence on behalf of neoliberalism but "*undermine[d]*," by way of a "refusal of obedience . . . based upon a recognition of the dignity and a presupposition of the equality of everyone."[44]

It is because May does not think that violence can succeed against neoliberalism's structural violence, and the violence of those who support neoliberalism, that he endorses nonviolence as the means to undermining it. This nonviolent undermining of neoliberalism's violence is, as a means, a "refusal of obedience." A refusal like this, in May's view, does not overthrow but undermines, because if neoliberalism openly uses violence against those who nonviolently refuse to be obedient, then the project of neoliberalism, as a moral, social, and political project, is shown to be an immoral, antisocial, political ideology that violently enforces individualism, privatization, and economic inequalities, which have the potential to weaken and damage the ideology of neoliberalism itself.

The assumption is that nonviolent refusal to obey undermines, forcing a change. Those against whom the intentional use of nonviolence is directed are either provoked to use violence against the nonviolent, and thereby reveal the violence of those the nonviolence is directed toward, or the sought change is brought about. This, in May's view, is not an overthrow, because an overthrow could count as violence, but an undermining. To undermine is to start from the foundations, from the ground up, with actions that are assumed to be nonviolent in the sense of paradigm cases of nonviolence that are intentionally performed without any action counting as a paradigm case of violence.

May's assumption is that an overthrow implies a kind of domination and destruction, which can be more easily accused of violence. To be nonviolent, according to May, is to undermine because a nonviolent action assumes the dignity and equality of all, thereby producing a situation of respectfulness, which neoliberalism would openly violate, if it were to use violence against a nonviolent resistance or movement. So in this sense, a nonviolent political action provokes that against which it is directed into transforming into something else, such as when the nonviolent political actions of Gandhi undermined British imperialism and of Dr. Martin Luther King Jr. undermined the oppressive forces that upheld segregation.

In contrast to May's definition of the refusal to be obedient as nonviolent, Sartre defines a refusal as a kind of violence because it destroys the expectation that one will be obedient. In his *Notebooks for an Ethics*, Sartre writes that "violence is not just the refusal of making use of something, it is the destruction of the possibility of such use for everyone, the refusal of *all* lawfulness."[45] This is because, as opposed to obedient actions that conform to law and are therefore nonviolent from the perspective of law, refusal to be obedient breaks lawfulness in general and is therefore a kind of violence. Sartre states that "every refusal is likely to be taken for a form of violence."[46] So the refusal of obedience characterized by May as nonviolent political action can mean that in relation to other things, such as lawfulness, the refusal is a kind of violence. There is a political and ideological disagreement concerning whether a refusal of disobedience counts as nonviolence or as violence. In order to see how this nonviolent political action can count as violence, May's definition of nonviolence is addressed next because the issue concerns whether nonviolent actions can be effective in any way without there being a possibility of their being interpreted as a kind of violence.

May defines "nonviolence as *political, economic, or social activity that challenges or resists a current political, economic, or social arrangement while respecting the dignity of its participants, adversaries and others*."[47] He adds that "nonviolence must reject not only violence but also threats of violence" because such threats "don't actually respect the dignity of others" and because such threats intend to interrupt a human life.[48] The nonviolent means used, in the sense that May intends, are human bodies. He states,

> In nonviolence, one does not express one's equality with a gun but rather with one's own body. It is oneself, not one's weapon, which is the vehicle of resistance. . . . Moreover, in nonviolence it is by standing up rather than knocking down another that expresses refusal. . . . That is a form of emancipation that comes not from what is granted by one's adversary but developed through one's own activity.[49]

Whether a body counts as a weapon is debatable, depending on what people do with their bodies. A person's body could itself be a threat to someone's dignity, particularly if it "expresses refusal." If someone is intentionally nonviolent for the sake of enacting paradigmatic, nonviolent actions, acting nonviolently as if it were a maxim, standing up and refusing through nonviolent action, then it is possible that someone may disagree and interpret an action like this as a kind of violence. If this conception of acting nonviolently on principle entailed an action completely devoid of violence, then because it is a matter of interpretation and political, ideological assumptions that lead a person to think an action is in accordance with a principle of nonviolence, there can be others who do not necessarily define the actions as nonviolent ones. A person's standing up, in the sense of emancipatory refusal, could be that which is interpreted by the adversary as a threat. One's own idea of nonviolence, no matter how strongly one intends to actualize it in concrete, paradigmatic nonviolent actions, does not guarantee the action will be defined as nonviolent by most people, particularly by the adversary.

No matter how morally wrong it might be for someone to be a white supremacist who aims to uphold the institution of segregation, the nonviolent direct actions of Dr. Martin Luther King Jr. could be experienced as violence by them. Nonviolent political actors put their bodies in the way of things going on as normal, interrupting that normal and bringing about an abnormal situation that establishes a new normal that some individuals may refuse to accept as normal. They might sit on a bus or at a lunch counter, for example. This new normal can itself be experienced as a kind of violence by those who wish to preserve the past. The nonviolent refusal of the old normal, as Sartre might put it, is violence against the lawfulness of the old normal. Once refused, nonviolence violently destroys the possibility of that old normal continuing to be normal.

However, May is careful to define nonviolent political actions as nonviolent *actions*, emphasizing that it is not merely the intention that matters but the action itself. That is, if an action is to count as a nonviolent political action, then it really must be nonviolent *as an action*, in relation to what counts as a nonviolent action. Walking down a sidewalk is a paradigm case of a nonviolent action. Most people are likely to define the action as nonviolent. It is not that one must intend to embody nonviolence in principle but that an action is nonviolent if it accords with the way that nonviolence is defined by most people. However, whether an action is nonviolent depends upon the things that a person relates the action to. If the action is related to the disruption of some defined normal way of things, then one can disagree and define a nonviolent action as a violent one. The nonviolent refusal *makes way* through the normal way of things that the actors wish to transform. This would be to extend nonviolence beyond the paradigm cases, requiring that actions also not disrupt something defined as normal. Whether an action is nonviolent is a matter of disagreement, despite agreements that there are paradigm cases of nonviolent actions. Their effectiveness at changing something is exactly the point at which perspectives emerge, interpreting the action that refuses obedience as violent or nonviolent.

May defines nonviolent actions that undermine as those that are equivalent to expressions of respect for the dignity of others. He writes that "to act with dignity in nonviolent action . . . involves treating someone with the proper respect . . . tying together the dignity of the nonviolent actor with that of his or her adversary."[50] May frames nonviolent political action as something that uses the treatment of others with respect as a means to "tying together the dignity of the nonviolent actor with that of his or her adversary." Dignity is tied together when everyone involved, including one's adversary, is recognized by protesters as commonly sharing

> *the ability to engage in projects and relationships that unfold over time; to be aware of one's death in a way that affects how one sees the arc of one's life; to have biological needs like food, shelter, and sleep; to have basic psychological needs like care and a sense of attachment to one's surroundings.*[51]

A body's nonviolent action that respects the dignity of the other is defined by May as equivalent to the respect for the other's living life toward death, with basic biological and psychological needs. If one does not act with respect for the life and needs of one's adversary so that this adversary will reciprocate with respect for the dignity of the nonviolent political actors, then one's action is not equivalent to a nonviolent political action that undermines by refusing obedience, as defined by May. Respect for the dignity of others, the presupposition that all equally have basic needs and a life to lead, is defined as central to how nonviolence is thought to work as a means of refusal that undermines and emancipates. But should an individual respect the dignity of an adversary who is physically attacking that individual? If the adversary is not giving up and continues to attack, despite the individual's enacted nonviolent refusal, does one simply stand there and continue to receive those attacks? If one only stands there, is one allowing violence to be used as a means against oneself for the sake of some higher goal? Can a person use self-defensive violence?

May answers "no":

> Nonviolent action requires that one not physically attack others, even in self-defense . . . [because] any form of violent self-defense involves a significant diminishing of respect for the dignity of the one attacked . . . [and t]o have to defend oneself violently is to be put in a situation where one can only retain one's own physical integrity by disrespecting the other.[52]

The respect for the dignity and equality of everyone is central to social solidarity and serves as a normative assumption that is enacted by nonviolent political action. This respect, as May defines it, is the highest value that is to be committed to no matter what happens during a political action. During such an action, if one is to express this respect, one cannot even utilize self-defensive violence because that would eliminate the physical integrity of the political action's actually expressing refusal in a nonviolent way. May's assumption is that the violence of the other, which might otherwise justify self-defense, should be refused so that it is not reciprocally returned against that other. This undermines the other by respecting that other even when the other directs violence against oneself. That is, the assumption is that by refusing violence and being nonviolent against violence, nonviolence can defeat violence because an action's expression of nonviolence is defined as equivalent to the expression of respect for dignity.

However, whether a nonviolent political action is equivalent to this expression of respect is disputable. An adversary's violent action may be a reaction to a kind of action that the so-called nonviolent political action put into use, particularly their refusal of obedience. If a so-called nonviolent political action interrupts the flow of traffic on a highway, for example, then the ability of people to lead their lives is cut off, if even momentarily, in such a way that some of those people might claim to have suffered some kind of violence. Perhaps, for example, someone cannot make it to their job and loses it as a result, or perhaps someone is in need of medical assistance but cannot make it to a hospital because of the nonviolent political action. A person performing a nonviolent political action has no control over what nonparticipants think of the action. Ideally, the nonviolent political action makes way for emergency vehicles, but if any mistake is made, or some individual does some miniscule thing, such as stepping off a sidewalk into a road, that they ought not to have done because the police had told the participants to "Stay on that sidewalk! Get off the road! I am only going to tell you once!" then the police and state can claim that the nonviolent political action provoked the police to react because lawful commands were disobeyed, which then led to the participants arguing with police, all of which can escalate into police violence against that nonviolent political action. At that point, it is not going to be obvious that the political action is nonviolent because there are only images of arrests, arguments, physical struggles, bodies aggressively confronting one another, and so on. In short, a nonviolent political action can appear as violence, given opposed political, ideological assumptions, as do the "mistakes" that can occur during a nonviolent political action.

Also, following the assumption that a body's action can count as a refusal, it can count as violence because it depends on the person acting and the person acted against, who are bound together, involved in a particular situation, interpreting actions as they see them. A person may be engaging in a sit-in, lying on the ground, doing nothing, but because the police have told this person that "the street must be cleared now," whether the person's action is nonviolent is disputable, given disagreements on what counts as violence. From the perspective of the police, refusal to perform actions commanded by the police is not necessarily a legitimate, nonviolent action. Each person's actions will be interpreted in their relationships with other things. A nonviolent political action can thus at the same time be a kind of violence, possibly as a provocation, as a violation of law or of some "normal," or perhaps due to some actor's aggressiveness, or because the actions of some actors failed to express respect for dignity.

An issue for May's theory of nonviolent resistance is that it is difficult to guarantee that the actions of the participants in a campaign or social-political movement will not be interpreted as violent. That is, there are disagreements concerning whether nonviolent political action really is nonviolent. One analysis might look at the total gestalt of the political action and then decide whether it is nonviolent, ignoring the particular actions of individuals, and instead focusing on the overall "action" and what it, as a totality, did as a means to some end. Another analysis might begin with each individual's actions, weighing the degree to which they are violent or nonviolent, and then adding these up to see whether the violence or nonviolence outweighed the other. Surely, there are other ways some kind of violence pertaining to a political action could be defined and measured, such as in terms of police arrests, property destruction, and negative economic impacts. But the point is that ensuring that a political action is nonviolent is difficult, if not impossible, because, beyond the paradigm cases, there are disagreements concerning what counts as violence and as nonviolence in the first place.

May's argument follows a logic of exception. X is a nonviolent political action, except when Y. Y is defined as actions that are *not* the embodiment of nonviolent refusal of obedience that express respect for dignity as a means to the goal of gaining the adversary's reciprocated respect. May's view seems to idealistically suggest that, if a person engaged in a political action does not embody the expression of respect for the dignity of the adversary in just the right way, then the person's political action is not nonviolent. One is required to embody and enact this respect for dignity. By definition, according to May, one cannot be nonviolent unless one's body expresses this respect. But there is no way to guarantee that the acts will be taken as this kind of expression by the adversary.

Note that, because one must act in the way May defines in order for one's action to count as a nonviolent political action, one cannot choose to act nonviolently in any way other than how May defines a nonviolent political action. This itself can be interpreted as an oppressive imposition of a normative expectation that we must act a particular way. If so, it could be interpreted as a kind of violence. No one is allowed to be a nonviolent political actor, unless one does it the way May defines.

We should again note that refusal can count as a kind of violence from other perspectives. Likewise with respect. For example, Merleau-Ponty condemns respecting those who disrespect you. He states,

> We only know of situated consciousnesses which blend themselves with the situation they take and are unable to complain at being identified with it or at the neglect of the incorruptible innocence of conscience. . . . [A]s soon as we begin to live, we lose the alibi of good intentions; we are what we do to others, we yield the right to be respected as noble souls. To respect one who does not respect others is ultimately to despise them; to abstain from violence toward the violent is to become their accomplice.[53]

The respect for an adversary's equality and dignity in relation to oneself that a nonviolent political action is supposed to express might be a good intention, and enacted, but this nonviolent respect still does something *against* those targeted people and institutions that the nonviolent political actions act against. They did not choose for any kind of political action to occur in relation to them. The protesters force them into a situation. The nonviolent political actors have *made their way through to confront their adversary in an antagonistic relationship*. If a person does not disrespect an adversary who disrespects them in at least a minimal way, then they are not authentically engaging in the relationship of disrespect that exists and might come to despise that adversary. Once the adversary is despised though, that is all that has happened. The adversary's disrespect and violence will remain. So Merleau-Ponty does not argue that one should respect those who disrespect others *because this does not work*. If kinds of violence are happening and people are disrespecting others, then respecting an adversary merely allows the kinds of violence and disrespect to continue, in Merleau-Ponty's view. This political, ideological perspective directly disputes May's requirement that adversaries be respected by protesters, even when they use violence against us.

Similarly, Sartre argues that respect *is* violence. In his *Being and Nothingness*, he argues that "respect for the Other's freedom is an empty word; even if we could assume the project of respecting this freedom, each attitude which we adopted with respect to the Other would be a violation of that freedom which we claimed to respect."[54] Freedom is violently violated, in Sartre's sense, because it is always treated as a thing whenever one is respectful toward it. There cannot be "*laissez-faire*" tolerance and respect for another person's freedom because in relation to one another, each individual limits the freedom of every other.[55] Each individual in relation to every other is forced into a world of an Other where that Other's respect and tolerance limit what each individual may do. Respect and tolerance restrict what is acceptable, and this violates freedom as a kind of violence. In terms of Sartrean existentialism, there is no escape from the fact that the freedom of consciousness sees others as they are in the world, as things, and to expect an Other to express respect and tolerate others is to impose an objectified existence as a thing onto the freedom of that person's consciousness, violently violating it. Respect as an imposition of an expectation is merely another means of domination over another and can be counted as a kind of violence.

However, May is focused on the equality of everyone, and not freedom, in the sense that "to act on the presupposition of equality is to act *as though one were already an equal* rather than *asking to be treated as an equal*."[56] Sartre means something very precise in his existential notion of the freedom of consciousness that transcends the existence of that person as an embodied thing, but for our purposes it suffices to capture his main point, which is that assuming a project of any kind and then respecting others *in relation to that project* is an imposition of that project and a violent violation of anyone who is not likewise persuaded by that project. Any universalization of such norms, even if they are defined as being nonviolent, might be experienced by some people as a violent objectification of their existence as an equal. Though May defines respect in relation to equality rather than freedom, it is no different because the expectation that an adversary acknowledges respect for equality can be experienced by that adversary as a kind of violence.

4.6.2 Active and Passive Equality: Challenging the Police Order

May defines two kinds of equality, passive and active, in his *The Political Thought of Jacques Rancière*.[57] May writes,

> Passive equality [is] the creation, preservation, or protection of equality by governmental institutions. The animating idea behind passive equality is that some form of equality is to be ensured by an institution for the sake of those whose equality is at stake. It is to be given, or at least protected, rather than taken or enacted by the subjects of equality.[58]

Passive equality is the passive reception of distributed justice or distributed equality, particularly in the sense of equal consideration.[59] This means that people do not "create, ensure, or protect their equality" but are merely recipients of equality. May writes, "inasmuch as we conceive our political space in terms of rights . . . , we conceive ourselves as passive. And inasmuch as we conceive that space in terms of equal rights, we conceive our equality as passive."[60] The passiveness of passive equality lies in that rights and equality are assumed as having been achieved and sustained through the distribution of these, which citizens passively receive as recipients. May agrees with Rancière's description of this passive equality as being a matter of "policing" and not of politics.[61]

"Policing" is the result of passive equality and the distribution of equality and rights. This is "the idea of the police as involving a social ordering that is enforced not merely by military-style intervention—armed men in uniforms—but more significantly by the idea of a proper social order."[62] This kind of policing "seeks . . . to put everything in its place, through allotment and through justification. The allotment is the distribution posited by the order. The justification . . . is the appeal to equality that founds the particular distribution."[63] This passive view of equality overlooks the significance of the active, creative struggles for equality and rights that were first required before any passive distribution could occur. May means to focus not on this passive reception of rights, "secured" through policing, but on the active "political moment of struggle itself" that challenges this.[64]

In contrast to passive equality, active equality is "political participation," which May defines as that which everyone can engage in.[65] In brief, "equality is not received. It is made . . . because to receive equality is already to be less than equal to the one who bestows it."[66] Democratic politics is political participation, enacted as a challenge, a "dissensus" in Rancière's terms, in relation to the police order.[67] The foundation for political participation is equality in the sense that each individual speaks from a position. Politics happens, in May's view, when "the traditional mechanism of what are usually called 'politics' are put into question." And it happens as "an action by the people, the demos, that intervenes upon [a] situation" from which they have been excluded.[68] In this sense, "a democratic politics is the appearance of that which has been excluded . . . manifests a people . . . [and] creates a political subject."[69] In short, "in the name of equality . . . , a demos arises that dissents from the position or positions its members have been allotted . . . disrupt[ing] the completeness of a police order through an activity that is in itself an expression of its own equality with those whose own position or actions seek to deny that equality."[70] Political expertise is not necessary for this enacted challenge to the "equal" identity individuals passively receive within a police order because everyone is equally intelligent, in the sense that Rancière means, namely that "anyone and everyone . . . is capable of speaking to one another, understanding one another, reasoning with one another."[71] "Being able to consider and act upon our world" is all that is required for one's being an equal.[72] Actually speaking words or having a particular level of intelligence and education is not necessary for being equal. In this sense of equality as being able to act upon and consider our world, this is "a form of active rather than passive equality."[73] Active equality is enacted equality and, as such, it is democratic politics, which "unif[ies] those who are oppressed and those who act alongside them and on their behalf into a single subject" such that a participant is not "a part that has no part" because her actions actively communicate equality to her oppressors.[74] Altogether, this democratic politics of participatory active equality is required for a progressive form of politics because it "concerns the ability of each of us, in concert with others, to engage in the project of a reflective reconstruction of lives."[75]

May also adds that democratic politics, as a collective action that emerges from the presupposition that participants are equal to their adversaries and the police order, must be "nonviolent political action."[76] However, nonviolence is not passiveness. Violent resistance is the route typically taken, he argues, because it is "the easy political option" that is the "natural temptation" that arises such that, when "one is dominated . . . one dominates; [and when] one is oppressed . . . one oppresses."[77] Nonviolent resistance, though, "reject[s] the type of thinking fostered by a police order [and] . . . requires the creation of a non-hierarchical space."[78] A collective action that is a nonviolent resistance does not react in the form of resentment but creates and is "defined by what [it does] rather than by that [which it] oppose[s]." In particular, a nonviolent, political, collective action presupposes equality, while "violent struggle requires one to choose between one's own worthiness and that of one's adversary."[79] Violence harms, which means that if violence is used, then who counts as deserving of harm, as less than equal, has been decided upon.[80] Violence will not work, in May's view, against a police order because it reestablishes a police order of inequality. For this reason, nonviolence is "the most likely path" to "a point of consensus," which is "an agreement on the equality of everyone in the [police] order itself."[81]

4.6.3 The Violence of Self-Preservation or the Violent Recreation of Inequality?

However, May adds that democratic political actions could use violence. He writes,

> There seems to be no bar to placing side by side the claims that one's adversary is one's equal and that, because of the adversary's refusal to recognize one's own equality, one must injure or kill her. The analogy here would be one of self-defense. To defend oneself against another does not require a denial of that other's equality. It requires instead an embrace of one's own. Self-protection is . . . the necessity of preserving oneself. So it is with a violent democratic struggle. The emergence of violence in such a struggle arises on the basis of a persistence in one's own equality, of the effort to maintain the expression of the presupposition of equality in the face of steadfast refusal to allow that expression. . . . [A]lthough the effect of violence may be a denial of the other, it is not because of the attempt to deny the other but to preserve one's own democratic expression that violence can be resorted to without violating the ethical strictures of a democratic politics. . . . [T]he appeal to violence in the context of democratic struggle lies on a razor's edge. The line between self-preservation and the denial of the equality of the other is a thin one. . . . [I]t is easy to ratify the destruction of the other out of anger or the denial one has suffered rather than for the preservation of one's democratic expression. The deeper the history of denial of equality, the stronger that temptation is. . . . By placing the emphasis of violent struggle on self-preservation rather than destruction of the other, it can help mitigate some of the more deleterious aspects of violent struggle. This provides no guarantee of safeguards against abuse.[82]

May's conception of equality in *Nonviolent Resistance* (2015) turns toward respect for dignity in a way not addressed seven years earlier in this work, *The Political Thought of Jacques Rancière: Creating Equality* (2008), as this quote expresses. However, the concern is similar. The later work conceives of this active equality in relation to nonviolent political resistance on the foundation of a presupposed equality concerning the dignity of others, namely that they have their own lives and needs, rather than on the equality of the ability to speak intelligently and live life in a way that affects the world. The nonviolence he expects of democratic politics, on the basis of presupposed equality and the refusal to dominate others in the way of a new police order, can turn to violence in the form of self-defense, or "self-protection" if the adversary persistently refuses the equality of the participants who act on the presupposition of equality. He indicates that the point at which this persistence exists is a "razor's edge" because there is a historical element that may be taken into consideration by those who engage in the political action. The razor edge difference between self-preservation and denial of the other's equality, through a use of violence, depends on historical factors and the specific situation in which the violence is used. If violence is used for self-preservation or denial of the other's equality depends on how it is related to other things that are not necessarily agreed upon. Whether the violent action is not productive of inequality or is the self-preservation of equality is not likely to be agreed upon. May's conception of nonviolent political actions thus depends on a political ideal.

May is particularly concerned with actual social-political movements from history, such as the Indian Independence Movement and Gandhi's insights into nonviolence as a means of protest, and the American Civil Rights Movement and Martin Luther King Jr.'s contributions to the study of nonviolence. However, in order for someone against whom a nonviolent political action is directed to acknowledge that the action is directed against the wrongness of their understanding of equality and freedom, such a person has to forfeit their understanding of equality and freedom. That is, the history of the British government in India and the judicial, police, and cultural systems of the south in the United States was forced to change its course so that oppression is explicitly on view for everyone to see *as oppression* and as wrong, thereby indicating that the institutions of occupation and segregation are themselves seen as things to be defeated. They are shown as that which breeds the possibility of injustices and violence. People are forced to acknowledge their own violence, which itself might be experienced as a kind of violence, no matter how nonviolent the action that forces these people to acknowledge their own violence happens to be.

However, the individuals who uphold oppressive laws need not have acknowledged that they were in the wrong. Instead, they were merely forced to succumb to the goals of the political action. It's not necessarily the case that racist segregationists suddenly had a change of heart. The nonviolent force used to make them acknowledge that they are wrong and to change course, eliminating segregation, is an interesting one in how it works, but can it work as nonviolence? Being forced by protesters to appear wrong in the eyes of the public has the potential to mobilize collectives of individuals in favor of and against the institutions that uphold those wrongs. If the targeted people and institutions are forced to see themselves as wrong, then whether this is a kind of violence or nonviolence is disputable. These people and institutions are imposed upon by the protests, even undermined, which means that even if they are wrong, the actions against them are not necessarily nonviolent. So it's not clear that the nonviolent respect of nonviolent political actions can be nonviolent in the first place, if it is to work against wrongs. Without coercion or provocation, which can themselves be experienced as kinds of violence, it is difficult to see how actions could nonviolently produce the kinds of social-political and economic transformations that May writes about.

In fact, in *Nonviolent Resistance*, May admits that it is highly unlikely for any campaign to be purely nonviolent. He argues that "a shove or a threat does not turn a nonviolent campaign into a violent one" but adds that "pure nonviolence is more an ideal than a description of certain campaigns. If we were to characterize only purely nonviolent campaigns as actually nonviolent, [May] suspect[s] that no campaign would find itself in that category."[83] So despite all his argumentation and the definitions he produces, he is not really defining nonviolent resistance as purely nonviolent. Whether a shove or threat turns a nonviolent political action into a violent one is debatable.

The issue, then, is that nonviolent means might not actually work as nonviolent means toward gaining goals. From the perspective of those against whom the campaign is directed, the "shove or threat" may be exactly that which transforms a nonviolent campaign into a violent one. For example, the media's coverage of the 2014 protests in Ferguson, Missouri, following police officer Darren Wilson's shooting of unarmed Michael Brown and their coverage of the 2015 protests in Baltimore, Maryland, following the death of Freddy Gray focus on the violence of collectives of individuals, describing those events as "violent," even though many participants were not intentionally violent. This was true of many of the Black Lives Matter protests as well as the January 6 insurrection in Washington, DC. The media tends to focus on the violence and, in turn, describes the entire event as violent. Whether one defines a political action as violent or nonviolent depends on one's focus and on that to which one relates the action. So what May defines is a kind of nonviolent violence that is, perhaps, less violent than other kinds of violence, such as the structural violence sustained by neoliberalism, but can count as a kind of violence nonetheless.

Last, May argues that because it is difficult to define violence, he only aims to indicate the kind of violence that nonviolent political actions aim to avoid. In fact, May admits that in order for a nonviolent political action to work, it has to be a kind of symbolic violence. On why a nonviolent political action counts as symbolic violence, May uses Slavoj Žižek's distinctions between subjective, systemic, and symbolic violence, discussed in the previous chapter.[84] May's concern is not primarily with how nonviolence can count as a kind of violence but with the kind of violence that nonviolent political action aims to avoid. Nonetheless, he defines nonviolent political actions as a kind of symbolic violence because, if they were not a kind of violence, then it would be difficult to see how they could work.

4.6.4 Nonviolence as Žižekian Symbolic Violence: The Nonviolent Violence of Jiu-Jitsu Maneuvers

In relation to the subjective, systemic, and symbolic kinds of violence defined by Slavoj Žižek, May argues that the kinds of violence rejected by a nonviolent political action are systemic and subjective, but not symbolic violence because he considers it a "stretch" to think of nonviolent political actions as not utilizing language.[85] If a nonviolent political action is to work at all, it has to at least communicate something. This means that the nonviolence that May defines is an action that aims to avoid physical, psychological, systemic, structural, and subjective violence, but that still counts as a kind of symbolic violence *because otherwise the nonviolent political action would not work.* In other words, the nonviolent political action defined by May still counts as a kind of violence because the purpose of a nonviolent political action is to demonstrate that an injustice exists, and this can only be communicated via linguistic, symbolic means, which themselves can be defined as kinds of violence, if they aim to undermine the status quo and establish a new "normal." In order to see how so-called nonviolent political actions are simultaneously symbolic violence, we turn to May's argument for how nonviolent political action works as a means.

The way in which a nonviolent political action works is described by May (who follows Gene Sharp on this) in terms of a "moral jiu-jitsu," which effectively "turns the ethical tables on an adversary, so that what had once appeared as justified actions or policies turns out to be an unjustified assault upon the dignity of those who resist them . . . [and] results in a convergence on a common moral view that includes protestors and adversaries on the same moral plane."[86] When a moral jiu-jitsu occurs, the adversary has a change of heart. May distinguishes moral jiu-jitsu from "political jiu-jitsu," which is capable of nonviolently forcing an adversary to involuntarily do something "without violating dignity or presupposing equality" and can occur as a nonviolent "refusal of obedience to and even the active disruption of an unjust political, economic, or social order."[87] With a political jiu-jitsu, the change sought by the nonviolent political actors occurs, but there is no change of heart among the adversaries. A moral political jiu-jitsu is a political one, but a political one is not necessarily a moral jiu-jitsu. May aims to retain the nonviolent ability of political actions to convince or force an adversary to admit that they are morally wrong, but the adversary against whom the nonviolent political action is directed can experience the action as symbolic violence, particularly if the nonviolent political actions have escalated to the point of forcing a new normal to come into existence. If this political or moral jiu-jitsu does not occur as symbolic violence, then it is difficult to see how nonviolent political action works at all. In such a situation, the adversary's position is forced to express itself as an abnormal kind of violence by the symbolic violence of the so-called nonviolent political action.

Merleau-Ponty's following statement reinforces the argument that May's definition of nonviolent political action shows that nonviolence could only work as a kind of violence, particularly as symbolic violence. Merleau-Ponty states,

> It is a law of human action that the present encroaches upon the future, the self upon other people. This intrusion is not only a fact of political life it also happens in private life. . . . In collective history the spiritual atoms train after them their historical role and are tied to one another by the threads of their actions; what is more, they are blended with the totality of actions, whether or not deliberate, which they exert upon others and the world so that there exists not a plurality of subjects, but an intersubjectivity, and that is why there exists a common measure of the evil inflicted upon certain people and of the good gotten out of it by others.[88]

Merleau-Ponty's point is that, in a world in which we cannot avoid affecting others as we pursue our projects, there is always the possibility that those pursuits that are good and nonviolent for one collective of individuals are evil and violent for others. Whether such an action succeeds at gaining its goal depends upon whether it makes those it is directed against acknowledge their own "wrongness," even if they do not believe they are wrong, and this can be considered symbolic violence.

4.7 RAWLS, MOUFFE, AND MERLEAU-PONTY: NONVIOLENT CIVIL DISOBEDIENCE AND POLITICAL LIBERALISM'S PLURALISM AS A KIND OF VIOLENCE

May's concern with equality and dignity as basic assumptions inherent to nonviolent political action reflect John Rawls's definition of nonviolent civil disobedience. The challenge to Rawls is whether the nonviolent civil disobedience that he defines is even possible. Rawls argues that nonviolent civil disobedience is that which arises when disagreement emerges, concerning "the principles of social cooperation among free and equal men."[89] He defines civil disobedience as

> a public, nonviolent, conscientious yet political act contrary to law usually done with the aim of bringing about a change in the law or policies of the government. By acting in this way one addresses the sense of justice of the majority of the community and declares that in one's considered opinion the principles of social cooperation among free and equal men are not being respected.[90]

For an action to count as nonviolent civil disobedience, it must also be "guided and justified by . . . the principles of justice," which are based on fairness, and "not . . . principles of personal morality or . . . religious doctrines . . . [nor] group or self-interest."[91] The action must be public, and *only* contrary to a particular law because justice and "principles of social cooperation among free and equal men are not being respected." Any action that is not guided and justified by the principles of justice defined by Rawlsian political liberalism cannot count as nonviolent civil disobedience. However, if nonviolent civil disobedience must be truly nonviolent, public, and guided by the principles of justice, and there is disagreement concerning what it means to be nonviolent beyond the paradigm cases, what it means for something to be public, or on what these principles of justice are, then it is not likely that an action could ever count as nonviolent civil disobedience without political, ideological disagreements arising.

In his *A Theory of Justice*, Rawls derives the principles of justice based on fairness from an assumed, fictional, "original position," in which participants are veiled from knowing anything about who and what they each are.[92] From this original position, two principles of justice are derived: "the first [that is, the liberty principle] requires equality in the assignment of basic rights and duties, while the second [that is, the difference principle] holds that social and economic inequalities, for example inequalities of wealth and authority, are just only if they result in compensating benefits for everyone, and in particular for the least advantaged members of society."[93] Agreement upon these two principles of justice is possible because none of the fictional participants know anything about themselves but instead seek rational and fair principles of justice that can attain among equals who are the same. In short, the original position veils from participants the conditions that could lead to envy. If a person has what others would want, then for those who do not have it, this is only fair on the assumption of Rawls's principles. Only nonviolent, public actions aimed toward these principles count as civil disobedience.

Rawls allows for nonviolent civil disobedience because he acknowledges that reasonable attempts to seek overlapping consensus do not always work, not even in a fictional state that is almost perfectly just. In *A Theory of Justice*, he states,

> By engaging in civil disobedience one intends . . . to address the sense of justice of the majority and to serve fair notice that in one's sincere and considered opinion the conditions of free cooperation are being violated. We are appealing to others to reconsider, to put themselves in our position, and to recognize that they cannot expect us to acquiesce indefinitely in the terms they impose upon us.[94]

However, like May's definition of nonviolent political actions, Rawlsian nonviolent civil disobedience does not seem to be possible other than as a theoretical abstraction from life. In particular, this appeal to others to reconsider and "to put themselves in our position" could be experienced by them as the kind of symbolic violence discussed earlier. If tables are turned, and these others are forced to reconsider that they do not actually understand or aim toward the principles of justice, then there is already a conflict concerning the kind of justice that is to be pursued, and the institution of the principles of justice defined by Rawls could itself be interpreted as violence, at least in the Žižekian, symbolic sense.

However, Rawls adds that "by resisting injustice within the limits of fidelity to law, [civil disobedience] serves to inhibit departures from justice and to correct them when they occur. A general disposition to engage in justified civil disobedience introduces stability into a well-ordered society, or one that is nearly just."[95] So Rawls assumes a society in which the principles of justice are upheld in common by everyone, and that in a just society, only those who are in some way denied equality or freedom will utilize civil disobedience nonviolently for the sake of upholding the principles of justice as he defines them. In other words, if someone is not engaging in nonviolent civil disobedience for the sake of upholding the principles of justice Rawls defines, then that person's actions do not count as legitimate nonviolent civil disobedience. Given that a person could conceive of justice differently, Rawlsian political liberalism is that which one cannot choose against. One can only act within the confines of the structures of justice that Rawls defines. In fact, Chantal Mouffe argues this and Merleau-Ponty implies it.

4.7.1 On Liberalism's Rejection of the Freedom to Choose against It

Chantal Mouffe argues that there is a presumed neutrality of Rawlsian-styled political liberalism, which is precisely the problem with political liberalism. In her "Political Liberalism: Neutrality and the Political," Mouffe argues that Rawls ignores the underlying conflict that results from the plurality of persons that is upheld by the principles of liberalism in the first place.[96] She states, "a liberal democratic regime, while fostering pluralism, does not put all values at the same level. It could not do so, since its very existence as a political form of government requires a specific ordering of values which precludes a total pluralism."[97] This means that, despite Rawls's intention that the participants agree upon neutral, rational principles of justice, the decision made in the original position behind the veil of ignorance rejects anyone's knowing who and what they are in the world and rejects anyone's being committed to anything other than political liberalism. Political liberalism's "neutrality" is, therefore, not neutral because there is no freedom to choose against it.

Likewise, Maurice Merleau-Ponty points out that liberalism contradicts itself. In his *Humanism and Terror*, he rejects liberalism in favor of communism precisely because liberalism's so-called humanism hides its violence. He states, "the dogmatic basis of liberalism . . . [is] the way it only grants certain liberties by taking away the freedom to choose against it."[98] Liberalism is contradictory because, "if I wish freedom for another person it is inevitable that even this wish will be seen by him as alien law; and so liberalism turns into violence." For one to make someone free, this freedom is imposed on that person, and the person cannot choose against that freedom. Imposed freedom is the opposite of freedom. In the end, Merleau-Ponty admits that "we are not accusing liberalism of being a system of violence; we reproach it with not seeing its own face in violence."[99] He decides in favor of communism's violence because, unlike liberalism, communism does not pretend as though it does not utilize violence for the sake of gaining freedom. Despite the fact that liberalism defines itself as the flag-bearer of humanism, its humanism becomes terror because it uses violence while hiding that it does so at the same time. This means that the principles of justice that Rawls considers to be constitutive of the legitimacy of political liberalism's neutral conditions for a nonviolent, pluralistic society turn out to be a mask that veils its own inclusion of violence against those who are against political liberalism. So the nonviolence of political liberalism's justice turns out to be a kind of imposed violence.

This also means that Rawls's expectation that one's nonviolent civil disobedience is not a refusal to be obedient to the principles of justice (which are not concretely actualized in any regime) because if one is not obedient to these principles of justice, then this eliminates the possibility of one's being nonviolently civilly disobedient. If anyone engages in civil disobedience, then it must be made clear during their action, presumably on the condition that the action is public, that the action communicates the intention to uphold the principles of justice. For this reason, civil disobedience is both obedient to the norms of justice and the laws outlined by a constitution that is supposed to uphold those norms and simultaneously disobedient in relation to some of those constitutional laws and norms. But because one is not supposed to be disobedient to the norms of justice but only when those norms do not exist in society, one's nonviolent civil disobedience could be considered a kind of violence because it is directed against people and institutions, not the principles of justice themselves. So Rawlsian nonviolent civil disobedience, unlike the nonviolent political actions defined by May in terms of symbolic violence and jiu-jitsu, is not merely a kind of violence but is *practically impossible*, given opposed ways of conceiving of how a collective of individuals acting disobediently in relation to some injustice can at the same time embody in their action the principles of justice. In short, if nonviolent civil disobedience must exclusively aim toward the two principles of justice defined by Rawls, and there is disagreement concerning those principles and how they are enacted by protesters, then whether civil disobedience is nonviolent is disputable.

4.8 ŽIŽEK ON THE VIOLENCE OF DOING NOTHING

Žižek also defines nonviolent actions in such a way that they seem barely possible, given symbolic, systemic, and subjective violence. In his book *Less than Nothing: Hegel and the Shadow of Dialectical Materialism*, Žižek describes a person's "standing still" and "doing nothing" as means to doing something because these can occur as "a sudden interruption of [the] movement" constitutive of "a harmonious[ly] functioning . . . Whole."[100] Intentionally standing still is one's doing something by doing nothing. The idea is that, "in order to effectively 'do nothing,' one should not 'stand still,' but be active [so that] . . . one is really active" when one purposely "stands still." The result, he argues, is that "this immobility causes havoc and chaos."[101]

Žižek means that symbolic and systemic violence, as well as the subjective violence that results from these, as discussed earlier, are interrupted by individuals who intentionally do not engage in the actions that reproduce them. Doing nothing is a means to this goal. In order not to be or to contribute to objective and subjective violence, one must really be nonviolent, and this requires intentionally using "doing nothing" as a means. Being nonviolent requires not being violent in any way at all, and this requires actively doing nothing. However, unlike May's definition of a nonviolent political action as a kind of symbolic violence, Žižek defines "doing nothing" as not being a kind of symbolic violence. So there is disagreement on how nonviolently doing nothing is a kind of violence. Furthermore, if standing still and doing nothing are intentionally done for a goal, and this nonaction disrupts, and results in "havoc and chaos," it is quite easy for others to interpret it as a kind of violence.

In his book *Violence: Six Sideways Reflections*, Žižek expands upon this idea of the nonviolence of doing nothing. He makes three points concerning the "lessons" learned from his discussion of violence in this book:

1. First, to chastise violence outright, to condemn it as "bad," is an ideological operation par excellence, a mystification which collaborates in rendering invisible the fundamental forms of social violence.

2. It is difficult to be really violent, to perform an act that violently disturbs the basic parameters of social life.
3. Violence is not a direct property of some acts, but is distributed between acts and their contexts, between activity and inactivity. The same act can count as violent or non-violent, depending on its context; sometimes a polite smile can be more violent than a brutal outburst.[102]

Here, he clearly states that violence can remain hidden, as his definitions of symbolic and systemic violence indicate. Also, that the same action can count as both nonviolent and as violent is not a contradiction, given that whether an action is of one kind or another depends upon a perspective from which it is contextually described and experienced. What counts as the nonviolent functioning of capitalistic structures of employment, for example, is not necessarily experienced as nonviolent by those who are the most exploited. Nonetheless, Žižek intends to conceive of a kind of act or event that transforms human relationships. Doing nothing is such an act, but only if it does something. So doing nothing is not literally *doing nothing* because there is something that is actively and purposely done by one's doing nothing for the sake of a transformation. Doing nothing is not acting when one would otherwise be expected or commanded to act, which upsets the framework of systemic and symbolic violence. Because the nothing that is done is a refusal to be obedient, it is a kind of violent nonviolence, and one that Žižek believes is capable of transforming social-political and economic structures.

Žižek also defines today's conflicts such that "mass killings are more and more legitimated in religious terms, while pacifism is predominantly atheist. It is the very belief in a higher divine goal which allows us to instrumentalise [*sic*] individuals, while atheism admits no such goal and thus refuses all forms of sacred sacrificing."[103] In this sense, Žižek opposes theorists who argue that there is a theological, transcendent element to the justification of nonviolent protest, perhaps as Dr. Martin Luther King Jr. does. His point is that the belief in deities easily justifies violence. Violence occurs for the sake of a religious goal. Because atheists do not believe in such things, there is no religious goal in relation to which they would be able to justify violent actions. Atheists tend to be less violent or more likely to reject violence than religious individuals. However, atheism's refusal of sacred sacrificing would itself be an atheistic, secular sort of sacrifice of oneself as well, and this indicates that the atheist who refuses sacrifice retains the role played by sacrifice in that the atheist sacrifices sacrifice by refusing it. So Žižek veils the fact that the atheist's pacifistic rejection of goals is itself a goal. Other goals are rejected for the sake of the goal of having no goal that instrumentalizes individuals toward "divine goals." It is in this sense that he secularizes the role of sacrifice played in theology. To see how Žižek's view disagrees with theologically framed justifications for nonviolence, we turn to Dr. Martin Luther King Jr.

4.9 KING'S THEOLOGICAL DEFINITION OF NONVIOLENT DIRECT ACTION IN RELATION TO JUSTICE

In his "Letter from a Birmingham Jail," King defines nonviolent direct action in a way that shows that it "seeks to create such a crisis and establish such creative tension that a community that has constantly refused to negotiate is forced to confront the issue."[104] He also writes that "there is a type of constructive, nonviolent tension which is necessary for growth. . . . The purpose of our direct action program is to create a situation so crisis packed that it will inevitably open the door to negotiation." The issue is that King frames the ability of a nonviolent direct action to produce a change in terms of this "creative tension" and "crisis" that is forced into existence. If "creative tension" and "crisis" are experienced *against* the expectations and desires of some individuals and institutions that the direct action is aimed at, then those individuals and institutions may decide that the nonviolent direct action is not nonviolent but perhaps a kind of provocative symbolic violence.

However, King aims to argue that, though the nonviolent direct action produces a crisis and creative tension, the crisis and tension are not the fault of the nonviolent actors. He states, "we who engage in nonviolent action are not the creators of tension. We merely bring to the surface the hidden tension that is already alive. We bring it out into the open where it can be seen and dealt with." So though the nonviolent direct action brings this tension to the surface, it is not the fault of the direct actions but is already there and is simply exposed by them as what it already is. Of course, from the perspective of racist segregationists, they might not see things this way and could still interpret the direct action as a violent one.

King's nonviolent actors are not doing something by doing nothing and are not atheists without a goal, in the sense defined by Žižek. Instead, King defines a distinction between just and unjust laws directly in relation to the existence of "the law of God." To eliminate God from King's argument would be to eliminate the distinction between just and unjust laws, which is needed for justifying nonviolent direct actions. Just laws are defined, by King, as equivalent to God's laws. Such a conception of justice also disagrees with Rawls's principles of justice, derived from an original position, behind a veil of ignorance, where fictional participants arrive at the principles of justice without any knowledge of a God or religion.

Nonetheless, King argues that "one has a moral responsibility to disobey unjust law" and "one has not only a legal but a moral responsibility to obey just laws." One has a legal and moral responsibility to obey just laws because these "square . . . with the moral law or the law of God," while "an unjust law is a code that is out of harmony with the moral law." So for King, segregation in particular is unjust because it immorally violates "the law of God" and "degrades human personality."

King also writes that segregation treats "persons [as] . . . things" and is "not only politically, economically and sociologically unsound, it is morally wrong and sinful." However, whether people see segregation as "morally wrong and sinful" and whether it is unsound in the ways described is disputable. Someone might argue that integration is unjust assimilation to white cultural norms, for example. To nonviolently act for and against laws because they do or do not square with God's laws is a matter of dispute because Žižek can reject religious justifications because it tends to mobilize people to act toward goals in ways that are not nonviolent but instead produce mass killings. That is, invoking God as a means to justifying nonviolent actions does not guarantee that the actors will be nonviolent, in Žižek's view. Insofar as individuals can disagree on what is just and unjust, godly and ungodly, the actions that they engage in can be violent or nonviolent depending on the context of their actions and their beliefs. So when King argues that "it is wrong to use immoral means to attain moral ends . . . [and] it is just as wrong, or perhaps even more so, to use moral means to preserve immoral ends," he means to argue in favor of the nonviolence of nonviolent direct actions as a moral means used toward moral ends, but because whether an action is nonviolent is disputable, whether the action is moral or immoral is also disputable.

May, Rawls, Žižek, and King, therefore, each define a kind of nonviolent action that is capable of transforming a social-political or economic status quo. How the action works, though, is not necessarily nonviolent, because in order for the action to work, it has to be capable of somehow making this transformation occur. The action itself has to *make way* by producing at least a political jiu-jitsu, or by upholding Rawls's principles of justice, or by doing nothing, or by bringing tension to the surface. The adversary's perspective can always interpret the action that *makes way* as not truly nonviolent, especially if the adversary sees the action as disruptive to a status quo norm that the adversary wants sustained. The transformation of the status quo itself can be defined as a kind of violence in relation to context and opposed political, ideological perspectives. Anyone or anything that the so-called nonviolent action is directed against can conclude that the action is not really nonviolent. So in the following, I briefly discuss Gil Bailie and Hannah Arendt's arguments for kinds of nonviolence as useful means toward defeating desires for vengeance and violence. Like May, Rawls, Žižek, and King, though, Arendt's and Bailie's definitions of kinds of actions as nonviolent indicate that these actions could only work if they are at least definable as some kind of violence from an opposed political, ideological perspective.

4.10 THE DESTRUCTIVE VIOLENCE OF NONVIOLENT PRAYER AND FORGIVENESS[105]

Following Girard's view, and a representative of the theological view Žižek likely disagrees with, Gil Bailie argues, in *Violence Unveiled: Humanity at the Crossroads*, that

> it was religion—archaic religion . . . [that] is humanity's astonishing instrument for turning murder and madness into a sacralized bulwark against madness and murder. More or less refined forms of this same recipe for generating social solidarity and lending it the requisite solemnity have played a part in cultural existence since the dawn of human culture.[106]

However, he focuses on the issue that "in the *foreseeable* future, neither religious mystification nor the solemn and quasi-religious causes of 'history' will sufficiently veil our violence from our own eyes nor keep us from seeing the faces of victims."[107] Bailie's worry is that it may happen that the religious veils that hide our own underlying desires for vengeful violence will become unveiled to the extent that the social solidarity brought about in relation to beneficial and maleficent kinds of violence will itself be threatened, in an apocalyptic ("unveiling") way. His view is that "the social stability of . . . cultures was determined to a considerable degree by the success with which they were able to experience and interpret the violence which brought them into being as holy."[108] Holy violence, that is, the sacred sacrifice that binds a society together, is beneficial, but Bailie's worry is that people are "floundering" at distinguishing between beneficial and maleficent kinds of violence.

Bailie defines the modern crisis in the following:

> In today's world, both the political right and the political left, if they are to remain morally coherent, must speak on behalf of victims. . . . The left justifies or excuses the violence committed by the victims of structural violence. . . . The right justifies the violence necessary to control crime and excuses its occasional excesses as regrettable but unavoidable. Looking abroad, where the right sees "freedom fighters," the left sees the forces of counter-revolutionary oppression. Where the left sees a liberation movement, the right sees terrorists. . . . It is a mistake to think of this as a merely political disagreement. Seen from a larger perspective, it is a society . . . floundering in its attempt to determine whether violence is destructive or beneficial. It is another symptom that we live

> in a world no longer able to make a coherent distinction between good and bad violence.[109]

Of course, Bailie assumes himself to have the correct distinction between good and bad violence. His answer to this modern crisis that lies in the failure of people knowing how to distinguish between kinds of violence is found in the Lord's Prayer, where humanity is instructed to genuinely pray not to be led into temptation because this is what secures "immunity to the contagion of desire."[110] In particular, Jesus had taught humanity to pray, "Lead us not into temptation."[111] This is similar to the last of the Ten Commandments, found in Exodus 20, which states, "you shall not covet your neighbor's house. You shall not covet your neighbor's wife, or his servant, man or woman, or his ox, or his donkeys, or anything that is his."[112] The similarity lies in that both tell us not to desire what others show us is desirable because otherwise the mimetic rivalry, defined by Girard, ensues and desires for vengeance increase. A person's earnest prayer not to be led into temptation is a nonviolent means to eliminating the envious desire that leads to mimetic rivalry and apocalyptic violence being unleashed.

Bailie adds that, for "innately religious beings" bound together by the violence that founds our culture's unity, there are two religious forms of transcendence that we must choose from: either engage in violence for the sake of transcending (and stopping) violence or engage in prayer for the sake of transcending (and stopping) violence. Bailie's solution to the modern crisis that is the failure to correctly distinguish between kinds of violence is this nonviolent prayer. However, this prayer, if it defeats violence by defeating desire, can be a kind of violence turned against oneself, given the disagreements concerning what counts as kinds of violence and nonviolence.

For example, prayer is assumed to work as a means to defeating temptations. If one has strong temptations, then against these, one prays relentlessly and earnestly in order to defeat the temptations. If one is not as strongly tempted to seek vengeance, then less prayer is needed to defeat these temptations. In this sense, the amount a person prays may depend on the strength of his temptations. The defeat of temptation, therefore, is achieved by one who prays by the *force* of their prayer. For this, I imagine a parent whose child has been brutally raped and murdered and strongly desires to harm or kill the rapist-murderer. If this parent's desires are very strong, to the point that they have difficulty not thinking about their desire, then they may have to pray intensely and quite often. Bailie assumes the prayer to be nonviolent but capable of defeating temptations that can lead to violence. Because the goal is to defeat temptation that potentially lead to violence, the use of this prayer can be experienced as one's doing violence against oneself, perhaps in terms of psychological or symbolic violence. If desires are successfully defeated by this prayer, and only violence is assumed to be capable of defeating violence, and there is disagreement concerning what counts as violence and whether nonviolence is possible, then this prayer can count as a kind of violence.

Similarly, Hannah Arendt argues in *The Human Condition* that forgiveness is efficacious because it violates one's desire for vengeance. She first assumes that violence is necessarily involved in anything that humans make. She writes, "it is true that violence, without which no fabrication could ever come to pass, has always played an important role in political schemes and thinking based upon an interpretation of action in terms of making."[113] Forgiveness can fabricate new relationships between humans, and this means that forgiveness may also involve violence. It involves violence because forgiveness violates the desire to seek vengeance, fabricating a novel relation to the one forgiven. She states, "forgiveness is the exact opposite of vengeance, which acts in the form of re-acting against an original trespass."[114] Rather than enacting their desire for vengeance, people can forgive one another for their trespasses, and thereby violate and eliminate this desire. As a means, forgiveness, like the sacrificial kinds of violence, can only work as a violation of the desire to seek vengeance, in accordance with one's idea of justice, or what kinds of relationships between people should be achieved. As with the prayer not to be led into temptation, truly forgiving someone means violating one's own desire for vengeance, and this may also occur as a kind of psychological or symbolic violence. So for this reason, forgiveness can be interpreted as a kind of violence in the same way as the prayer not to be led into temptation.

4.11 CONCLUSION

Here, it has been argued that, given context, perspectives, and political, ideological disagreements, what counts as a nonviolent means can count as violence. Disagreements concerning how nonviolence works as a means have been outlined, demonstrating the ways in which nonviolence can be defined as a kind of violence. Ideologically speaking, theorists produce premises for the sake of demonstrating that nonviolence works as nonviolence, but how these premises unfold in actual, concrete actions is not necessarily considered by the adversary who can always interpret an otherwise nonviolent action as a kind of violence. Though there are the core paradigm cases of nonviolence, and though there are also commonsense views of nonviolence, when nonviolence (and violence) is defined as equivalent to other things, such as respect for dignity, equality, principles of justice, the result of scapegoating violence, and doing nothing, political disagreements emerge. Because even doing nothing, forgiveness and the prayer not to be led into temptation can themselves be considered kinds of violence, the weight of the argument leans toward nonviolent actions, refusals to act, and the intention to do nothing always possibly counting as kinds of violence. Violent nonviolence is possible because whether a use of means is nonviolent depends upon the contexts related to that use of means, as well as the goals toward which the means are utilized. Because there are diverse contexts in relation to which actions, as means, can be considered violent or nonviolent, and because there is disagreement concerning the goals toward which nonviolence is utilized, it is always possible to define what would otherwise be considered nonviolence as a kind of violence. So for these reasons, nonviolence, like the concept of violence, is an essentially contested concept for which no politically neutral definition is possible. There are paradigm cases of violence and nonviolence that individuals agree upon, but the wrongness of violence and the not-wrongness of nonviolence are extended beyond these paradigm cases in their politicizing ideological arguments, which can result in formations of collectives of individuals in relation to visions of some good. From the perspective of the person who defines nonviolence, that person's political and ideological assumptions influence how nonviolence is evaluated and opposed political ideologies can evaluate that nonviolence as a kind of violence.

NOTES

1. Maurice Merleau-Ponty, *Humanism and Terror: An Essay on the Communist Problem*, trans. John O'Neill (Boston: Beacon Press, 1990), 109.
2. Ibid., 35.
3. Ibid., 96.
4. Ibid., 28.
5. Ibid., 107.
6. George Bush, "Address to a Joint Session of Congress and the American People," September 20, 2001, accessed January 13, 2023, https://georgewbush-whitehouse.archives.gov/news/releases/2001/09/20010920-8.html.
7. Osama bin Laden, "Declaration of War Against the Americans Occupying the Land of the Two Holy Places: Expel the Polytheists from the Arabian Peninsula," in *On Violence*, ed. Bruce B. Lawrence and Aisha Karim (Durham: Duke University Press), 540–44.
8. Merleau-Ponty, *Humanism and Terror*, 110.
9. Ibid., 13.
10. René Girard, *Violence and the Sacred*, trans. Patrick Henry (Baltimore: John Hopkins University Press, 1977), 20.
11. Ibid., 23.
12. Ibid., 27.
13. Ibid., 21.
14. Ibid., 181.

15. Ibid., 144.
16. Ibid.
17. Ibid., 145.
18. Ibid.
19. Ibid., 146–47.
20. Ibid., 146.
21. Ibid., 147.
22. Ibid.
23. Ibid., 148.
24. Ibid., 151.
25. Ibid., 81.
26. Ibid., 15.
27. Ibid., 151.
28. Ibid., 148.
29. Ibid., 49.
30. Ibid., 152.
31. Girard interchangeably uses the terms "surrogate" and "scapegoat." Both terms are equally appropriate, as will become clear shortly, because the sacrificed victim is a substitution for everyone else and because the victim bears the blame attributed to him/her by everyone else.
32. Ibid., 220.
33. Ibid., 131.
34. Ibid., 22.
35. Ibid., 25.
36. Todd May, *Nonviolent Resistance: A Philosophical Introduction* (Malden: Polity, 2015), 166–67.
37. Ibid., 167. See David Harvey, *A Brief History of Neoliberalism* (Oxford: Oxford University Press, 2007), 19.
38. Ibid., 169. See also Brad Evans and Henry Giroux, who scrutinize neoliberalism in a comparable way, particularly emphasizing the point that those who cannot or who refuse to participate in "casino capitalism" (the consumption of one thing after another for the sake of consumption itself) are condemned, though they already live impoverished lives. In short, neoliberal ideology blames victims, and this is neoliberal violence. Giroux and Evans write, "Neoliberal power is unmediated in its effects on people as it operates throughout the global space of unregulated flows. Whereas in an earlier industrial period capital was largely rooted and peoples migrated, for the most part today capital flows while peoples are contained. What becomes of sovereignty in this economically driven environment is a military and policing protectorate put to the service of global capital in ways that work by condemning the already condemned. At the same time, neoliberal ideology, policies, and modes of governing are normalized as if there is no outside or alternative to capitalism. As corporate power replaces political sovereignty, politics becomes an extension of war and all public spaces are transformed into battle zones. Not only are all vestiges of the social contract, the safety net, and institutions of democracy under siege, but so too are all public spheres that support non-market values such as trust, critical dialogue, and solidarity. . . . Paul

Buchheit is right in arguing that 'privatizers believe that any form of working together as a community is anti-American. To them, individual achievement is all that matters. They're now applying their winner-take-all profit motive to our children.' They are also punishing those individuals, groups, and institutions that refuse the individualized and cut throat values of a market-driven casino capitalism." Brad Evans and Henry Giroux, "Critique of Violence," in *Disposable Futures: The Seduction of Violence in the Age of the Spectacle* (San Francisco: City Lights Publishers, 2015), 2.

39. May, *Nonviolent Resistance*, 169.
40. Ibid., 170.
41. Ibid., 171.
42. Ibid., 175.
43. Ibid., 176.
44. Ibid.
45. Jean-Paul Sartre, *Notebooks for an Ethics*, trans. David Pellauer (Chicago: The University of Chicago Press, 1992), 182.
46. Ibid., 210.
47. May, *Nonviolent Resistance*, 59.
48. Ibid., 62.
49. Ibid., 155–56.
50. Ibid., 111.
51. Ibid., 117; May's emphasis.
52. Ibid., 54.
53. Merleau-Ponty, *Humanism and Terror*, 109.
54. Jean-Paul Sartre, *Being and Nothingness*, translated by Hazel E. Barnes (New York: Washington Square Press, 1992), 531.
55. Ibid., 530.
56. May, *Nonviolent Resistance*, 154.
57. Todd May, *The Political Thought of Jacques Rancière: Creating Equality* (Edinburgh: Edinburgh University Press, 2008), 1–77.
58. Ibid., 3.
59. Ibid., 31.
60. Ibid., 33.
61. Ibid., 40.
62. Ibid., 42.
63. Ibid., 47.
64. Ibid., 34.
65. Ibid., 29.
66. Ibid., 71.
67. Ibid., 47.
68. Ibid., 49.
69. Ibid.
70. Ibid.
71. Ibid., 57.
72. May follows Rancière's argument that equality does not imply sameness, identification, or unification but "declassification," in the sense that the equality of

the ability to speak on, act on and about our world occurs from different positions. Active equality declassifies because democratic politics is based on "a heterogeneity to the established police order that is not recuperable in the form of a different police order." The ability to speak, conceived of as a basic common denominator, binds people together heterogeneously, not attributing any one identity or distributing particular kinds of equality in the way of passive equality. This is expressive of May's anarchistic rejection of all kinds of domination. There is only difference because homogeneous identifications and unifications are those imposed by oppressive police orders, which May rejects. May conceives of anarchism as "reducing liberty to equality" because equality is a presupposition of both liberty as the ability "for one to create a life [that] . . . is to go in the direction one seeks to take it," and as ownership over one's own life. "Equal intelligence [is] required to create a meaningful life," so, equality precedes liberty. See pp. 64 and 89–91.

73. Ibid., 53.

74. Ibid., 55.

75. Ibid., 60.

76. Ibid., 134.

77. Ibid., 135.

78. Ibid.

79. Ibid., 136.

80. Ibid., 137.

81. Ibid., 138.

82. Ibid., 138–39.

83. May, *Nonviolent Resistance*, 37.

84. Žižek, *Violence*, 1–2. For a more in-depth description of the kinds of violence Žižek defines, see the previous chapter.

85. May, *Nonviolent Resistance*, 34–35. Žižek, as indicated in the previous chapter, argues that objective violence consists of symbolic and systemic violence, both of which are conditions for a "zero-level" "normal" against which actions are subjective violence because they are "abnormal." Symbolic violence occurs linguistically, as a form of communication, when linguistic expressions represent things as superior and inferior. Systemic violence is the "often catastrophic consequences of the smooth functioning of our economic and political systems." See pp. 1–2, 9, 12–13, and 67–68 of Žižek's *Violence*.

86. Ibid., 163. See Gene Sharp's *How Nonviolent Struggle Works* (East Boston, MA: The Albert Einstein Institution, 2013).

87. Ibid., 163.

88. Merleau-Ponty, *Humanism and Terror*, 110.

89. John Rawls, *A Theory of Justice* (Cambridge: The Belknap Press of Harvard University Press, 1999), 320.

90. Ibid., 320, especially footnote 19. It is true that Rawls acknowledges other theorists' work on civil disobedience, such as that produced by H. A. Bedau, Henry David Thoreau, Dr. Martin Luther King Jr., and Howard Zinn. He asserts that he "do[es] not at all mean to say only [his definition of nonviolent civil disobedience] . . . is ever justified in a democratic state." Rawls concedes that other kinds of dissent can be

justifiable, but the point here is to analyze definitions and their implications, particularly that they lead to political and ideological disagreements.

91. Ibid., 321.
92. Ibid., 11.
93. Ibid., 13.
94. Ibid., 335–36.
95. Ibid., 336.
96. Chantal Mouffe, "Political Liberalism: Neutrality and the Political," *Ratio Juris* 7 (1994): 314–24.
97. Ibid., 324.
98. Merleau-Ponty, *Humanism and Terror*, 35.
99. Ibid., 35n11.
100. Slavoj Žižek, *Less than Nothing: Hegel and the Shadow of Dialectical Materialism* (New York: Verso, 2012), 946–47.
101. Ibid., 947.
102. Žižek, *Violence*, 206–7, and 213.
103. Ibid., 135.
104. Martin Luther King Jr., "Letter from a Birmingham Jail" (speech given April 16, 1963), Stanford University, The Martin Luther King Jr. Research and Education Institute, accessed January 13, 2023, https://kinginstitute.stanford.edu/sites/mlk/files/letterfrombirmingham_wwcw_0.pdf.
105. In this section, I also draw on ideas and passages that appeared earlier in my paper "The Efficacy of Scapegoating and Revolutionary Violence," in *Philosophy, Culture, and Traditions: A Journal of the World Union of Catholic Philosophical Societies*, ed. William Sweet, 10 (2014): 203–19. I am grateful to the editors of the journal for permission to draw on this material here.
106. Gil Bailie, *Violence Unveiled: Humanity at the Crossroads* (New York: Crossroad Publishing Company, 2002 [originally 1995]), 16.
107. Ibid., 16; Bailie's emphasis.
108. Ibid.
109. Ibid., 54. Bailie describes "structural violence" as "the deprivations and indignities to which the poor, the underprivileged, racial minorities, and those habituated and socialized to ghetto life are often subjected."
110. Ibid., 207, 270.
111. Ibid., 270.
112. Ibid., 144.
113. Hannah Arendt, *The Human Condition* (Chicago: The University of Chicago Press, 1974 [originally 1958]), 228.
114. Ibid., 240.

Conclusion

I have argued that distinctions between kinds of violence, including nonviolence, extend the paradigm case core conception of violence and nonviolence. Nonviolence is a kind of violence, though it generally produces less harm and destruction because it aims to avoid subjective, physical, psychological, systemic, and structural violence. But if nonviolence is to work, it's likely that it will be experienced by the adversary as a kind of symbolic or linguistic violence. When the concept of violence is extended by theorists beyond the paradigm cases of violence and nonviolence that most everyone agrees upon, violence and nonviolence are essentially contested concepts for which no politically neutral definition is possible. It is difficult to establish this as a matter of principle, but I have shown that, inductively, the major philosophical theories of violence and nonviolence depend on political preferences that are themselves highly contestable. A general reason for this might be that violence is, in the paradigm cases where its wrongness is evident and uncontested, an interpersonal, relational act; notions of violence that extend the concept but claim equivalence with the moral opprobrium attached to the paradigm cases of violence also involve interpersonal or, more broadly, social consequences of the acts construed as violence. Theorists discussed here evaluate violence negatively, but in doing so, they produce justifications for other kinds of violence, and in doing so, they put into question the wrongness of violence. Likewise with nonviolence. Theorists tend to evaluate it positively, but in doing so, they produce justifications for defined kinds of nonviolent actions, which themselves can be evaluated negatively by the adversaries against whom the nonviolent actions are directed. The positive evaluation of nonviolence is thus put into question by those people, policies, laws, and institutions that the nonviolent direct actions target.

Opposed political ideologies disagree on when an action counts as a kind of violence or as a kind of nonviolence, even though there is agreement concerning paradigm cases. Except for these paradigm cases, justifications for violence, and distinctions between kinds of violence (including nonviolence) rely on relationships to other things, which are themselves contested, such as defense, freedom, justice, power, equality, and dignity. These are normative terms that characterize social outcomes; to act on these terms is to act politically; to act politically is to act in terms of political values or ideas. Such actors mean *to be* these values and ideas and to enact them and their consequences in the world. The "Stop the Steal" ideology, for example, which has emerged since Donald Trump lost the presidential election to Joe Biden, was embodied by individuals in public on January 6, 2021, and had consequences, some of which were the result of paradigm cases of violence, such as beatings, pushes, shootings, and so on. There are collectives of individuals who interpret what occurred as legitimate. They believe in the "Stop the Steal" ideology, while others disagree. Whether the violence was justified on that day and what kind of violence it was is a matter of political, ideological disagreement for which there may be no possible resolution. It is a difficult task to try to change the beliefs of individuals, particularly when they live in politicized relationships with others who share the same ideological beliefs. The same can be said of other events, such as the Black Lives Matter protests that occurred across the United States and in other countries, such as in South Africa, Japan, Ireland, England, Denmark, and elsewhere. The political ideology that says that people of color are not afforded the same justice as others is highly disputed, some embracing this ideology and acting on it during these protests, while others reject it, arguing that "All Lives Matter." This has led to confrontations that themselves turned violent. There is evidence that Black Lives Matter protests did sometimes occur violently, in the sense of the paradigm cases, as did some of the All Lives Matter counter-protests. The question often asked is, "Who started it?" And it is difficult to draw conclusions with certainty because most people were not there, and we can only rely on video recordings and testimonies. And even if evidence could be presented, it is often the case that people would deny it or simply not believe it because the evidence didn't support their political, ideological perspective. As Bailie says, perhaps people are failing to distinguish between good and bad violence, though I wouldn't go so far as to say that this isn't just a political disagreement. It's a political disagreement par excellence because conceptions of kinds of violence, including nonviolence, are nonneutrally political and ideological.

I have not argued here that any distinction between kinds of violence and nonviolence is preferable. Instead, it has only been indicated, through an inductive analysis of some of the available philosophical accounts of violence and nonviolence, that the paradigm cases of violence and nonviolence serve as the core exemplars in relation to which disagreements arise, but that extended concepts of violence and nonviolence depend on political values or ideas and ideologies. Political ideologies oppose one another, and the kinds of violence defined and justified by a political ideology opposes that of another political ideology. This indicates two things.

First, in order to avoid the rhetorical pull of political ideologies, paradigm cases of violence and nonviolence should be the focus of philosophical speculation in political philosophy. The focus should tarry with negative evaluations of violence as wrongs, no matter how political philosophy occurs. The focus should remain on positive evaluations of nonviolence too. Surely, the perspectives of victims of violence and the perspectives of the people and institutions targeted by nonviolent actions matter, even if we disagree with them. Accounting for the disagreements matter. To reject another perspectival interpretation may result in something worse. Most people consider paradigm examples of violence to be wrong. So how do we stop them from occurring? What direction do we pursue? What policy? Using violence is one conceivable way but does not seem to get the job done when aiming to thwart violence. Perhaps, instead of embracing political ideologies so strongly to the point that people engage in paradigm acts of violence, skepticism is needed. To undertake defining, justifying, and legitimizing extended notions of violence is an attempt to rhetorically convince people to engage in actions that they reject. The paradigm cases of violence are wrong without the influence of any political ideology defining them as wrong. Their wrongness is politically neutral. No political ideology is needed by anyone for convincing people that it is wrong for one person to intentionally behead another person for the sake of causing harm and destruction. The reasons the person has for this violence do not change the fact that it is wrong to do this. Political ideologies tend to be fantasies ideologically believed to be facts, but they are not facts in the sense that it is a fact that a triangle has three sides. Rather political ideologies do themselves, as a matter of fact, conjure norms and descriptions of things that people believe in and desire. However, those norms and descriptions are not necessarily true. Political ideologies can be convincing and effective, particularly when they tell people that they can be secured from violence, if only they believe in and act upon a particular political ideology, but political ideologies remain political ideologies, that is, they are only factual insofar as they exist and are enacted in the world. Otherwise, a political ideology can always be replaced and wither away into history as fewer and fewer individuals embrace and act upon it.

Second, the distinctions between kinds of violence defined by every political ideology are essentially contested. *Every* political ideology is suspect, particularly because they define themselves as superior in relation to others. Each political ideology aims to justify its own uses of violence against opposed political ideologies. Each positively values the kinds of violence that serve to uphold its political ideology. These evaluations produce conditions for enmity and violent conflicts that are paradigm cases of violence.

If political philosophy is to move away from actual, paradigm cases of violence, then it would need to root a theory of violence in something other than contested political concepts. This is where the paradigm case core conception of violence may be the most useful, particularly because it reveals the commonly agreed upon wrongness of examples of violence. However, the question is whether such a political philosophy could be. Is it possible for a political philosophy to avoid reproducing conditions for violence even if it, from the start, affirms the wrongness of violence and in its development aims to avoid justifying kinds of violence as legitimate? Perhaps an ahistorical, nontraditional, global, and nonviolent kind of cooperation could serve as the foundation for a future political philosophy, but it may be difficult for this kind of cooperation to avoid counting as a kind of violence or for a politically neutral argument to be made for it. However, in consideration of the fact that no political ideology is neutral, there is a choice of which political ideology to choose to believe in as legitimate and to enact. Yet doing so is likely to reproduce conditions for violence, reflecting the historical tragedy of humanity's existence in its relationships. Obviously, people usually obediently cooperate, going along, working with others. But the key, historical moments that occur when conflict emerges in relation to noteworthy events and developments will continue to bear violence as collectives of politicized individuals fight to defend their political ideological beliefs.

From here, the future project that this points to concerns the question whether it is possible for a novel political philosophy to be developed that simultaneously addresses the wrongness of paradigm cases of violence and avoids justifying kinds of violence. Given that political ideologies tend to describe kinds of violence as justified, this novel political philosophy would have to address issues that arise when considering how violence can be avoided in such a way that the political philosophy does not reproduce a logic of domination or a logic of exception in relation to kinds of violence. We can inductively list examples of paradigm cases of violence and say these should never occur. Most people want to be protected against them. But this does not solve the problem of justifiable violence or of whether it is possible to construct a theory that does not itself lead to and justify political conflict. There remains the problem of what to do when paradigm cases of violence do occur. There also remains the problem that systems, structures, language, and so many other things can be interpreted as kinds of violence. Claims made by people who say that they suffer a kind of violence that cannot be seen with the eyes should be provided a charitable hearing and not shut down. There will be disagreement in relation to their claims, but that's just how things are and why public discourse concerning kinds of violence is essential. An ideal vision for a political philosophy focused on cooperation and supporting everyone's needs would have to ensure that most people are sufficiently and thoroughly educated on violence and nonviolence so that they can see why political ideologies should be considered from a skeptical perspective. What is needed is a premise that grounds a new political ideology and that can be enacted in the world with little to no possibility of oppression, exploitation, domination, or violence resulting. But this appears to be an impossible task, and there is a limit to what we can do about violence. A multicultural pluralism seems like an excellent approach, insofar as individuals, cultures, and so on are free to express themselves insofar as they do so without paradigm cases of violence, but this approach suffers those who reject multicultural pluralism from the start. A participatory democracy likewise seems like it could be a successful approach, but again, there are people who reject this, and it is pragmatically difficult to involve everyone in decision making whenever they would prefer to be involved. A political philosophy focused on nonviolence as the primary assumption, which altogether rejects any use or justification of paradigm cases of violence, while also acknowledging that nonviolent political actions can be experienced as kinds of violence, could be what is needed. However, how can such a political philosophy suggest means of nonviolent defense when those who enact it are violently attacked? Are they supposed to simply suffer their victimization and not fight back? If violence is to be avoided because it is wrong, and those with this political philosophy refuse to justify or engage in violence to the extent that they refuse to defend themselves, then perhaps this suffering is what is needed, given that it is this suffering that is hoped to generate the moral or at least the political jiu-jitsu that would convert adversaries who are against nonviolence. However, that may mean that more violence will nonetheless inevitably occur.

References

Arendt, Hanna. *The Human Condition*. Chicago: The University of Chicago Press, 1974 (originally 1958).

Arendt, Hannah. "Ideology and Terror: A Novel Form of Government." *The Review of Politics* 15, no. 3 (July 1953): 303–27.

Arendt, Hanna. *On Violence*. New York: Harcourt, Inc., 1970.

Arendt, Hanna. "Race-Thinking before Racism." *The Review of Politics* 6, no. 1 (January 1944): 36–73.

Bailie, Gil. *Violence Unveiled: Humanity at the Crossroads*. New York: Crossroad Publishing Company, 2002 (originally 1995).

Bakunin, Mikhail. *The Political Philosophy of Bakunin: Scientific Anarchism*. Edited by G. P. Maximoff. New York: The Free Press, 1953.

Benjamin, Walter. "Critique of Violence." In *Reflections: Essays, Aphorisms, Autobiographical Writings*, edited by Peter Demetz, 277–300. New York: Shocken, 1986.

Bergson, Henri. *Time and Free Will: An Essay on the Immediate Data of Consciousness*. Translated by F. L. Pogson. London: George Allen & Unwin Limited, 1950.

bin Laden, Osama. "Declaration of War Against the Americans Occupying the Land of the Two Holy Places: Expel the Polytheists from the Arabian Peninsula." In *On Violence*, edited by Bruce B. Lawrence and Aisha Karim, 540–44. Durham: Duke University Press.

Brennan, Jason. "When May We Kill Government Agents? In Defense of Moral Parity." *Social Philosophy and Policy* 32 (2016): 40–61.

Bufacchi, Vittorio. "Violence." In *International Encyclopedia of Ethics*, edited by H. Lafollette. Hoboken: Wiley-Blackwell, 2013. https://doi.org/10.1002/9781444367072.wbiee146

Bush, George. "Address to a Joint Session of Congress and the American People." September 20, 2001. Accessed January 13, 2023. https://georgewbush-whitehouse.archives.gov/news/releases/2001/09/20010920-8.html.

Butler, Judith. "Rethinking Vulnerability and Resistance." In *Vulnerability in Resistance*, edited by Judith Butler, Zeynep Gambetti, and Leticia Sabsay, 12–27. Durham: Duke University Press, 2016.

Butler, Judith. "Violence, Mourning, Politics." *Studies in Gender and Sexuality* 4 (2003): 9–37.

de Haan, Willem. "Violence as an Essentially Contested Concept." In *Violence in Europe: Historical and Contemporary Perspectives*, edited by Sophie Body-Gendrot and Pieter Spierenburg, 27–40. New York: Springer-Verlag, 2008).

Derrida, Jacques. "Force de Loi: le 'Fondement Mystique de l'Autorité'" (Force of Law: The "Mystical Foundation of Authority"). *Cardoza Law Review*, translated by Mary Quaintance 11 (1990): 919–1045.

Erlenbusch, Verena. "Notes on Violence: Benjamin's Relevance for the Study of Terrorism." *Journal of Global Ethics* 6 (2010): 167–78.

Evans, Brad, and Henry Giroux. "Critique of Violence." In *Disposable Futures: The Seduction of Violence in the Age of the Spectacle*, 1–12. San Francisco: City Lights Publishers, 2015.

Foot, Philippa. "The Problem of Abortion and the Doctrine of the Double Effect." *Oxford Review* 5 (1967): 1–5.

Gallie, Walter Bryce. "Essentially Contested Concepts." *Proceedings of the Aristotelian Society* 56 (1955–1956): 167–98.

Garver, Newton. "What Violence Is." In *Violence: A Philosophical Anthology*, edited by Vittorio Bufacchi. New York: Palgrave Macmillan, 2009.

Girard, René. *Violence and the Sacred.* Translated by Patrick Henry. Baltimore: John Hopkins University Press, 1977.

Greene, Joshua. *Moral Tribes: Emotion, Reason, and the Gap between Us and Them.* New York: Penguin Books, 2013.

Harvey, David. *A Brief History of Neoliberalism.* Oxford: Oxford University Press, 2007.

Hobbes, Thomas. *Leviathan: With Selected Variants from the Latin Edition of 1668.* Edited by Edwin Curley. Indianapolis: Hackett Publishing Company, 1994.

Kant, Immanuel. "The Metaphysics of Morals." In *Practical Philosophy*, edited by Paul Guyer and Allen W. Wood, 353–604. New York: Cambridge University Press, 1999.

Kant, Immanuel. "On the Common Saying: That May Be Correct in Theory, but It Is of No Use in Practice." In *Practical Philosophy*, translated by Mary J. Gregor, edited by Paul Guyer and Allen W. Wood, 273–310. New York: Cambridge University Press, 1999.

Kant, Immanuel. *Perpetual Peace.* Edited by Lewis White Beck. New York: Macmillan Publishing Company, 1957.

King, Martin Luther, Jr. "Letter from a Birmingham Jail." Speech given April 16, 1963. Stanford University, The Martin Luther King Jr. Research and Education Institute. Accessed January 13, 2023. https://kinginstitute.stanford.edu/sites/mlk/files/letterfrombirmingham_wwcw_0.pdf.

LaFollette, Hugh, ed. *International Encyclopedia of Ethics.* Hoboken: Wiley-Blackwell, 2013.

Lewis, Charlton Thomas. *An Elementary Latin Dictionary.* New York: American Book Company, 1890.

Lichtheim, George. "The Concept of Ideology." *History and Theory* 4 (1965): 164–95.

Machiavelli, Niccolò. *The Prince*. New York: Penguin Books, 2005.

MacIntyre, Alasdair. "The Essential Contestability of Some Social Concepts." *Ethics* 84 (1973): 1–9.

May, Todd. *Nonviolent Resistance: A Philosophical Introduction*. Malden: Polity, 2015.

May, Todd. *The Political Thought of Jacques Rancière: Creating Equality*. Edinburgh: Edinburgh University Press, 2008.

McCreery, Gregory. "The Efficacy of Scapegoating and Revolutionary Violence." *Philosophy, Culture, and Traditions: A Journal of the World Union of Catholic Philosophical Societies*, edited by William Sweet, 10 (2014): 203–19.

McCreery, Gregory. "On the Politicization of Violence within Reductive and Non-Reductive Accounts of Violence." *Human Studies* 43 (2020): 269–89.

Merleau-Ponty, Maurice. *Humanism and Terror: An Essay on the Communist Problem*. Translated by John O'Neill. Boston: Beacon Press, 1990.

Mouffe, Chantal. "Political Liberalism: Neutrality and the Political." *Ratio Juris* 7 (1994): 314–24.

Nagel, Thomas. "What Is Wrong with Terrorism?" *Project Syndicate*, November 19, 2002. Accessed January 13, 2023. https://www.project-syndicate.org/commentary/what-is-wrong-with-terrorism.

O'Brien, Kevin J. *The Violence of Climate Change: Lessons of Resistance from Nonviolent Activists*. Washington, DC: Georgetown University Press, 2017.

Putnam, Hilary. "Is Semantics Possible?" *Metaphilosophy* 1 (1970): 187–201.

Rancière, Jacques. *Disagreement: Politics and Philosophy*. Translated by Julie Rose. Minneapolis: University of Minnesota Press, 1999.

Rawls, John. *A Theory of Justice*. Cambridge: The Belknap Press of Harvard University Press, 1999.

Robespierre, Maximilien. "Robespierre February 1794: Justification of the Use of Terror." Accessed January 13, 2023. https://www.marxists.org/history/france/revolution/robespierre/1794/terror.htm.

Sartre, Jean-Paul Sartre. *Being and Nothingness*. Translated by Hazel E. Barnes. New York: Washington Square Press, 1992.

Sartre, Jean-Paul. *Critique of Dialectical Reason, Vol. II*. Translated by Quintin Hoare. New York: Verso, 1991.

Sartre, Jean-Paul. *Notebooks for an Ethics*. Translated by David Pellauer. Chicago: The University of Chicago Press, 1992.

Sartre, Jean-Paul. Preface to *The Wretched of the Earth* by Frantz Fanon, translated by Richard Philcox, xliii–lxii. New York: Grove Press, 2004 (originally 1963).

Schinkel, Willem. "Regimes of Violence and the *Trias Violentiae*." *European Journal of Social Theory* 16 (2013): 310–25.

Schmitt, Carl. *The Concept of the Political*. Translated by George Schwab. Chicago: The University of Chicago Press, 2007.

Schütz, Alfred. "Common-Sense and Scientific Interpretation of Human Action." *Collected Papers 1: The Problems of Social Reality*. Edited by M. Natanson. Boston: Martinus Nijhoff, 1962.

Sharp, Gene. *How Nonviolent Struggle Works*. East Boston, MA: The Albert Einstein Institution, 2013.

Smith, Ted A. *Weird John Brown: Divine Violence and the Limits of Ethics*. Stanford: Stanford University Press, 2015.

Sorel, Georg. *Reflections on Violence*. Translated by T. E. Hulme and J. Roth. New York: Collier Books, 1974.

Staudigl, Michael. "Topics, Problems, and Potentials of a Phenomenological Analysis of Violence." In *Phenomenologies of Violence*, edited by Michael Staudigl, 1–34. Leiden: Brill, 2013.

Staudigl, Michael. "Towards a Relational Phenomenology of Violence." *Human Studies* 36 (2013): 43–66.

Stein, Edith. *The Collected Works of Edith Stein, Volume Three: On the Problem of Empathy*. Translated by W. Stein. Washington, DC: ICS Publications, 1989.

Stråth, Bo. "Ideology and Conceptual History." In *The Oxford Handbook of Political Ideologies*, edited by Michael Freeden, Lyman Tower Sargent, and Marc Stears, 3–19. New York: Oxford University Press, 2013.

Stråth, Bo. "Ideology and History." *Journal of Political Ideologies* 11 (2006): 23–42.

Thomson, Judith Jarvis. "Killing, Letting Die, and the Trolley Problem." *The Monist* 104 (1976): 204–17.

Thomson, Judith Jarvis. "The Trolley Problem." *Yale Law Journal* 94 (1985): 1395–415.

Thomson, Judith Jarvis. "Turning the Trolley." *Philosophy and Public Affairs* 36 (2008): 359–74.

Treitschke, Heinrich von. *Politics*. Translated by Arthur James Balfour. New York: The MacMillan Company, 1916.

Truman, Harry S. "Radio Report to the American People on the Potsdam Conference." *Harry S. Truman Library & Museum*. Accessed January 13, 2023. https://www.trumanlibrary.gov/soundrecording-records/sr61-37-radio-report-american-people-potsdam-conference.

Votel, Joseph. "Department of Defense Press Briefing by Army General Joseph Votel, Commander, U.S. Central Command." Press Briefing, April 29, 2016. US Department of Defense. Accessed January 13, 2023. http://www.defense.gov/News/Transcripts/Transcript-View/Article/746686/department-of-defense-press-briefing-by-army-general-joseph-votel-commander-us.

Waismann, Friedrich, D. M. McKinnon, and W. C. Kneal. "Symposium: Verifiability." *Proceedings of the Aristotelian Society, Supplementary Volumes* 19 (1945): 101–64.

Warren, Karen. "The Power and Promise of Ecological Feminism." In *Environmental Ethics: Readings in Theory and Application*, sixth edition, edited by Louis P. Pojman and Paul Pojman, 589–605. Boston: Wadsworth, 2012.

Weber, Max. "The Profession and Vocation of Politics." In *Weber: Political Writings*, edited by Peter Lassman and Ronald Speirs, 309–69. New York: Cambridge University Press, 1994.

Williams, Howard. *Kant's Critique of Hobbes: Sovereignty and Cosmopolitanism*. Cardiff: University Wales Press, 2003.

WHO Global Consultation on Violence and Health. Violence: A Public Health Priority. WHO/EHA/SPI.POA.2. Geneva: WHO, 1996.

Žižek, Slavoj. *Less than Nothing: Hegel and the Shadow of Dialectical Materialism*. New York: Verso, 2012.

Žižek, Slavoj. *Violence: Six Sideways Reflections*. New York: Picador, 2008.

Index

About the Author

Gregory (Greg) McCreery lives in Tampa, Florida, and has been teaching for the University of South Florida's Judy Genshaft Honors College, the Department of Philosophy, and the School of Interdisciplinary Global Studies for over ten years in Tampa and St. Petersburg, as well as for Hillsborough Community College, Ybor City. His teaching is devoted to political philosophy, applied ethics, and controversial issues, particularly within the areas of political conflict, authoritarianism, nonviolent civil disobedience, environmental ethics, biomedical ethics, and racial issues. He is married with two children, Celeste and Sebastian, enjoys the arts, playing music, outdoor recreation, and ancient philosophical practices that address the mind-body relationship, such as found in Yoga.